Doing Business in China

Tim Ambler and Morgen Witzel

London and New York

First published 2000
by Routledge
11 New Fetter Lane, London EC4P 4EE

Simultaneously published in the USA and Canada
by Routledge
29 West 35th Street, New York, NY 10001

Routledge is an imprint of the Taylor & Francis Group

© 2000 Tim Ambler and Morgen Witzel

Typeset in Baskerville by Taylor & Francis Books Ltd
Printed and bound in Great Britain by
TJ International Ltd, Padstow, Cornwall

British Library Cataloguing in Publication Data
A catalogue record for this book is available from the British Library

Library of Congress Cataloging in Publication Data
Ambler, Tim.
Doing business in China / Tim Ambler and Morgen Witzel.
p. cm.
Includes bibliographical references and index.
1. China–Economic conditions–1976- 2. China–Economic policy–1976-
3. Investments, Foreign–China. 4. International business
enterprises–China. I. Witzel, Morgen. II. Title.
HC427 .A593 2000
330.951–dc21

99-086052

ISBN 0–415–22329–6 (Pbk)
ISBN 0–415–22328–8 (Hbk)

Contents

Foreword

I was flattered and honoured to be asked to write this foreword. Then I remembered with humility the words of a distinguished former colleague in the Foreign Service: 'There is no such thing as a Western "expert" on China, only varying degrees of ignorance.'

When considering the vastness and variety of China, I often remind myself of the hoary old story about the six blind men who were introduced to an elephant for the first time. Each was asked what it was. The first, who was stroking one of the elephant's legs, declared it to be a tree. The second, at the rear, felt the elephant's tail and announced it to be a rope. The third and fourth thought that the tusk and the ear were, respectively, a weapon and a carpet. 'Nonsense', cried the fifth, pushing against the beast's side, 'it's a wall'. 'Rubbish', said the last as he handled the elephant's trunk, 'you are all wrong. It's a hosepipe'. None of them could comprehend that they were in the presence of an elephant.

Most Westerners, on encountering China for the first time, are rather like the blind men. We see only a small part of the country, and form our views of the country and its people based on those few impressions. Very often, those impressions have little to do with the 'real' China. Seeking to understand China, as I know from my own experience, is a long-term process.

China, with its great size and vast population, has always been something of a mystery to the West. In the eighteenth century, China was admired for its civilisation, philosophy and taste. This turned to contempt in the nineteenth century as the weakness of the Manchu dynasty was exposed. As China recovered its national dignity in the mid-twentieth century, the West began to exhibit anxiety and fear. There has been a gulf between us, based in part on geographical distance but also in the vast differences between our cultures, our languages and customs, and our education systems and ways of thinking. Historically, the differences between China and the West have too often led to suspicion, mistrust and conflict.

However, in the past few decades that has begun to change. In 1979, China launched the first of its economic reforms. With hindsight, this may come to be seen as one of the most important events of the twentieth century, after the triumph of the Chinese Revolution in 1949. The effect, within just a few years, has been to bring China out of its long isolation. Prosperity has increased steadily, and hundreds of millions of people have been lifted out of poverty. Suddenly, China has become a major player in the world economy. Its gross domestic product is already one of the largest in the world, although per capita income remains low because the pie has to be shared by 1.3 billion inhabitants. Even with the recessionary effects of the recent Asia crisis, growth has continued, and is now picking up speed once more.

China is committed to joining the family of nations, as the current negotiations over membership of the World Trade Organisation clearly show. The present government has pledged that China will be modernised by the middle of this century, to the extent of reaching the standard of living presently enjoyed by a medium-sized European country today. Already a major player in the world economy, China's could soon become an influential force, joining the old triad of Japan, the USA and the European Union helping to shape the pattern of world trade and economic policy. Further, the nature of the Chinese economy will continue to change, with more sectors becoming open to foreign investment, greater deregulation, and, with continued steady management, a fully convertible currency all scheduled for implementation over the next decade or so.

China is regarded today by Western businesses as a market for high-technology goods and as a source of low-cost manufacturing facilities. This too will change. China's own high-tech businesses are going from strength to strength; its consumer and software industries in particular are growing rapidly. One of the fascinating aspects of China today is that while part of its economy remains almost pre-industrial, especially in the more remote rural regions, other parts are moving rapidly into the post-industrial age.

The opportunities for Western business in all this should of course be obvious. Indeed, as this book suggests, the question for most business should not be 'should we go to China?', but rather 'can we afford *not* to go to China?' Or at the very least, 'can we afford *not* to give serious and careful examination to the prospects of trading with China?' Given China's prominence in many business sectors and the rapid growth occurring in others, can any company which claims to be global afford not to have a stake in China?

No one can pretend that entering the China market is an easy business.

But developments in China are moving along at great speed. Once a Western business takes the critical decision to enter China, it would be better to enter soon; later, with competition growing at a very rapid pace, may be too late.

In this book, Tim Ambler and Morgen Witzel have produced a serious and thoughtful book for managers contemplating the problems of entering China for the first time. This is neither a how-to guide nor a 'complete' description of China. Even if the latter were possible within the confines of a single volume, as the authors point out, few managers would have time to digest all the information it would contain. As for how-to guides, given the diversity and variety of the Chinese economy, it is impossible to produce such a guide that would be relevant for all managers all the time.

What *Doing Business in China* does instead is provide readers with a series of frameworks for learning about China. It urges managers first of all to develop at least a basic knowledge of Chinese history and culture before going to China, and to continue to learn about these things while there. History and culture are still vitally important in modern China, and by learning about them one will come a little closer to understanding the Chinese. The book then details some of the frameworks for strategy making and relationship building used by the Chinese, including the all-import concept of *guànxi*. For those planning to market their products in China and/or set up offices and plants in China, the book goes on to describe some of the strategies and methods which may be used, and highlights important areas where Chinese and Western practices and attitudes diverge. Finally, the book points out the important links between the People's Republic of China and the overseas Chinese, and suggests that Western business people need to consider the latter when establishing businesses and building relationships.

This is an exciting time, not just for business people but for the world community in general. The emergence of China signals the beginning of a new era. Those Western businesses already involved in China have helped, through their investment and influence, to bring that era about. The next generation of managers will help see China's economy and society become more and more integrated with those of the rest of the world. It is to them that this book is commended.

Sir Alan Donald
March 2000

Acknowledgements

Books are always collaborative ventures, and this one is more than most. Our many friends and colleagues, most of whom know far more about China than we ever will, have been incredibly generous with their time and knowledge, and we must offer our deepest thanks to Sir Alan Donald KCMG, Ian Rae, C.F. Li, Ken Campbell, Zinan Liu and Tian Jun, who supported our course at London Business School and came year after year to speak to our students and share their vast store of knowledge and experience. Giles Chance, Malcolm Warner, Michael Yahuda, Simon Powell, Rod Wye and many others also joined us from time to time. Between them, they have many hundreds of years of experience of China and things Chinese, and we are honoured that they should have shared so much with us.

Special thanks should be tendered to John Beyer, former director of the China-Britain Trade Group (now China-Britain Business Council), who visited the class and has been of great help in many other ways. His deputy, Mandi Robinson, has also been invaluable, particularly when giving feedback on the first year of the course. James Glasse provided valuable comments on the final draft and, in general, we should like to thank all the CBTG/CBBC staff for their assistance over the years.

At London Business School, our warmest thanks to go Wang Xiucun, who visited us on sabbatical from Beijing for a year, co-taught the course with us, and corrected with great kindness and politeness our more crass errors on things Chinese. Other assistance and material came from George Tian, Jonathan Thompson, Zhang Jing and Vivan Li Fang. Ken Simmons and the late Philip Law also contributed advice and ideas.

Material for cases came from many sources. Our thanks go to Giles Chance, Greg Harris, Geoff Mills, Li Xuemin, Shan Jinglong, Gabrielle Sentilhes, T.Y. Wong, Jonathan Patrick, Larry Renaldi, Chen Derong, Jin

Shen Yu, Michael Zhu and the staff of the Sun and Moon Spreading Company for their generously given help.

At Routledge our thanks go to Vicki Smith, who first commissioned the work, Craig Fowlie who has seen it through and also to Allison Bell and Ann O' Quigley.

Last but not least, we would like to thank our students, the hundred or so men and women from all over the globe who took the 'Doing Business in China' course and contributed so much to it, year after year. Without them, this book would not have been possible.

Tim Ambler
Morgen Witzel
March 2000

Note on References

Most of the works referred to in endnotes can be found in the annotated bibliography, and have therefore simply been referred to by the author and date of publication. However, full citations are given in the endnotes for more general works as these do not appear in the bibliography, which is intended to be a research tool for managers and students of business in China.

Introduction

What does anybody here know of China? Even those Europeans who have been in that Empire are almost as ignorant of it as the rest of us. Everything is covered by a veil, through which a glimpse of what is within may occasionally be caught, a glimpse just sufficient to set the imagination to work and more likely to mislead than inform.

(Lord Maccartney *c.* 1790)

This is a big canvas, much of it still dark. Personal impressions are sometimes vivid, always incontestable; but they illuminate only part of the scene, and from one angle only. They are also outsiders' impressions. We each construct our vision of China from the limited materials available to us, from our direct experience and reading, our memories of certain conversations and scenes; and we cling tenaciously to it. But it remains China through a foreigner's distorting glass. The real China, whatever that may be, eludes us.

(Sir Percy Craddock 1994)

This book grew out of a second-year MBA course at the London Business School, which we taught from 1995. At that time of great prospects for business in China itself and in East Asia as a whole, no course at any European business school, and only a handful in the USA, provided a fundamental review of the differences between doing business in China and the West. Despite all the interest, and despite the Asian boom, Western, especially British, managers were not being adequately trained or prepared for the challenges of doing business there.

Many aspects of China have changed in the five years since then and the details will change again before the ink is dry on this page. We realised that we had to address the underlying Chinese mental maps – not the ever-changing rules and structures. We had to provide our students with understanding at a level that would see them through their business careers. British intellectuals, as shown above, make the same findings two hundred years on and we would not be that surprised by another ambassador being equally amazed in 2194. The accounts of Lord Maccartney's first British trade mission to China, from India, two hundred years ago are easily recognised by today's business visitor. China is constantly changing and yet it is always the same.

So what has emerged is a rather more profound study of business in China than is available from the instant guides. It is addressed to business people going there, be they Western or Asian, and to their colleagues who sit in the home office and fail to understand why they are not bringing the goods back by Friday. Almost all expatriates in China complain of this lack of understanding but few prepared themselves or their colleagues for the realities of business in China ahead of time. Bearing in mind the size of the future Chinese market and their likely influence in world trade, we suggest that there are few managers anywhere who can afford to ignore this challenge.

Part of what makes China unfamiliar is its culture and its history, which have given the Chinese people mental processes, outlooks and attitudes that can sometimes be very different from those with which Westerners are imbued. These differences often create misunderstandings and serve as powerful barriers, hindering or preventing Western and Chinese business people from working together. One has the impression that the Chinese are working harder on understanding Western business approaches than the reverse. Do not assume they will all convert any more than Japan did after World War II. Much more likely is the retention, as in Japan, of traditional ways alongside the international. The consequence is that it has been much easier for Japan to penetrate Western markets than vice versa. Expect the same again, only more so, with China.

But, to the Westerner prepared to devote the time to understanding China, many of these differences can be overcome or got round. The reward, for those who succeed, is good relationships with Chinese partners, access to new markets and/or sources of supply, and entrée into Chinese business networks. All of these can be powerful sources of competitive advantage.

While this book discusses marketing and advertising, organisation behaviour and the mechanics of joint ventures in China, they are placed in the context of Chinese history, philosophy and culture. These form the essential backdrop against which business in modern China makes sense. A greater understanding of China not only helps to explain *how* things happen in that vast, complex and diverse country, but it can also suggest reasons *why* they happen, and why they might (or might not) happen again.

Differences between China and the West provide the rationale for this book but the similarities are growing fast. More and more Western techniques and practices can be usefully replicated in China. There is much to be said, as Wall's ice cream, the Unilever subsidiary, did in Beijing, for starting with the usual market entry formula and only changing it when you have to. Second, and a little more esoterically, by looking at these common features from a Chinese perspective, we learn more about the things we already do. In other words, by learning how to do business in China, we can also improve what we do in the West.

This book, therefore, has several purposes. For those business people who deal directly with China, as traders, investors, expatriate managers or partners, it provides an introduction. For their colleagues, it provides some explanation of why things may take so long, why people come before business, why legalistic or contractual thinking has so little place and of the kind of help that expatriates and visitors will need. For teachers and trainers, the book can serve as a textbook. We have included some short cases and examples. In the past, China has contributed many of the world's most useful inventions – from paper to spaghetti to explosives – and it will provide many more in the future. In one sense or another, we are all students of China. To the extent that this book contributes to mutual understanding, it will have served its purpose.

Why China?

In 1995, China's post-economic-reform boom was at its height. This was the time of the 'Wild East', with double digit growth (and inflation) in China and Southeast Asia. Shanghai's Pudong district had some of the most expensive real estate on the face of the planet. Western companies were scrambling to get in, often exhibiting a mentality reminiscent of the nineteenth-century gold rushes. The reason for interest in China was obvious: it was the place to go to make money.

Since then, the Asia crisis of 1997–8 temporarily knocked the stuffing out of the Southeast and East Asian economies, with knock-on consequences for China as well. Within China, the problems of economic expansion continue, not least the ongoing crisis of the state-owned enterprises (SOEs). Most make losses and there is a long tail that cannot be closed for social reasons more than economic. Private capital is understandably reluctant to take on the burden. The 1998 spy scandal in the United States highlighted the sensitivity of relations between the two countries. Enthusiasm for China has, for the time at least, diminished a little. Some pundits, journalists and economists question whether investing in China is worth the risk.

But it is not sensible to ignore China. Indeed, from a Western standpoint, it never has been. Since the days of the spice trade in the Middle Ages, trade between Western Europe on the one hand and China and Southeast Asia on the other has been vital to Western economic growth. Profits made from trade with the Orient helped kick-start the Industrial

Revolution. The search for trade routes to China led to the founding of empires. US independence followed an incident with Chinese tea in Boston harbour. The Americas themselves were 'discovered' and colonised by European seamen and traders whose first objective was to find a sea route to China. Like it or not, we are linked to China; and our general ignorance of the people and nation that have done so much to shape our own way of life is not to our credit.

Today, China is on the verge of becoming an economic superpower. Depending on how the figures are calculated, China may already be in the league of top ten nations in terms of gross national product. It has the world's largest population (1.2 billion, expected to peak at 1.6 billion around the middle of the twenty-first century). It is the third largest nation in terms of land mass (3.7 million m^2; 9.6 million km^2). When China finally does join the World Trade Organisation, which may be soon, it will be a major power in that organisation. When it makes its currency fully convertible, it will be able with justice to ask for membership of the G7 club of nations. Within two decades, barring disaster, China will be challenging Japan, the USA and Western Europe for global economic power. The giant is awake – and flexing its muscles.

China's development as a major player in the world economy is often compared with India's. China's population growth is under better control and India will probably become the most populous nation. China seems cursed by a boom–bust character relative to India, much as the PRC government tries to control it. By the time investment in China becomes an imperative, it is too late and one has to wait for the next cycle. Unfortunately, like London buses, all the opportunities arrive together and there's not another for ages.

So long as China's economy continues to grow in this fashion, there will be opportunities for individual businesses to make money. The passing of the overheated 'gold rush' days of the early 1990s is a good thing. There may be fewer quick profits to be made, but the prospects for firms that are able and willing to invest for the long term, build relationships and embed themselves in China have probably never been better.

Whilst China may become the world's dominant trading nation and economic powerhouse in the new century, that is far from certain. The last two decades have seen good and stable government but the period before included the disastrous Cultural Revolution. Whether the central government can retain effective and enlightened economic and other disciplines over the provinces and municipalities as well as the by-then privatised (not that the Chinese accept the term) commercial sectors remains to be seen. Two clouds on the horizon are corruption and inequitable wealth distribution.

Corruption affects many aspects of business in China, as it has since ancient times. We will return to that throughout the book. Foreigners have to be especially careful as some business people have the underlying idea that, as foreigners ripped off China in the past, they are now fair game. The wealth problem is still in the future but it seems likely that China will generate many mega-billionaires at the same time as most of the population continues to live near the bread-, or rice-, line. One only has to look at the US, Brazil and India for examples of economic development being accompanied by extremes of wealth distribution: the bigger the country, the wider the disparity. Compare Hongkong with Switzerland and one finds a similar disparity but not due to size. To what extent the relatively fatalistic social fabric will stand the strain, remains to be seen.

Two centuries ago, getting to China meant travelling in a cramped, uncomfortable ship and eating bad food for several months. Today, getting to China means travelling in a cramped, uncomfortable airline seat and eating bad food, but only for nine or ten hours. The question should not be, why China? but rather, is there any reason for *not* going to China?

The Overseas Chinese

There are fifty-five million ethnic Chinese outside mainland China, concentrated mainly in the countries of Southeast Asia including Malaysia, Indonesia, Thailand, Singapore, Taiwan, the Philippines, Vietnam, Cambodia, Laos and Burma. Other smaller communities exist around the world. Taken together, these *huaqiao* communities are a powerful economic force; were they a nation in their own right, their gross national product would be two-thirds that of Japan. In many of the countries which host them, they dominate the local economy, even though in every case except Taiwan, widely considered part of China anyway, and Singapore they are a minority ethnic group.

There are close ties between *huaqiao* communities in these different countries and, importantly, there are also close ties between them and the homeland, mainland China. The overseas Chinese have already played an important role in the economic growth of China since the reform process began, and despite the blip of the Asia crisis of 1997–8, they will continue to do so. Their contribution has included not only investment capital but management expertise, gathered in the often rough-and-tumble free markets of Southeast Asia during the decades when the Chinese were immured in the Maoist command economy system. Any look at business in China today must consider these vibrant, volatile, powerful communities and their sometimes uneasy relationship with the motherland.

The focus of this book is on the People's Republic of China, and throughout the book when we refer to 'China' we generally mean the PRC.

But we do refer regularly to the overseas Chinese, sometimes for comparison and sometimes for contrast. This book is *not* a detailed guide to doing business in Malaysia, Indonesia, Singapore *et al.* (although Chapter 9 gives an overview of these countries), but it does describe the affinities that the *huaqiao* communities have with China. Generally these take place on two levels:

1   Cultural; the residents of the Chinese mainland and the overseas Chinese communities continue to share a strong cultural bond, and despite different regulations, market conditions and so on, their ways of doing business remain fundamentally similar.
2   Business; particularly since economic reform began, but before that as well, overseas Chinese and their mainland cousins have done business together and made money together. Since reform, the overseas Chinese (including the Taiwanese) have been by far and away the largest investors in China, far outstripping the efforts of the USA, Europe, or even Japan.

Why another book on China?

As anyone studying or researching business in China will have realised, there are hundreds of books, and probably thousands of magazine and journal articles, in print. Does the world really need another book on China?

Indeed, there are a number of highly useful books, all of which illuminate some aspect of the problems of doing business in China. (In Chapter 1, we discuss some of the various types of recently published literature on China and make suggestions for further reading.) There are, for example, a number of 'road maps', books which help the first-time entrant to China figure out where to go and who to see when planning a first venture there. Likewise, there are books on etiquette and negotiation styles which explain some of the cultural hurdles to be crossed. Along with these are a few – far too few – memoirs by business people, telling what happened to them in their early years in China: *Beijing Jeep* (Mann 1989) and the excellent *Barefoot in the Boardroom* (Purves 1991) are examples. We need more of these tell-it-as-it-was accounts, especially as those above are a little dated. The large and often excellent body of academic work covers economics, organisational behaviour, corporate governance (joint ventures) and foreign trade. Very few, if any, deal with marketing, i.e. the basic business of making money.

There is also much that is of limited use. While few in the West really know China, that does not seem to restrict the number of opinions. Particularly in books on Chinese politics and in books by journalists, not to mention journalism in general, one can hear as one reads the sound of axes being ground. The Chinese mostly dislike these books, not because the facts are inaccurate but because they have been selected in ways they do not recognise. Fifty years ago, a group of British businessmen were proposing the first-ever trade mission to 'Red China'. The most senior was summoned by their Foreign Minister, Sir Anthony Eden, and advised not to take part. Sir Alfred Owen responded 'If you will take care of the politics, we will take care of the trade'.[1] We do not suggest that politics and trade are wholly divisible but the focus of this book is on the latter.

This book has two main aims. First, we want to take a broad view of doing business and managing organisations in China, bringing together the various accounts and surveys mentioned above. This approach is broad-based and holistic. Doing business in China, as indeed anywhere else, requires us to combine personal experience *and* macro-level knowledge. Personal experience, on subjects such as markets, negotiation styles, etiquette and so on, is necessary in the first instance, in order to deal with the people and things encountered in daily life in China. Personal knowledge helps us know *what* to do. Macro-level knowledge, on the other hand, provides depth to personal experience and explains *why* things happen and why particular responses may be more appropriate. As we shall see in the next few chapters in particular, macro-level knowledge is extremely important when doing business in China.

Following on from this, our second aim is to suggest particular areas where readers should focus attention. This is important: China is far too vast and complex a subject for there to be 'one big book about China' which tells you all you need to know. Chapter 1 discusses sources of knowledge about China, but if you are going to China to do business, even on a small scale, some sort of personal learning about the country and its inhabitants is essential.

What the business person needs to know

Some of the questions, which first-time business visitors to China ask, include:

- Where do I find information about China?
- How do I determine if there is a market for my firm's products/services in China?
- Where should I make my first point of entry?
- Do I need a Chinese business partner, or should I go it alone?
- If I decide I want a partner, how do I go about getting one?
- How do I deal with the language barrier?
- How do I market my products/services in China?
- How do I recruit staff in China?
- How will I personally adjust to living in China?

And these are some of the questions which *should* be asked:

* What will my Chinese business partners expect of me?
* What ethical issues might I encounter when doing business in China?
* Are there advantages to becoming involved in the overseas Chinese network, rather than going straight into China?
* When establishing a joint venture with a Chinese partner, what conditions should I insist on? Is it imperative that I retain control?
* How will I deal with various levels of government in China?
* How will I establish good relations with suppliers? with customers?
* Having recruited trained and skilled staff, how will I keep them?
* How should Western subsidiaries in China be structured? Can I expect my Chinese managers and staff to work to Western methods and principles?
* Why is my company going into China in the first place, and what does it hope to gain/expect to achieve?

We cannot anticipate every question and are well aware of the dangers of claiming any expertise for ourselves in matters Chinese. The more one learns about China, the less one actually seems to know. We do, however, claim the expertise of others. During the years that the London Business School course has run, and throughout the development of this book, many Chinese and Western students, academics and business people have contributed greatly. We are in their debt.

May we also claim your expertise? If you have a cautionary tale, or consider what we say to be misleading in any respect, please e-mail us at: *Tambler@lbs.ac.uk* or *wblock@centrenet.co.uk*. We would be glad to hear from you. Our students can only gain.

David Hall and Roger Ames (1998: 30–1), in a fine introduction to Chinese philosophy, note that the Chinese character *zhi*, which means 'knowledge' or 'wisdom', also has connotations of enjoyment. Knowledge and happiness in Chinese thinking are mutually dependent. This is probably true on a practical level as well. The more knowledgeable about China, the easier life becomes. Business decisions will become less stressful, and relationships with Chinese partners will become less tricky. Doing business in China becomes not only profitable but enjoyable. Achieving both profit and enjoyment in your China venture is success by anyone's standards.

Note

1   Timberlake, Percy (1994) *The Story of the Icebreakers in China*, London: The 48 Group Club.

Part I

1   The road to Cathay

it is certain that in the course of time, and at an increasing pace, China will tend to become industrialised. There is likely to be sustained demand for capital goods and, concurrently with it, a demand for consumer goods in which the emphasis will swing in the direction of high quality specialised products as China succeeds in producing more consumer goods for herself. ... In the course of time, a great and profitable trade can flow between our two countries.

Report on the UK Board of Trade Mission to China in 1946

There are few remarks concerning China of which the exact opposite cannot be said with equal truth. The fact is that 'China' and the 'Chinese' are words which embrace so vast a subject that any attempt to deliberate details inevitably obscures the main features of the subject ... China, like statistics, can be made to supply apparent proof for any preconceived notion.

(Stephen King-Hall, *Western Civilization and the Far East*, 1924)

The Board of Trade Report, produced just after the end of World War II in Asia but while Chiang Kai-shek and Mao Zedong were still slugging it out, was remarkably prophetic. It outlines a message for China hopefuls which is just as true more than fifty years later: be sure China wants you. This chapter looks at the first steps to China market entry. Topics covered include research before the first visit; options for visiting; finding business partners; using a staging post (i.e. making a first base in one of the other East or Southeast Asian countries); and the decision to enter.

Research before the first visit

Most businesses thinking of entering the China market already have one of the following:

- a product or service that they think would sell in China;
- a product or service that might be sourced from China;
- both of the above.

In other words, they are extending their current business. Strategically, the least risky option is to take a winning formula and roll it out into another market, adjusting to suit local conditions. It is unusual for a foreign entrepreneur to start his or her first business in China, although examples do exist. As one would expect, Chinese government at all levels and business are much more welcoming to those creating new exports for them than those seeking to enter their market. They are also more welcoming to those bringing goods of strategic value to China – high technology and infrastructure, for example – than consumer brands like drinks. For the purpose of this exposition, we adopt the most difficult case, market entry, leaving the reader to adapt the comments for sourcing. This book therefore assumes that an existing business is being expanded into the China market, but most of the ideas and information are relevant to China sourcing and new start-ups as well.

What sorts of research does the first-time business person need to do? The first thing most people think of is market research. Ideally, of course, when setting up a new business with the aim of selling in China, the manager would want to know things such as the likely demand for the firm's products and services, whether customers will pay the asking price, and whether they will do so more or less on time.

None of this can be discovered for China (or any other export market) by prior market research. It may be somewhat radical, but our view is that market research is largely useless in determining commercial opportunities – how much business there *will* be, or what people *will* buy and at what price. Research can establish *current facts*; it cannot provide hypothetical future data. Furthermore, as we will see in Chapter 7, market research and statistics are less reliable in China than, say, Europe or North America.

Contrary to popular belief, there is never a 'gap' in the market for a new product or service. Rather, good innovations create their own 'gaps'. Research will not provide an answer. If research shows that equivalent products or services already exist, the nay-sayers will tell you that the market is already satisfied. If the equivalent does *not* exist, then they will tell you there can be no demand. In principle China has a market for any good product, though intangible services are more difficult. There are, after all, more than 1.2 billion people in China; and while it is a dead certainty that not all of them will want your offering, some of them probably will. The questions are, how many, and where are they? And (this may be the killer) how much will they pay?

There are, of course, benefits in doing market research before deciding to launch or, better, the appropriate marketing mix for the launch. A snapshot of the present puts future knowledge into perspective. Nevertheless, there can be few, if any, situations which justify commissioning new market research before the first China visit. Good first impressions require the appearance of being knowledgeable but that can be gained from already published sources – Euromonitor, for example. We have met managers going to China, and even taking up expatriate postings, who have read nothing at all. That is not only foolish; it is rude to Chinese hosts.

First-time business visitors have this problem – they will discover most of what they need to know in China itself. Even if they had the time intensively to study before hand, their study will make little useful impression until they have confronted the reality. Yet no business person, Chinese or otherwise, wants to spend time educating a novice when they could be out making money for themselves.[1] Where is the balance? Apart from the visit arrangements, this or another introductory book, together with a quick review of published market information (see below), should be enough.

Given the competing demands on most people's time, there is always a problem of how much information is enough. If one is visiting the Isle of Man from Iowa, the locals would forgive a lack of grasp of the finer points of the Manx socio-economic situation. If one is visiting Northern Ireland, on the other hand, ignorance of the fundamental political situation could create very serious trouble. China is somewhere between these two extremes: ignorance is unlikely to lead to physical risk, but it will result in loss of face. As the largest country with the longest surviving civilisation, China is, from the perspective of most of its inhabitants, the centre of the universe.

Before the first visit, then, one should therefore achieve (1) a basic understanding of the sector markets in which one is interested, and (2) some general knowledge and an understanding of social sensibilities.

Market facts

Thirty years ago, getting market information for China was almost impossible; today, there is an embarrassment of data but not, unfortunately, of riches. Much of the information is unreliable and one soon learns to ask the same questions of many different people. Accurate statistics about China are notoriously hard to come by, and Chinese analysts will admit to 20 per cent or wider variances. Some see statistics as more of an art than a science: the figures are intended to paint a picture, not to be used exactly.

The problems of getting useful information from the World Wide Web (noted below) reflect a broader problem. Both China itself and the rest of the world publish more statistics about the Chinese economy and trade than anyone can assimilate. They may be out of date or even intentionally misleading. Disraeli famously remarked that there are lies, damned lies, and then there are statistics. Market research companies are now required to share their findings with the relevant ministry before they show them to clients. The reasoning is obscure, but the suspicion is that the authorities are sensitive to unfavourable findings.

Some places to start include (the examples given are from the UK and the USA, but similar sources are available in most countries and now also on the Web):[2]

- specialist information providers
- home government
- home embassy in China
- home-country professionals and businesses
- dedicated trade bodies
- Chinese embassies abroad
- Chinese businesses abroad
- The Web

Specialist information providers   These include businesses and organisations such as the Economist Intelligence Unit (EIU) and Euromonitor. These will provide a range of special reports and databases.[3] For instance, the EIU published a 'China connection series' with guides to the four main commercial regions in the autumn of 1994, though these like so many other published sources are now getting a little long in the tooth. Euromonitor's excellent Directory and Sourcebook are a 'must' for any company entering the market. Occasionally you will find these reports on the shelf or online at business schools or institutional libraries. Many of these organisations also have websites.

Home government   Most governments of countries that actively trade with China will provide information and assistance to exporters. In Britain, the Department of Trade and Industry (DTI) has established an Export Marketing Information Centre with databanks, terminals and staff to help.[4] They provide 'Hints to Exporters Visiting' for most major countries, including China, for around £8 each. The DTI will also advise on any subsidies available for smaller firms wishing to export to China.[5] The US Department of Commerce offers similar facilities, as do trade ministries in most Western countries. The Great Britain China Centre has a free comprehensive library, and other countries maintain similar resources.

Home embassy in China   One of the jobs of embassies abroad is to help their government's nationals make contacts and establish relationships with clients and partners. Some embassies are better at this than others. The US Embassy in Beijing has an extensive commercial section, though the current level of political tension between China and the USA needs to be considered. The British Embassy in Peking (as they continue to call it; they do not call Rome 'Roma' either) has since the 1980s been proactive and helpful. Again, the current political situation may have a bearing.

Home-country professionals and businesses   This category includes banks, lawyers, accountants and consultants, including both specialist 'China' consultancies like Clifford Chance and A.T. Kearney and international firms with a presence in China like Andersen Consulting, Price Waterhouse Coopers and Ernst & Young. How much information they will provide before the meter starts making expensive noises depends on your existing and potential relationship with them. Many of the larger firms (including Clifford Chance, A.T. Kearney, Andersen Consulting and PWC) publish useful reports on business in China, available free or for a small fee. Many of these firms also have excellent websites.

These organisations are also valuable in that they tend to have, on staff or as advisers, people with considerable personal experience of China. Reading about China is one thing: hearing about it from someone who has already 'seen it and done it' is another. For a small fee or sometimes even just the cost of a good lunch, you can learn a lot in a short time. Finally, all the major organisations and many of the smaller ones have representative offices in China, which can usefully provide further information and make introductions during the visit.

Dedicated trade bodies   These include both government-sponsored groups such as the US-China Business Council and the China-Britain Business Council (CBBC, previously called the 'China-Britain Trade Group'), and private bodies such as the American Chamber of Commerce in China. These have many of the advantages of the firms we noted above, except their fees tend to be lower. The CBBC, for example, has a compact but comprehensive library (for members), of books, journals, magazines, trade reports and cuttings. Its principal function is to promote British trade through connecting Chinese and British business partners, and to this end it organises business trips to China and helps act as a *hongniang* (go-between) to match British and Chinese firms. Other similar bodies exist in most Western European countries. The reciprocal to these Western bodies is The China Council for the Promotion of International Trade (CCPIT) which is primarily interested in exporting from China, not those wishing to sell goods there.

Chinese embassies abroad   The Chinese Embassy is basically there to deal with the host government, not individual businesses, and still less individual managers. In particular cases, through contacts perhaps, information may be provided. Their subsidiary units may be helpful if the enquiry happens to strike a chord with a current Chinese need. The initial approach may need a contact who can arrange introductions to the right people.

Chinese businesses abroad   Once upon a time, the Bank of China and other Chinese businesses abroad, such as import–export corporations, were all affiliated to the relevant government ministries. Under the old system, all imports and exports flowed through them, or at least the paperwork did. Today, the ties to government have been loosened and business deals are done either through Hongkong or Taiwan, or, increasingly, directly with the West. Some have established their own representatives in major markets such as the UK and the USA. Again, a personal introduction is advisable; but if you can make your first direct Chinese contacts before you go, so much the better.

The Web   The virtual anarchy which we know and love as the Internet provides some good sites with up-to-date information. For every one such site there are 99 containing rubbish, out-of-date or incorrect statistics, short and fairly useless 'overviews', and rants by various groups of cranks. Squarely in the latter category falls the otherwise useful site put up by the Central Intelligence Agency, whose overviews of the political and economic situation in China nearly always conclude (with a note of wistful hope) that China is doomed.

Some of the organisations noted above, such as the EIU and Euromonitor, have very good websites with useful macro- and micro-level information. The University of Vienna has a useful website with a large number of links to business and economic sources concerning China. *Asia Business Journal* also has a good site, though downloading can sometimes be tricky. Hongkong University also has many useful links.

Websites come and websites go, but at time of writing, some of the most useful sources for businesses are www.business-china.com, www.chinesebusinessworld.com and www.net-trade.com; the latter has a large Far East business directory. The *South China Morning Post*'s business pages can be found at www.scmp.com, and useful information can sometimes be gained from *China Daily* on www.chinadaily.com. The Ministry of Foreign Trade and Economic Co-operation (MOFTEC) maintains a website at www.moftec.gov.cn.

What facts should be available from the above sources? The size of the market perhaps, the extent to which products sold in it are domestic or imported, and if the latter, which countries are exporting to China. With luck, you may discover which companies now lead the market, which competitors are already in China, and how long they have been there. You may also discover which parts of China have been penetrated by the competition. This can be useful, as China is a big place: presence in Guangdong may not inhibit any first-mover advantage in other provinces. Success or failure in one place may not indicate success or failure in another Chinese market.

A favourite topic of many China hands concerns the number of 'markets' there are in China, given the geographical and cultural diversity of the country. While a province-by-province separation is convenient and used by Chinese domestic marketers, even these groupings are so large as to allow many 'markets' to exist within them (see Chapter 2 for more on this). Any cake ultimately divides into as many pieces as you care to cut it into. Realistically, each product has to consider the market characteristics necessary for its own situation (number of consumers, spending power per consumer, extent of competition, likely pricing and costs) in order to assess the minimum size of an entry market. From this starting point, one can then move to consider how many conurbations or other regions in China have the required characteristics, that is, how many markets there are for that product. Then one can start choosing target markets, although with care, and keeping options open. The short answer is that your market should be dictated by the resources available: the fewer the resources the smaller the territory. No matter how clear a picture you may think you have, reality may differ once you are on the ground.

What is less likely to be available? Information about consumers, retailers, pricing, packaging, distribution, availability, promotions and advertising are all unlikely to be found in your home country except in very general terms, unless you are able to network through to market research firms with China offices (see Chapter 7 for more on market research in China). Otherwise, you will need to visit China to see the situation for yourself.

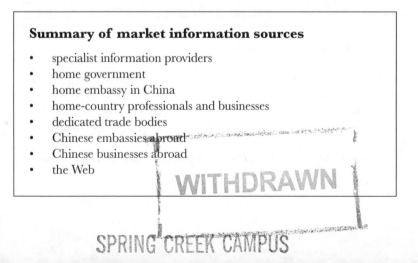

Summary of market information sources

- specialist information providers
- home government
- home embassy in China
- home-country professionals and businesses
- dedicated trade bodies
- Chinese embassies abroad
- Chinese businesses abroad
- the Web

General knowledge and sensibilities

Chinese hosts would prefer (but do not necessarily expect) the visitor to have some knowledge of:

- geography, recent history and economic reform;
- culture and etiquette, notably on matters of the table;
- power, i.e. who is who in organisations, governments and ministries, as distinct from politics.

Readers of international media will find regular briefings on the overall political and socio-economic situation hard to avoid, but these should be treated with care. The Western press irritates the Chinese, and so media coverage provides a good list of topics to avoid. This does not just refer to government and Communist Party officials; as noted above, many ordinary Chinese find Western reportage of events in China biased. This particularly applies to Western press coverage of issues such as human rights, where many Chinese believe the Western media is particularly hypocritical (see Chapter 2 on Chinese attitudes to the West).[6]

Up-to-date geographies of China are hard to find, and many are fairly technical geography textbooks; but even out-of-date works will give information about land forms, climate and so on, should you need to know them.[7] Basic geographies can be found in many of the best short histories of China.[8] More detailed geographical information is available in Baedeker, which provides details including population and climate for every province, city and town of any size in China.

Edwin Moise's *Modern China: A History* provides an excellent summary of recent history, while Charles Hucker's *China to 1850: A Short History* covers imperial China succinctly and intelligently (but he uses Wade-Giles rather than pinyin spellings). We also suggest Ray Huang's *A Macro History of China*. Apart from these, good overview histories are hard to come by.

Five books to choose from

With enough time to spare, the following will give a flavour of the past:

Jonathan Spence, *God's Chinese Son*. Fascinating account of the Taiping rebellion that almost destroyed China in the nineteenth century.

T.H. White, *In Search of History*. White had close personal contact

---

with Mao Zedong, Zhou Enlai and the other leaders of the
Communist revolution.
Sterling Seagrave, *The Soong Dynasty*. History of a remarkable family
whose members, between them, helped shape the history of twen-
tieth-century China and Taiwan.
Robert van Gulik, *The Chinese Lake Murders*. Fiction set in the Song
dynasty, immaculately researched, full of a sense of time and place,
and more fun than Pearl S. Buck.
Cao Xueqin, *Dream of the Red Chamber*. The classic Chinese novel of
all time, the tale of a wealthy Suzhou family's slide into decay and
decline.

Economic reform seems to be another subject on which *everyone* in the West
has an opinion. In Chapter 2 we provide a very brief summary of the
reform programme to date, and browsing among the works listed in the
bibliography will provide more detail. One problem is that, given the pace
of reform, even the best books tend to be out of date by the time they hit
the bookshelves. This is especially true of central changes: Zhu Rongji cut
50 per cent of the headcount of PRC government ministries within a few
weeks of assuming office as prime minister. On the other hand, though,
there may be months or years between a reform measure being announced
in Beijing and implementation in the provinces.

Food plays an important role in Chinese culture, and it is probably
worth acquiring some familiarity with it. No restaurants in any Chinatown
will prepare the visitor for food in China though they will provide some
idea of the regional variation. They will also help provide dexterity with
chopsticks, worth acquiring if weight loss during the first visit is to be
minimised.

A lot is written and said by Westerners about alcohol consumption,
particularly the practice of repeated toasts during and after a meal. We
suggest that the more macho views on this subject can be treated with
scepticism. Teetotallers will not be forced to drink, if they simply make
their position clear, politely, from the outset. No one will think any the less
of them.

Finally, a health warning: briefings and books like this one usually
provide long lists stating how much executives must learn before visiting
China, to the point of inducing total paralysis. There can never be enough
time in a busy manager's schedule to learn all this stuff before departing.
(In fact, having fallen into the same trap, we then removed most of our
own suggestions while this book was in draft.) There is no need to be over-

prepared. Natural courtesy will nearly always suffice. More important is to be friendly, to be alert, and above all, to keep an open mind.

If time is short, just browse this book and any of the better tourist guides, such as *Lonely Planet*, which cover the essentials.

Options for visiting

Broadly, there are five types of first visits:

*   trade missions, led by Chambers of Commerce, trade bodies or trade associations;
*   co-operative missions, with perhaps from three to five people from different companies sharing costs;
*   fairs, exhibitions and trade shows;
*   bought-in expertise;
*   individual.

Trade missions

These are a specialism of the dedicated trade bodies we discussed above. They offer several advantages, including both the opportunity to network like-minded businesses from your own country, and access to a wider variety of Chinese contacts than might otherwise be possible. Costs will be lower and may well be subsidised by your own government. Most of the hassle involved in setting up meetings, accommodation and travel is taken care of by the sponsoring body. More importantly, tuition about China is, in effect, provided as one goes along.

Missions have an advantage in that Chinese hosts prefer groups to individuals, though this is becoming less true. An official delegation has a reassuring cohesion and substantive image, particularly if the sponsoring body has good relationships and reputation. Groups tend to have established seniority rankings and go-betweens. This enables the hosts to understand who is who within the group context, and make judgements as to which members are most valuable.

Less good is that time may have to be given to activities and subjects one might rather avoid. As groups are becoming more regional and specialised, keeping distance from direct competitors (welcomed by China of course) increases. A group always travels more slowly than an individual. This will partly depend on the balance of initiative and interest on the Chinese and UK sides. Missions may be organised by trade sector or geographic destination(s). To minimise these problems, schedules are generally tailor-made. In the UK, the China-Britain Business Council usually meets with companies joining a trade mission for a couple of hours, well before the mission departs for China. The company's entry strategy is discussed (and perhaps challenged), and then personal appointments are made in line with that. The group travels together and meets up in the evenings, but each individual may pursue his/her own agenda.

A trade mission might best be treated more as a reconnaissance than with the expectation of finding the right partner, still less finalising a deal. On the other hand, as the mission sponsor's local offices organise the local arrangements, sensitive briefing can help line up reasonable prospects. Trade missions are usually only a first step, but they can help open doors and establish relationships which will bloom in the future.

It is no bad thing to treat these missions as opportunities for people watching, as distinct from business finding. Try to develop the 'golden eye', the origins of which expression lie in the ancient story of the Monkey King. In essence, the golden eye allows you to distinguish real people from ghosts. Most bureaucracies in any country are filled with 'ghosts'. Of the huge number you will meet on a mission, only some will be 'real' and only some of those may become friends and partners. The ability to use the golden eye is far more likely to determine market entry success than any economic analysis.

As the focus moves from bureaucracies to market trading, group missions are becoming less important.

Co-operative missions

Co-operative missions are similar to trade missions but are more tailored. This means less time spent on boring activities but, probably, less access to top officials. It is unlikely that you will know compatible businesses wanting to visit China at the same time, but there are consultants who will put interested business together and help with the administration. Some of these specialise in working with smaller firms, and will generally do their best to help keep costs down.

Fairs, exhibitions and trade shows

Fairs and exhibitions are the modern equivalent of the markets along the silk road of Marco Polo's day. Handled skilfully, they are not just places to exchange goods or services for money but centres of information and the beginnings of friendships. They can also go horribly wrong; there are plenty of tales of sitting in a cavernous hall for a week, surrounded by people who don't want to know, with nothing to fill in the time except calculate how much this experience is costing. However, a little advance spadework can avoid this fate. As one tactic, consider organising a reception (perhaps jointly to spread costs) for other compatible exhibitors and potential customers. Send out personal invitations ahead of time, using local business directories; telephone first to try to learn personal names, rather than just inviting 'The Marketing Director'. A formal personal invitation card is highly regarded. Guests will also be favourably impressed if the attention they get on arrival is personal, intensive and enjoyable for them. It should be like an invitation to one's own home.

Companies planning an exhibition in China should always ensure that the exhibition organiser has the right links with the relevant Chinese authorities and that the show has been endorsed at the right (high) level.

In more high-tech sectors, the technical seminar has replaced the fair. Travel is simplified since, in theory, the customers come to you. Government agencies may be able to help defray some of the costs in these cases, as most Western governments are keen to support anything connected with high-tech. Another advantage of technical seminars is the involvement of the ubiquitous Chinese research institutes. These bodies are a bridge between Chinese industry and academia, and provide much of the leading thinking for Chinese commerce. Here, a successful approach in making contacts may be to stress knowledge transfer rather than commerce; this approach is more likely to succeed in getting the more senior and/or more technical brains of the institute to attend. Of course, the potential downside is that one may end up transferring knowledge without generating business for oneself.

The Guangzhou Trade Fair is the grandfather of them all and also the largest, with over 5,000 exhibitors. Many other regional or sector-specific trade fairs have sprung up since the mid-1980s (organisations like Euromonitor provide lists of these, and some also advertise directly on the World Wide Web). Fairs can be extremely good ways of getting one's foot in the door but, as with trade missions, they do not necessarily result in immediate business.

An associated concept, not really a trade fair, is to participate in or host 'technical' lectures to explain how the products are made, tested and used. There is an insatiable thirst for knowledge, especially anything which can be seen as technology transfer.

Bought-in (or borrowed) expertise

Many larger firms prefer to buy, either directly or indirectly, the expertise they need in order to gain entry. They may prefer to avoid official and semi-official events and visits for a number of reasons. Bespoke tours may be better targeted and more relevant to the company's needs; they will probably also be more enjoyable. They are almost certainly a better use of time, but they are also likely to be the most expensive option. Bespoke visits and tours can be arranged through:

- consultants, either the major international firms or small China specialists, depending on preference;
- overseas Chinese entrepreneurs with whom contact is already established;
- organisations such as the China-Britain Business Council and others previously mentioned;
- existing businesses in Greater China contacted similarly.

This is the classic Chinese method, using one's existing network to effect new introductions; in other words, developing or using *guànxì* (relationships).[9] In many circumstances, it is the best solution. Certainly it applies the local system to the local market. However, the hazards are those of any networking solution: the intermediaries may only pass on what they want you to know. Wang's brother in Chengdu is not necessarily the best wholesaler in Chengdu. Objectivity and independence may be hard to achieve. Once the contacts have been made, it may be too late to consider alternatives. Therefore, it is very important to find the right intermediary in the first place.

Selecting the right mode of introduction largely depends on the quality, integrity and relevance of the intermediary, and the cost. McKinsey is not cheap, but then a Hongkong Mr Five Per Cent, a 'bag company' (an entrepreneur whose only asset is his brief case) may ultimately cost more. The expertise and contacts displayed by a sole consultant may be brilliant; they may also be ephemeral or substantive. Again, as a newcomer, it can be very difficult to tell. There is much to be said for joining forces with a compatible business, if you can find one.

The networking approach is potentially the best, but it is also potentially the worst. Getting the right partner from the start can lead to a dream relationship; getting the wrong one can land you in a nightmare of which there are all too many examples. Get to know potential partners well before agreeing anything substantive, still less signing anything; homework on partners is *much* more important than homework on the market. Good partners will keep the new entrant out of trouble and bad ones will land them in it, whatever the state of the market. We discuss this further in Chapters 4 and 5.

Individual

Small firms will not generally be able to buy or borrow expertise described above. However, there is nothing to stop anyone getting on a plane and going.

Solo travel in China is getting easier, and if all you want to do is to go and look around, a tourist visa (depending on where you come from) is the best and cheapest option. Most Western travel companies have relationships with private Chinese agents. If all else fails, the state-owned China International Travel Service will book packages and organise tourist visas. Solo travellers can also contact consultancies or organisations like the China-Britain Business Council whose local offices will, for a fee, organise a translator and a schedule of meetings with their contacts.

For business visits, an official 'host' is still needed for visa purposes. You will need the host in China to issue a letter of invitation, which must accompany your visa application. Be warned that, while you are in China, the government will regard the host company or organisation as responsible for you. If the host is genuinely interested in your mission and provides substantive help, life then becomes much easier.

Finding a host to invite you, though, can sometimes be an adventure in its own right. One of the problems is that, unless one has been properly introduced by suitable intermediaries, one often does not exist in the minds of Chinese companies. Someone answering a ringing phone in a Chinese office will not necessarily feel any obligation to pass on a message or do a favour for an unknown voice. Letters, messages and faxes are unlikely to get any response unless contact has already been initiated. To complicate life, a letter/fax about a future event may not be deemed worth a response until immediately before that event. Silence probably means 'no'; but it may also mean that a reply is not yet necessary.

If introductions can be made from the home country and if appointments have been confirmed, then the individual visit may prove the most direct (and the most cost-effective) mode of entry. Certainly it is the most flexible. China's better hotels now meet all of a solo business person's needs, and transport is fairly easy. Be warned that appointments need to be reconfirmed once on Chinese soil: one materialises from being a foreign 'ghost' only in stages.

Finding business partners

It should be obvious by now that some sort of partnership arrangement is essential in the first instance. As we will discuss later in the book, business in China functions primarily on a relationship basis, whether we are talking about customers, suppliers, joint venture partners or even local government officials.

What about finding a partner before going to China? As we have seen, desk research and coming up with lists of potential contacts is easy; it is much harder to get a foot in the door so as to actually discuss business with them. Make use of go-betweens wherever possible, such as the China-Britain Business Council or other organisations described above. They have the local knowledge, reputation and *guànxì* to be taken seriously, whereas the visitor is just a ghost.

Ultimately, though, the job has to be done in the field. The first meetings with go-betweens, hosts and other contacts may not yield anything more than a few names. Track these down, using existing relationships to build new ones. Exploit the system: contacts lead to contacts. This will take time, and it will be hard work, but a few days in China will equate to several weeks of research at home. With these new relationships, depth matters more than quantity.

Staging post v. direct entry

One common question is whether to go directly into China, or whether to set up a 'staging post' in another country in the region or in the Hongkong SAR (Special Autonomous Region), and then use this as a base for expansion into China itself at a later date. In the 1980s and into the early 1990s the indirect option was popular, but more recently firms have tended to go directly into China, even in some cases using China as a base for expansion into other parts of East and Southeast Asia.

In part, the decision depends on the firm's future goals and present situation. Which markets matter most and which are most immediate? These are not the same question. If small, quick paybacks are crucial, China will be riskier than other parts of Asia. It would be a mistake to neglect the large and potentially lucrative populations and markets of Taiwan, Malaysia and Thailand, or even the somewhat more difficult cases like Indonesia and the Philippines. When considering potential markets and market requirements as above, these should be put into the mix as well, along with the potential for growth and expansion. Largely, though, this decision is a strategic one, and it needs to be taken with an eye to the longer term.

Firms with existing bases in the region, especially Hongkong and Taiwan, will be tempted to expand into China or other countries from there. They may be right to do so: costs are incremental, existing staff will already have contacts, communication will be easier, distances are less and the administration is already in place.

But there are also problems with this strategy:

- Individual staging posts are usually closely linked to one particular area of China (for example, Hongkong with Guangdong). Too close a tie with one region can obscure vision of the others.
- Mainland Chinese usually prefer to deal direct with American or European firms rather than with their regional branches. China is important; being routed via a branch office rather than dealing directly with headquarters is unflattering.
- Taiwanese, Hongkong and Singaporean, to name but three, are unpopular in PRC and are seen by some Chinese as untrustworthy, arrogant and stupid [!] respectively. These stereotypes are of course ridiculous, but they do affect perceptions and need to be borne in mind.
- The communications channel between headquarters and the China office acquires an extra link. This can lead to inefficiency and confusion.
- There may be conflicts of interest with existing businesses and clients.

Neither option is wholly right or wholly wrong. Certainly where an offshore office already exists, for cost reasons it makes sense for the regional office to do some of the research and preliminary groundwork. The principal contacts, however, tend to be better made directly between the head office and China itself. The decision and the implementation can both be very sensitive on a number of levels, including external politics and internal sensitivities within the firm, particularly if the firm employs a number of Chinese managers and staff. Tread carefully.

Sino Infrastructure

As an encouraging example of diving straight into the deep end, here is what one young man with a brand new MBA achieved straight off the reel.

In 1994, Geoff Mills was preparing to create a new infrastructure development business in China. On the one side, there were many British engineering and building companies and consultancies looking for work in China. On the Chinese side, infrastructure development was welcomed, provided finance could be arranged at a minimal cost. There was some dissatisfaction in the UK construction industry with the Chinese 'opportunity'. Since the advent of the open-door policy, most of the big firms had been involved in tendering, yet most of the contracts were still going to Chinese firms.

After researching the British firms involved, Mills thought he could put together an arrangement which would aid British firms in tendering. However, he faced two principal problems. British firms would only enter into a partnership with him if there was evidence of the arrangement including Chinese customers. The latter, in turn, were interested but would only come on board if British firms were already committed.

Mills needed a partner in China to help him link the two together. He was fortunate in having a well-connected friend in Hongkong who was able to advise him on options. These were:

- team up with a trading company such as Jardine Matheson;
- team up with Chinese contractors in hopes of getting these to establish partnerships with their British rivals;
- team up with 'design institutes', Chinese government offices that oversaw the technical design of projects once project approval had been given;
- team up with the People's Liberation Army, then a powerful and growing commercial force.

Mills himself had no China background, little or no Chinese, and few contacts outside Hongkong. What he had was an idea which he knew would work. Through patience and persistence, he was able to establish links with some of the important design institutes. These, in turn, gave the venture the seal of approval which persuaded both Chinese clients and British contractors to come aboard. Mills's main problem now is how to manage expansion.

The decision to enter

The decision to enter the China market should not be made on the basis of one visit. At best, this visit will introduce key people and increase your stock of knowledge about the country. Leads need following up with further visits. Expect to make three visits before deciding whether China market entry is feasible or desirable. If one visit is all that can be risked, then do not go at all.[10] This is not wasting time; it is building relationships. Deciding *before* understanding the calibre of relationships, however effective that may seem, is unwise. That said, if some non-committing orders can be filled, so much the better.

Establishing a base in China is not to be done overnight. It takes time to build relationships with clients, partners and others with whom mutual trust can grow. Trust is not an on/off switch. The Chinese use small matters (punctuality, for example) to test commitment. As the tests get bigger and are satisfactorily met, trust grows. The visitor's behaviour and actions on almost every level will be scrutinised by Chinese hosts in an attempt to determine trustworthiness. If suitable relationships are proving elusive, one should consider pulling back and rethinking one's approach. What is putting out the bad vibes? Get help from a Chinese expert.

First encounters with China may be more discouraging than motivating. Sometimes the reverse applies: the welcome mat conceals traps. First impressions in China tend to be even more misleading than usual; after all, this is a culture that itself distrusts first impressions. As one colleague has commented,

> In China, you need to check, check and double check everything. If you think everything is going okay, the chances are that you have been misinformed or disinformed ... humility is vital – without being a soft touch – a delicate balancing act indeed.

Last of all, a programme of visits needs a clear and realistic set of desired outcomes. Colleagues need a shared view of the minimum conditions for entry; in other words, what results constitute 'go' and 'no go'. Benchmarks for a visit make it possible to assess whether it has been successful. On the other hand, serendipity must be given a chance. One Western firm went to China to sell cheese-making equipment (optimistic, in a non-cheese-eating society), and came back with orders for a bean curd plant, which turned out to require similar equipment. Amazing things turn up if one is alert to them. Be prepared to seize chances as they come.

China is the largest and most difficult market a business can enter. If it is not also the most difficult decision, you are either very lucky, or you may be missing something. Too often in the past, the latter has been the case. The last two decades are full of tales of firms that thought they had a lucrative business deal in China sewn up, only for the whole thing to evaporate almost before the wheels of their planes had touched the ground back home.

Are we being unduly pessimistic? No: this is realism. The decision to enter the China is fraught with risk. However, there are ways and means of laying off that risk. Success is never guaranteed, but should be more likely with the following:

- Do homework before the visit; not market data and macro-economic conditions, so much as researching contacts. Cultural and historical reading is good but limited by time.
- Work out in advance where to go, and what to achieve.

- Pick a suitable visit type, whether as part of a trade mission or larger group, or as a solo venture.
- Trivial as they may seem, worry about the diplomatic niceties. Pack samples, literature and small gifts. Your contacts will want to take something tangible from your meetings. Get your business cards ('name cards') printed on the back in Chinese – PRC Chinese, not the traditional characters still used by overseas Chinese. Take a whole box.
- Be prepared for the process to take time. Don't commit without being as certain as possible about your partners.

Inevitably, many of the details in a book like this will prove ephemeral. Names and facts change fast. At the more fundamental level, though, China does not change at all. The success of market entry depends far more on harmonising these fundamental understandings and values than any passing knowledge of current affairs.

Entering overseas Chinese markets

With some provisos, given the differing political, economic and social conditions in their host countries, much of what was said above applies also to the overseas Chinese business communities elsewhere in East Asia. Although some of these communities are hundreds of years old, all still have much in common with Chinese culture, often more than with their host culture. Conditions for the foreigner can be comparatively easy or comparatively hard, depending on the country. For British and American business people, for example, Malaysia, Singapore and the Philippines offer a greater chance of English being spoken and understood by potential contacts. This can help in the initial stages, though the comments we make later in the book about the importance of translation will still apply here.

Decisions about pre-market analysis and point of entry apply elsewhere in Southeast Asia just as noted above. (Note we are talking here about dealing with the Chinese business communities in these countries only; dealings with *bumiputra* Malay or Javanese Indonesian businesses require a different set of cultural assumptions.) So too does the importance of having at least some background knowledge before you go. Finally, we would stress the importance of developing partnerships in the local community. These are still Chinese cultures, and the emphasis on relationships is at least as strong – indeed, in some cases much stronger – than in the PRC.

Notes

1 See Chapter 7 for more on market research in China.
2 For a longer list of UK organisations which can offer advice and assistance, see Porter and Robinson 1994. De Keijzer 1994 does the same for the USA. Be warned that both of these are getting a little dated; confirm contact details before trying the suggested organisations.
3 It is warned that prices can vary from organisation to organisation; some of these can be quite expensive.
4 The address is Room 134, Kingsgate House, 66–74 Victoria Street, London SW1E 6SW.
5 We are informed that the quality of the advice varies, but it is worth exploring.
6 Everyone has a right to their own opinions on contentious issues such as human rights. We simply urge caution when it comes to when and where you express these views. It is perfectly possible that an injudicious opinion will offend your hosts even if they are broadly in agreement with you. Remember the American saying, 'My country right or wrong'; it applies in China as well.
7 Shabad 1972 is an example.
8 Hucker 1978; Moise 1994.
9 This is an important concept, developed in more detail in Chapter 4 but referred to throughout the book.
10 This advice is more didactic than realistic: China is never so determinist. Luck may strike first time. A Chinese importer may approach the exporter's home office in the first place, saving the immediate need to travel and search. We are not suggesting you won't get lucky; we are suggesting you be prepared for a long haul.

2 Through a glass darkly

China from a Western perspective

To regard a nation's mentality as a fixed monolith is to run counter to the truth that variety is the law of nature.

(Zhou Lisheng in *Westerners Through Chinese Eyes*)

No matter how much is read about China[1] ultimately one has to go there. But on arrival, China is too vast to comprehend. Many of the sights and experiences are too unfamiliar to make sense. Inevitably this brings us back to the books to make sense of it all. In visiting the China offices of expatriates, look at their bookshelves. Those without books on China will not be staying long. Personal experience and macro-level knowledge are complementary; one needs the other. The best learning blends personal experience and the researches and experiences of others in a single mix.

We will return to what is *essential* at the end of the chapter, but for the moment, let us assume the basics outlined in the last chapter. The Chinese, as we said, are justly proud of their long history and great culture, and expect foreigners to respect these things. Here we amplify:

- the *geography* of China (where things are);
- the *history* of China (*why* things are);
- the *ethnic make-up* of China (who the Chinese are);
- the *culture* of China, with reference to particularly important points such as language, food, literature and the arts;
- the current government of China and the *political situation*;
- the Chinese *economy* and its future prospects;
- Chinese *attitudes* to the West (both official and unofficial).

Geography

China's contrasts are nowhere more visible than on the map. Virtually every extreme of terrain is present, from the rich coastal plains of the east to the barren mountains and deserts of the west. Contrary to our usual image of a teeming, crowded China, mountains and deserts predominate; much of China is a barely populated wilderness, and only about 13 per cent of its vast surface is arable land.

Geographers, economists and others seeking to segment China have approached the task in different ways. Geographers have tended to divide the country into three from north to south: north China includes the valley of the Huang He (Yellow) River and the north China plain, 'central China' is centred on the valley of the Chang Jiang (Yangtze) River and the coastal provinces around Shanghai; and 'south China', mainly mountainous but with a rich coastal plain, stretches from Guangzhou (Canton) to the Gulf of Tonkin and the Vietnamese border.

Economists also favour a tripartite division, but from east to west. First there is the relatively rich coastal region, which had the first Special Economic Zones (SEZs) and the greatest amount of foreign direct investment; then there is the central zone, which has been slower to develop but is now receiving attention, especially around cities like Wuhan; then there is the west, including Sichuan, which has received comparatively little investment, and the wilderness regions of Tibet and Xinjiang. The major differences between these regions concern things such as economic output and per capita income, both of which tend to be higher in the east than the west. (Though by 1999, 29 of the 31 provinces and municipalities had investment zones (now called 'ETDZ'), averaging about six each. The divisions are beginning to break down.)

Both these divisions have their utility, but for the first-time business person they can still be a bit daunting. After all, we are dealing with a country any one of whose provinces is the equivalent to a fair-sized European state; Sichuan has a population equivalent to France and Italy combined, or all of the states of the USA west of the Mississippi and south of New York combined.

The following breakdown might be more useful. It divides the country a little more exactly by region, with the divisions reflecting some economic and culture distinctions as well. We dwell on this at some length, as there are no good up-to-date geographies of China on the market at the moment. In our scheme, there are twelve distinct regions:

1   **The north**, including Beijing and Tianjin cities and Hebei, Shandong and part of Henan provinces. Population: *c.* 250 million. This is the second most densely populated area of China and contains several major cities (including the capital), much rich agricultural land and a lot of heavy and light industry. The climate is temperate, though winters can be cold and harsh.

2   **The Huang He valley** and the north-west, including Shanxi, Shaanxi and part of Henan provinces, the eastern part of Gansu province and the Ningxia autonomous region. Population: *c.* 138 million. This is the ancient heartland of China, including in its bounds the 'yellow earth' country where the first Chinese civilisation emerged. The western part of this area has some minority Turkish ethnic groups, and Ningxia is home to a large proportion of China's Hui (Moslem) people. Climate consists of cold harsh winters and hot dry summers.

3   **The east coast**, including the city of Shanghai – China's largest – and Jiangsu and northern Zheijiang provinces. Population: *c.* 132 million. This is the most densely populated area of the country, with some of the richest agricultural land particularly in the delta of the Chang Jiang (Yangtze) River. Apart from Shanghai there are also a number of large urban manufacturing centres, including Nanjing, Wuxi, Suzhou and Hangzhou. The cities are growing rapidly, encroaching on the agricultural land as they do so. Climate is generally moderate, though winters can be very wet.

4   **The Dongting Hu and the lower Chiang Jiang valley**, including Anhui, Hubei, Jiangxi and Hunan provinces. Population: *c.* 156 million people. This again is rich agricultural land studded with industrial centres, the largest of which is Wuhan. This area was largely overlooked in the first wave of economic growth, but is now receiving increasing levels of investment. The climate is comparatively moderate.

5   **The upper Chang Jiang**, including the province of Sichuan. Population: *c.* 130 million. Cut off from the lower valley by the Dabla Shan mountains, Sichuan was once rich and prosperous but has fallen behind in recent years. Current Chinese government efforts are targeted at reviving Sichuan's economy. Sichuan has a distinctive sub-culture, history and cuisine of its own.

6   **The southeast coast**, including Fujian and southern Zhejiang. Population: *c.* 58 million. This heavily mountainous region faces the sea, and until fairly recently was almost entirely dependent on shipping and fishing. It too has its own regional sub-culture. Some of the first SEZs were located here, giving a considerable boost to the local economy. Parts of the region are also heavily militarised as Taiwan continues to occupy several islands just offshore.

7   **The far south**, including Guangdong and Hainan provinces and the eastern part of the Guangxi autonomous region. Population: *c.* 110 million. This area, almost cut off from the rest of China by the Nan Shan (Southern Mountains) is sometimes referred to collectively as Lingnan (South of the Mountains). Population densities are much

lower than in the north. The economy is booming, thanks in large part to the presence of Hongkong and some early SEZs like Shenzhen, Shantou and Hainan. Guangdong is the centre of the Yue (Cantonese) language region and has its own sub-culture and cuisine. Guangxi is the home of the Zhuang ethnic group. The climate is sub-tropical with heavy rains in the monsoon season.

8   **The far southwest**, including western Guangxi and the provinces of Guizhou and Yunnan. Population: *c.* 104 million. This region is very mountainous, ranging from the lower mountains along the Vietnamese border south of Nanning to the high ranges bordering on Tibet to the west. Timber and mining are major industries but agriculture is also important in the deep valleys around Guiyang and Kunming. The area has considerable strategic importance in Chinese military planning. The population includes about fifty different ethnic groups. The climate is sub-tropical in the valleys, harsh in the high mountains.

9   **Manchuria** (the northeast), including Liaoning, Jilin and Heilongjiang, provinces. Population: *c.* 124 million. An industrial powerhouse, Manchuria has China's largest oilfields and a number of major manufacturing centres including Harbin, Jilin, Changchun, Shenyang, Fushun, Anshan and Dalian. The Manchu and Han Chinese ethnic groups are effectively intermingled, but there are Mongolian groups in the west and several hundred thousand Russians, descended from White Russian refugees, around Harbin; these retain their own language, restaurants and even vodka distilleries. The climate is harsh and cold in winter, dry in summer.

10   **Mongolia**, encompassed by the Nei Mongol autonomous region. Population: *c.* 22 million people. The major centre is the capital, Hohhot; elsewhere, there are scattered towns and mining, but most of the area is given over to pastoral herding much as it has always been. There is a Han Chinese majority, most of whom are comparatively recent emigrants; the rest are of Mongol descent. Hot dry summers give way to bitterly cold winters.

11   **Turkestan**, as the West still sometimes calls it, including most of Qinghai and Gansu provinces and the Xinjiang Uigur autonomous region. Population: *c.* 45 million. As in Mongolia, the majority of the population are now Han Chinese, but these are concentrated in cities such as Urumqi. The rural population are largely Turkish. Much of this vast area is almost entirely uninhabited, such as the Tarim Basin and the Takla Makan desert. Again, the climate ranges from hot dry summers to cold hard winters.

12   **Tibet**, including the Xizang autonomous region and part of Qinghai province. Population: *c.* 3 million. High, mountains, bleak and largely

uninhabited. Tibet has its own culture and history, and was largely independent until occupied by China in the 1950s; its status continues to be the subject of dispute and protest both inside Tibet and out.

That, briefly and with much generalising, is China in physical terms. The major conclusion is that China is far from being a unified, monolithic whole. There are vast differences in terms of geography, climate, culture and economy between its regions.

Any one of the regions above could possibly make a useful entry point for China; all of them have markets large enough for most companies' needs, at least initially. The question is, which one do you choose?

If these divisions are too complicated, trying the following very quick segmentation:

1   **The Beijing region**. Highly populous and relatively well-off, the centre of political power. People are considered rather dull by other Chinese.

2   **The Shanghai region**. Very populous, rich and proud of it. Motto: 'In Shanghai we make the money, in Beijing they spend it.'

3   **The Guangdong region**. Southern, with different language and different attitudes; considered rather brash and loud by other Chinese. Includes the first SEZs, and a long track record of foreign investment.

4   **The Wuhan region**. The central heartland around the lower Chang Jiang valley, well-populated and industralised, looking forward to catching up to the better-off coastal regions.

5   **The west**. Sichuan, distinctive with its mouldering high-tech industries, sub-tropical climate and fiery cooking. Populous and eager to reap the benefits of economic reform.

6   **Manchuria**. Often overlooked by Western investors, but rich in raw resources and industry.

7   **The rest**. The highlands, mountains and deserts, often empty and desolate, but with some large population centres; many non-Chinese ethnic groups inhabit these regions.

History

A 'concise history of China' is almost an oxymoron, but there are few useful ones to be found in bookshops and on library shelves; we recommended a few in Chapter 1. Most textbooks divide Chinese history into periods determined largely by the ruling dynasty, and the display box below gives a brief resumé of these, with some notes for those too busy to read more deeply. They are, of course, artificial divisions imposed by later historians, but they are widely accepted and do give an easy framework for getting to grips with the vastness of Chinese history.

Western business people are notoriously reluctant to study history, usually citing some version of Henry Ford's dictum that 'history is bunk' (with pleasing irony, Ford himself has now become a major historical figure) and maintaining that the past is not relevant to the needs of modern managers and businesses. Even if this were true, China represents a special case. In China, history is very important indeed, and it is taken seriously by almost everyone. Even more than the need to understand how China became what it is today, the Westerner needs to recognise what historian W.F. Jenner calls 'the tyranny of history', the powerful influence of the past on the Chinese national psyche. The Chinese remember their history well, and react to it.[2]

This point cannot be emphasised too strongly. In China, history is important if only for the reason that *the Chinese themselves believe it is*. Recognising this is key to understanding China.

Chinese history in a nutshell

- Ancient period. Chinese civilisation was established along the Yellow River; the legendary king Huangdi (Yellow Emperor) probably flourished around the 25th century BC.
- Xian dynasty, *c.* 21–*c.*16th BC. The first Chinese state of note.
- Shang dynasty, *c.*16–11th BC. Bronze working and horse-drawn chariots were introduced.
- Western Zhou dynasty, *c.* 11th century–770 BC. This is the era of the fabled sage-kings of ancient China who so influenced Confucius, King Wen and the Duke of Zhou. This period laid the groundwork for much of later Chinese culture and society.
- Spring and Autumn period, 770–481 BC. This period saw China politically divided but culturally rich, with many competing artistic and philosophical schools. Confucius, Mengzi

---

(Mencius), Laozi (Lao Tzu) and Xunzi (Guan Tzu) were all active, and many classics of Chinese literature date from this time.

- Warring States period, 403–221 BC. The rich and powerful states of north China fought each other for supremacy almost continuously for two centuries. The master strategist Sunzi (Sun Tzu) was active in this period.

- Qin dynasty, 221–207 BC. The civil wars ended with the unification of China by its first true emperor, the powerful Qin Shi Huangdi, who suppressed dissent, reformed society, expanded imperial rule into southern China and began works such as the Great Wall. He has been described by some historians as a bloodthirsty tyrant, but modern China still shows many influences of his rule.

- Western Han dynasty 206 BC–24 AD. Qin's heirs were not able to keep the throne, and the strong monarch of the Han dynasty consolidated the empire. This was a period of economic prosperity and cultural greatness.

- Eastern Han dynasty, 25–220. After the brief usurpation of Wang Mang, the Han resumed their rule, but their power was much weakened. Ultimately the empire slid into chaos and broke apart.

- Three Kingdoms period, 220–265. As in the earlier Warring States period, the country was fragmented and several states fought each other for control.

- Jin dynasty, 265–420. China was briefly reunited under the dynasty of Western Jin (265–316) before breaking apart again under Eastern Jin dynasty.

- Southern and Northern dynasties, 420–589. Several emperors built their dynasties, but could not last. China was fragmented, with much conflict and many smaller states attempting to break away.

- Sui dynasty, 581–618. This dynasty reunited China, but collapsed when the Emperor Wen was defeated by the Koreans and the Turks.

- Tang dynasty, 618–907. Picking up the pieces after the Sui, the Tang dynasty restored order and its emperors expanded China's power and prestige.

- Five dynasties and Ten Kingdoms 907–979. When the Tang dynasty collapsed, China fragmented into more warring states. Foreign invaders, mainly Turkish and Mongol tribes from the north, increased the pressure.

continued

- Song dynasty, 960–1279. The Song were able to reunite China for a time, but the pressure from the northern invaders was becoming intense, and the Jurchen tribe ultimately drove the Song into the south in 1127. China was divided once more.
- Yuan dynasty, 1271–1368. Kubilai Khan's Mongols conquered all of China and united it. This was actually a time of some prosperity, with China opened up to foreign trade.
- Ming dynasty, 1368–1644. After the Mongol empire disintegrated, the Ming dynasty took control and swiftly reunited China. Culturally and economically, China reached a high level during the Ming dynasty.
- Qing dynasty, 1644–1911. The Ming dynasty gradually decayed and was replaced by the Manchu tribes from the northeast, who conquered all of China in a series of military campaigns lasting about twenty years. The first Manchu emperors, Kangzi and his grandson Qianlong, were great figures who between them ruled China for 135 years (1661–1796). Kangzi was a warrior and conqueror, and under his rule China reached its greatest extent, occupying its ancient enemies in Mongolia, Turkestan and Tibet. (The Tibetans were singled out as they had been allies of the Mongols and remained implacable enemies of China.) Qianglong was poet, artist and builder; in Beijing, many of the buildings in the Forbidden City and the Bei Hai park were built to his direction.

After the fall of the empire:

- Republic of China, 1912–1949. Established by Sun Yat-Sen, it quickly collapsed into feuding provinces ruled by warlords, until Chiang Kai-Shek was able to impose a form of unity in the late 1920s. The Japanese invasion (1933–45) then tore much of the country apart. After the success of the Communist Revolution of 1949, the government of the Republic of China went into exile on Taiwan.
- People's Republic of China, 1949–. Established by Mao Zedong and the victorious Communists in 1949, the PRC has undergone many changes, including the Cultural Revolution of the 1960s and 1970s, and the economic reform process which began in 1978.

Beyond the bare framework of names and dates, however, there are some powerful themes in Chinese history, which are still alive today and which do have an indirect and often a direct bearing on the business environment. The following aspects of Chinese history should form essential parts of the business person's body of macro-knowledge.

The integrity of China

Many Chinese, probably the majority, believe implicitly in the territorial integrity of China. They are often rather hazier about where the boundaries should be drawn. The Han heartland of north China has been the core of Chinese political entities for millennia, but the south and especially the southwest, with its large non-Han populations, entered the Chinese fold only later. Other areas, such as Manchuria, Taiwan, Tibet and the Turkish far west, only became attached to China in the last five hundred years. Still other areas once under Chinese rule, like Vietnam, are independent today. Where, then, should the boundaries of China lie? This is a subject for some debate among China's political leaders, and a source of concern in some quarters in the West, especially the USA. It is important to remember that the PRC's claims to, for example, Taiwan are meant seriously and are part of an emotional attachment that many Chinese feel to the integrity of their homeland. Sabre rattling from the West will not change this view over the long term.

The threat from the outside world

Textbooks on business, politics or economics in China seldom miss a chance to point out that many Chinese dislike and mistrust foreigners, referring to them as 'barbarians' or 'foreign devils'. This point is often overstated. In fact, throughout Chinese history there has been a continuous interchange with the outside world in which not only goods but ideas were imported and found a place in some part of Chinese society. In former centuries, Buddhism, Christianity and Islam were imported in this way. In the nineteenth century, critical Chinese saw the weakness of their country, and concluded that its best strategy was to learn from the West and became more like it (a view reinforced by the success of Japan, which did exactly this). The revolution that toppled the Qing dynasty was motivated by the desire of its leaders to make China more 'Western', and the Communists too recognised the need for contact with the West; it was Mao who opined that China should learn from the West, apply that knowledge which seemed relevant to the Chinese situation, and discard the rest. Even during the height of the Cultural Revolution many Western companies were trading quietly with China.

Setting aside specific examples of distrust (the present Chinese government probably distrusts the US government at least as much as the latter does the former, for example), the major concern of most Chinese is not the presence of foreigners, but the impact they may have on Chinese culture and society. It is important to recognise that China's views of the outside world have been formed over centuries of often unhappy history. In the early centuries, China's primary external contacts were with Turkish, Mongol and Tibetan nomad raiders from the north and west and Japanese pirates to the east. These forces brought disorder and chaos; at times, the invaders even occupied China and ruled it. In fact, for more than half of the last thousand years, part or all of China has been ruled by a foreign power. The Manchus of the Qing dynasty adopted much of Chinese culture but remained a distinct ethnic group who controlled nearly all the political power in the country; in 1912 with the fall of the empire, there were massacres of Manchus in the south, where local Chinese took revenge for two and half centuries of foreign oppression.

More recently, contacts with the West have often been equally unhappy. The Ming dynasty restricted foreign traders to a narrow point of entry around Guangzhou, where they had to do business with local middlemen; this state of affairs lasted until a combination of opium and modern artillery blasted open the doors of China in the 1830s, and the Western nations began to impose their authority. The damage opium did to Chinese society in the nineteenth century has never been properly assessed, but the memory of the opium trade remains vivid today. The Westerners also spread ideas, which could be just as dangerous as drugs. In the 1850s Hong Xiuquan, a young Hakka man from the south who had just failed his civil service exams, had a nervous breakdown and became convinced that he was the younger brother of the Christian God. Armed with a partial Chinese translation of the Old Testament and a series of prophetic visions, he began converting his fellows. The result was the Taiping Rebellion (1853–60), which laid waste to central China and cost at least twenty million lives.

In this century, foreign meddling in China has occurred; US and other Western backing for Chiang Kai-Shek and the Guomindang was bitterly resented by many Chinese, and then came the Japanese invasion with its immense destruction and loss of life. The Rape of Nanking, which may have resulted in as many as 100,000 deaths, was but the best-publicised of many such incidents.

And yet, the foreigner going to China is nearly always treated hospitably and with great politeness. Surely the question should be, not, why do the Chinese distrust foreigners, but why after the last thousand years are they willing to speak to us at all? The simple answer usually given is that we have things that China wants, such as investment capital and technology; this is true, of course, but is far from being the whole picture.

The Chinese do not hate or fear foreigners. They are, from bitter experience, wary of the influence that foreigners bring. Contact with the outside world can bring instability and chaos, two things that most Chinese fear most of all.

The fear of chaos

China is (we'll say it again) vast and complex, but it is also fragile. The economy was, and to a large extent still is, dependent on agriculture. Foreign invasion, internal unrest and natural disaster can easily disrupt the agrarian economy, and when they did in the past, the result was disaster. At the end of the Han dynasty period, the population of China was about 60 million. By the end of the wars of the Three Kingdoms period, sixty years later, the population had fallen by one half. By the time the Ming dynasty took power, fourteen centuries later, the population was still only 60 million; all the natural increase had been swallowed up in the bloody cycle of war, invasion, earthquake and flood. Small wonder that in classical Chinese thought, heaven is populated by a celestial bureaucracy which attempts to maintain order and keep out the demons who bring chaos.

Order is a primary social and political goal in China; it may even be the most important goal. Government policy on the economy, the reform of state enterprises, the welfare system and many other areas can look inconsistent and changeable, until you realise this simple truth: one of the government's chief policy goals is the promotion of stability. The economic reform programme began with this in mind, and economic growth and diversification continue to be focused on this. No organisation – least of all a foreign business – whose activities seriously threaten stability will be tolerated for long.

The authority of the state

To defend against chaos, on earth as in heaven, China has erected formidable government and administrative structures. The Qin emperor, bringing order and unity to China after the chaos of the Warring States period, set the pattern followed by every ruler of China since, including the Communists: a strong, authoritarian administration and bureaucracy, pyramidal in structure, with the emperor himself at its head. In Neo-Confucian thinking (see Chapter 3), the state had a structure similar to that of the family; the emperor/father owed a duty of care to his subjects, who in turn owed him unquestioning obedience. Only through this mutual bond could order be maintained.

With some modifications, this theory has stood the test of time. Incoming dynasties, or in this century, the Communist Party, usually assumed power with a great deal of moral credit, as they were perceived to be able to clean up corruption, unite the country, oust foreign invaders and so on. Over time, of course, people start to become more cynical about their rulers and the bonds grow weaker. But criticism of rulers in China almost never means that people want to change the system by which they are governed; what they usually want is the same system but a change of ruler. Sun Yat-Sen got this badly wrong in 1912 when he tried to replace the empire with a republic; the experiment lasted just a year before authoritarian rule returned under Yuan Shikai and then Chiang Kai-Shek. Today, some Western observers interpret growing criticism of the Communist Party in China as a desire for democracy. This seems unlikely; what the average Chinese wants is a strong, honest leader who will guarantee stability, peace and prosperity.

The just revolutionary

Paradoxically, despite the fear of chaos and desire for stability, Chinese history is full of revolutionary movements and secret societies, from the Red Eyebrows rebel movement which overthrew the usurper Wang Mang and restored the Han dynasty in the first century AD, to the Buddhist-influenced White Lotus Society which rebelled repeatedly against the Qing in the eighteenth century. As dynasties grow weaker, such groups proliferate; the end of the nineteenth century saw hundreds of such groups springing up around China, the most famous of whom were the Boxers.

With very few exceptions – such as the special case of the Taiping, which was a religious movement apparently seeking radical change – these movements were all conservative. They did not want to change the system; they wanted to remove rulers who were perceived to be incapable of ruling. Most had roots in ancient philosophical movements such as Buddhism, Daoism and Confucian thought. There are strong similarities in ideology/theology, at least, between the White Lotus Society and the Falun Gong, a sect banned in China in mid-1999.

The most successful of the 'just revolutionaries' were, of course, the Communists. Their programme did include a radical revision of the structures by which China was governed and ruled, and they were quick to distinguish their form of authoritarian rule from that of the empire. Nevertheless, their goals were largely the same as earlier movements; to restore stability and stop the forces of anarchy. The same motivation can be glimpsed behind Deng's economic reforms.

The presence of these movements serves to remind us that although stability is desired in China, it cannot always be guaranteed. Any weakening of central power is nearly always accompanied by local unrest, the purpose of which is usually, and paradoxically, to restore order.

---

10 key figures in Chinese history

1   Duke of Zhou. The ancient sage-king of China, widely referred to by Confucius as a fount of moral authority.

2   Confucius. The greatest philosopher of the East, he constructed a moral and social system which continues to serve as the foundation for Chinese society.

3   Qin Shi Huangdi. The first true emperor of China, he founded the Chinese bureaucracy and established its long-lasting system of government.

4   Zhuge Liang. A counsellor in one of the warring states of the Three Kingdoms era, he has become a legend for his cunning strategy and statecraft harnessed to a strong moral purpose and sense of the duties of the state.

5   Zhu Xi. One of the greatest of the later philosophers, his Neo-Confucian synthesis of earlier thought was the basis of the moral and political regeneration of China by the Tang and then the Ming, and remains the basis of modern Chinese philosophy and education.

6   Qianlong. Probably the last truly great Chinese emperor, a warrior, poet and builder, who received the first British embassy to China in 1798.

7   Cixi. Imperial concubine and later dowager empress who held China together after the Taiping Rebellion and in the face of Western invasions and internal unrest. Her death was the signal for the empire to collapse.

8   Sun Yat-Sen. Chinese Christian, married to a Chinese-American wife, he admired the West and attempted to make China into a republic. Many of his followers in the Guomindang movement were descendants of Taiping rebels.

9   Mao Zedong. The most important figure in modern China, founder of the Chinese Communist Party and leader of it until his death in 1976. He established the modern Chinese state.

continued

10   Deng Xiaoping. Mao's successor and architect of the economic reforms that begin in 1979. He has been demonised by many in the West as an authoritarian and repressive ruler. On the other hand, in China his economic reforms have lifted half a billion people out of poverty. How will history judge him?

Ethnicity and language

China is dominated by the Han ethnic group, both culturally and in terms of numbers, but the country is by no means homogeneous. There are dozens of distinctive ethnic groups. Most are dispersed around the periphery of the country, though there are exceptions such as the Hakka, who still live in central and southern China. The Hakka may be descendants of the original inhabitants of south China before the Han conquest.

Another group worth mentioning are Hui, a generic name for Chinese Moslems (as distinct from the Moslem Turkish population of Xinjiang). Most of the 3–4 million ethnic Chinese Moslems live in the Ningxia autonomous region, but there are several hundred thousand living in their own district in southwest Beijing (you know you have entered the Moslem quarter when the butchers shops begin displaying beef instead of pork in their windows). Huo Da's novel *The Jade King* is an excellent introduction to the lives of the Beijing Moslems.

Ethnicity in China expresses itself most obviously in terms of language. There are 205 living languages in China, more than in Europe. Mandarin, or more correctly Pudtonghua ('the people's language'), has been the standard dialect of Beijing and lower Huang He regions since the Manchu conquest. It was adopted in the late nineteenth century as the *lingua franca* for the administration and the elite. Hu, spoken in Shanghai and the eastern regions, and Yue, commonly known as Cantonese and spoken in the south, are very widely spoken, but Minbei (spoken in Fujian), Xiang, Gan and Hakka are also common in some regions. Taiwan also has its own language, Minnan (a variant of Minbei), and most overseas Chinese communities speak either Minbei or Yue. Some of these languages have more in common than others. There is considerable difference between Mandarin with its four tones and Yue/Cantonese with six tones; the difference has been described as greater than that between Spanish and French.

There have been attempts to standardise spoken language. In the imperial period, *wenyen*, a very formal and ornate spoken language directly related to the written language, was used by bureaucrats and scholars, but was unintelligible to ordinary Chinese. Late in the nineteenth century *wenyen* was abandoned in favour of *baihua*, literally 'plain speech', and it was at this point that Mandarin was adopted as the *guoyu*, or national language. The use of Mandarin as a standard language was continued under the Guomindang and the Communists, and it is spoken by nearly all well-educated people. According to *China Daily* (7 September 1999), Pudtonghua is now spoken by 80 per cent of people in the major cities. However, it remains a second language for a large percentage of the population.

All this refers only to spoken language. In terms of *written* language, all Chinese use almost the same characters. Thus a Pudtonghua-speaker and a Yue-speaker may not be able to understand what each other is saying, but they can communicate in writing. This has obvious implications for business, particularly in areas such as advertising.

Culture

The Han Chinese culture is an ancient one, and nearly all Chinese, including many who are not themselves of Han ethnic descent, are extremely proud of it. Unlike in the West, where we see our history as marked by distinctive breaks – the fall of Rome, the Protestant Reformation, the American Declaration of Independence – the Chinese see their history as a continuous process, disrupted but never entirely interrupted by foreign occupation and conquest. The emphasis on stability means that some things such as styles of art and architecture have evolved only slowly over thousands of years.

China has a scientific, artistic and literary tradition that is as old as its civilisation. Bronze working, carving of jade and ivory, silk weaving and embroidery, painting and calligraphy go back at least as far as the Zhou era, and possibly further. Chinese literary traditions span three thousand years, from the ancient classics such as the *Yijing*, the *Daodejing*, the *Analects* of Confucius, the *Spring and Autumn Annals* and the works of Sunzi, through to the great poets and novelists of the past millennium. Luo Guanzhong's *The Three Kingdoms* (fourteenth century) is an epic tale of the fragmentation of China after the fall of the Han dynasty, focusing on the heroic figure of counsellor Zhuge Liang. *Flowers in the Mirror*, by Li Ruzhen (nineteenth century) is a satire which compares to *Gulliver's Travels*. Most famous of all, the *Dream of the Red Chamber* by Cao Xueqin in the seventeenth century recounts how a great family falls into decay and declines in fortune. The book has remained popular since its inception – in the late nineteenth century, Cixi had several rooms in the Forbidden City decorated with scenes from it – if for no other reason than that its story has been seen as a metaphor for China's own woes.

The Chinese, or at least those in mainland China, tend to think of all Chinese, including the *huaqiao* (overseas Chinese), as being part of the same cultural family. Feelings among the *huaqiao* themselves are a little more mixed, but the majority in East and South Asia, at least, feel a strong kinship with the Chinese of the PRC, even if they may have no wish to be politically associated with it.

Yet again, reinforcing the point above, Chinese culture itself is by no means monolithic. There are regional differences, not only in the various ethnic groups but among the Han themselves. The regions are very proud of their distinctive styles of cuisine, different attitudes to life, different regional histories and so on. Different regions are perceived differently; Guangzhou people are thought of as stylish, outgoing, sometimes brash; Beijing people are perceived as sometimes dull and lacking in sense of humour; Shanghai people are perceived as being industrious and hard-working. These perceptions are about as accurate as similar stereotypes anywhere in the world: the point is, they exist. And they may say as much about the beholders as the observed.

Even managers have to eat

Food is an important part of Chinese culture, so much so that cuisine is sometimes called the ninth art. Eight traditional styles of Chinese cuisine survive, each named after its home region:

- Shandong: from the northeast, this style features seafood and emphasises stir-frying and deep-frying.
- Guangdong: this style, popular in the West, emphasises fresh ingredients and rapid cooking to seal in the flavours.
- Sichuan: this complex style uses many different pungent spices, and can be very hot.
- Jiangsu: the cooking of the Shanghai region, it emphasises salty and sweet flavours, with many stocks, sauces and thick soups.
- Zhejiang: this style features seafood and is noted for its slow-cooked stews.
- Hunan: this style also features slow cooking, stewing or steaming, with food often heavily spiced.
- Anhui: this style uses plenty of oil when cooking, and deep fried and heavy sauces feature.
- Fujian: this style features seafood and often marinates dishes in wine to achieve sour-sweet flavours.

Aficionados of cuisine point out that although Beijing does have a tradition of cooking in the Imperial Court style, it does not have a style of cuisine of its own. This is strenuously denied by Beijing people.

Government and political situation

Since 1949, China has been a one-party state, governed by the Communist Party of China. The central government is in Beijing, but under it there are twenty-three provinces, four self-governing municipalities and five autonomous regions (Guangxi, Nei Mongol, Ningxia, Xinjiang Uygur and Xizang (Tibet)) directly under the central government and one special administrative region (Hongkong). Guangxi and Ningxia were created out of former provinces in 1958, around two major ethnic groups, the Chuang (Zhuang) and the Hui, or Chinese Moslems. Below the level of the provinces there are more tiers of government, at county, township and village level in rural areas and city, district and neighbourhood levels in cities.

This organisation is largely the same as it has been for centuries. At the level of the provinces, there was a bit of cutting and pasting in the 1950s and 1960s: Chinese-majority areas of Mongolia were added to the Manchurian provinces, and several old provinces in the heartland were abolished. Otherwise, the hierarchy of administration is much as it has always been.

Before 1911, China was ruled centrally from its capital (most recently Beijing) by the emperor, whose will was done by the civil service bureaucracy which effectively ran China. The bureaucracy was selected through competitive examinations which were reasonably democratic, though as has been pointed out, only the wealthier families could afford the education needed to pass the exams. Only about 1 in every 2 million Chinese succeeded in joining the ranks of the bureaucracy. The short-lived republic of Sun Yat-Sen attempted to create a Western-style government, but this collapsed in the era of warlordism. Chiang Kai-Shek ran his portions of China any way he could; the Guomindang did establish a bureaucracy, but it was notoriously inefficient and even more notoriously corrupt.

The Communists swept to power, like virtually every revolutionary movement in China before them, promising to restore order, which meant effective government and administration. By and large, they did so. Most unbiased studies of China after 1949 have concluded that, except for short periods of time such as during the Cultural Revolution, China has been well run. The things that have been important to the Chinese people – peace, safety in their own homes, freedom from crime and, more recently, economic prosperity – have for the most part been delivered.

The economic reform movement has necessarily set in train events that have loosened the ties between the people and the state. Opening up the labour market, for example, has meant greater freedom of movement. The agricultural reforms of 1978 leased farmland to the farmers. The centrally planning system has been gradually replaced by market mechanisms. There were fears from the outset that these freedoms would create the potential for disorder. Certainly there are problems in China today, such as homelessness and rising crime, which were not noticeable two decades ago; these are often blamed on the growing populations of migrant workers in the large cities, rural people who have come to the cities in the hopes of making more money. Increasing economic inequalities are also partly responsible for greater labour unrest; according to some reports, there are around 100,000 industrial disputes in China each year, and a few turn violent. Finally, corruption, though far from universal (and well below the levels found in some Asian countries) is on the increase.

Despite these and other signs, which many Chinese do find deeply worrying, there is at present no great call for the present system to be over-turned. In part, this is due to a fear that any alternative system of government might well be worse. Older Chinese remember the Guomindang era, World War II and the Cultural Revolution, and are willing to pay almost any price to retain stability. And, almost everyone can see across the border into Russia, and the dire consequences of a hasty and ill-thought through reform programme. The Chinese have chosen to reform slowly and cautiously, and it is hard to blame them.

Some observers have claimed that the Chinese are fundamentally disin-terested in politics. This may be true in part; there is none of the passion for politics that one finds in daily life in Italy or France, for example. To this extent the Chinese may be more like Americans, in that most prefer that politics does not intrude itself into their daily lives and that politicians leave them in peace. This does not mean, however, that the Chinese are incapable of taking an interest in politics; indeed, Mao was able to politi-cise the Chinese, especially the rural population, very effectively in the years leading up to the revolution. As Chinese history, both imperial and more recent, shows, the Chinese expect certain things of their rulers, and when the latter fail to deliver, they are more than capable of setting them aside.

Will this happen? Privately, many Chinese believe political reform will come ultimately on the back of economic reform; for example, the legisla-tive body, the National Peoples Congress, which formerly did little beyond rubber-stamping measures introduced by the executive arm of government, is now showing signs of wanting to consider and debate them. Any such change, though, is likely to be very slow. Today's government prefers to stress continuity.

Economy

> It doesn't matter if the cat is black or white, so long as it catches mice.
>
> (Deng Xiaoping)

Most books on China devote large sections, even whole chapters, to the Chinese economy. We do not, for three basic reasons:

1   there are already plenty of sources on this subject, and for those who desperately want to know, statistics on the gross industrial output of Anhui province can almost certainly be found somewhere on the Internet, if not in print;
2   a lot of economic forecasting concerning China is little more than guess-work, and even Chinese economists will cheerfully tell you that the margin of error in their figures could be anything up to 10 per cent;
3   in a country and economy the size of China's, macro-economic data are of only limited use for the business person.

This is in no way meant to be offensive to economists (indeed, some of our best friends are economists), but for the business person with limited time to research China, we caution against spending too much of that time trying to figure out what the Chinese economy has done/is doing/will do. Macro-economic data *are* useful in terms of identifying trends, and it is well to keep an eye on things like the inflation figures, especially locally. Really, though, the Chinese economy can be summed up as follows:

* it is big
* it is getting bigger.

The main, and perhaps only, business person's interest in the economic situation is the price, or inflation, and demand relationship. At the time of writing (late 1999) both are stagnating and that has profound consequences for investment and marketing. Media prices, for example, may even drop in 2000 after years of rapid growth but that is driven more by decreasing demand than increasing supply. Five years ago, inflation was the big danger; today it is deflation, with falling prices and consumer demand, but five years hence it will more than likely be inflation once more.

The Maoist approach to economic management was to plan *everything*. Setting quotas and measuring production allowed state planners to allocate resources with a view to matching food production with population requirements. Industrial investment was planned in exacting detail, with resources often dictated by the requirements of military strategy. Key industries were often dispersed over many provinces, so that, should some provinces be overrun by an invader, China would still have an industrial capability. The railway network was rebuilt with a view to moving troops and material quickly from one threatened frontier to another.

Again, by and large, this system worked. China experienced rapid economic growth in the 1950s and early 1960s, faltering during the Great Leap Forward, and then going backwards during the Cultural Revolution disaster; but that was ideological, not economic. However, there were problems. Fast though food production increased, it could not keep pace with the rising population, and by the early 1970s China was importing food. Food could only be paid for if China had something to export, but many of its traditional export industries such as textiles were in dire need of modernisation. Also, largely isolated as it was from the West, China did not have access to much of the technology that its industry and its army needed.

By the end of the Cultural Revolution it had become apparent to many of China's leaders and planners that the planned economy was increasingly unable to meet the needs of the state. So, quite pragmatically, the decision was taken to experiment with market reforms, initially in the tightly defined Special Economic Zones along the coast, then in the coastal areas more generally, and finally on a nationwide basis. It was quickly seen that the market system could deliver more than the centrally planned system. Almost immediately after land reform gave the farmers ownership of their fields and the right to sell their crops for cash, agricultural output doubled. Private industrial enterprises were soon seen to be far more efficient and productive than most (state) firms, and the open door policy allowed foreign investment and technology to provide a further stimulus to the economy.

Deng's statement quoted at the head of this section is often cited as evidence that he was a pragmatist rather than an ideologue. Well aware of the dangers inherent in the free market, he was convinced that the benefits outweighed the risks. (In similar vein, when asked about the prospect of foreign business influences leading to corruption, Deng responded, 'When one opens the door, one must expect that a few flies will get in.')

The important thing for the business person is this: China's long-term goals have not really changed. The aim is still to create a strong, self-sufficient, prosperous, independent state. The free market is encouraged because it delivers these things. If it were to show signs of failing to do so, or if the costs were start to outweigh the benefits, China's leaders would likely dump the free market as unceremoniously as they dumped the planned economy. The problems, as noted in the introduction, are corruption and the disparity in incomes. New Socialism in China faces the same ideological compromises as New Labour in Britain.

Over the short term, the government of China faces a number of problems. How it deals with these will impact directly on the business environment.

The problem of managing growth   There should have been little doubt that the slackening of controls on foreign investment and internal entrepreneurship would lead to economic growth; that was after all the plan. But the Chinese government was badly wrong-footed by the rapid growth of 1993 and 1994, and now admits that it may have moved too fast. Rigid controls to slow down the overheating of the economy worked, although on the reverse side of the coin they put off some foreign investors. Then came the Asia crisis, and the economy started to slow faster than expected. At the same time, increasing unemployment was reducing consumer confidence. Now, urgent attempts to reflate are underway. The Chinese have discovered that economic management in free markets is largely crisis management. Getting the economy on an even keel is difficult, and will likely become more so.

The problem of regulation   This is one of the biggest problems facing foreign businesses. The Chinese government wishes to keep control of the pace of economic reform, to ensure that there is no corresponding social breakdown or unrest. Foreign companies investing in China wish to earn profits. Not surprisingly, the two objectives collide on a regular basis. Equally unsurprisingly, the Chinese authorities use regulation as the principal tool to control the economy. On a single day in 1996, over 140 joint ventures were abruptly terminated by the authorities in the city of Tianjin, for a variety of reasons ranging from lack of profitability, incompatibility between partners and fraud. Increasingly, China's regulations are coming into conflict with those of other countries. China is attempting to harmonise, but this too is a slow and difficult process.

The problem of reforming state industries   Economic planning in Mao's China involved the centralisation and concentration of many industries. Ball bearings were concentrated in the Nei Mongol, while defence industries went to Sichuan. Most of these heavy industries were designed to produce goods for internal consumption only. Most were also hopelessly inefficient. The remaining industrial sectors, those depending on agriculture, remain as affected as ever by the vagaries of the weather. Of the heavy and light industries, there were in 1990 over 11,000 large and medium state enterprises in China. Of these, about 5,000 have now closed or merged. Most of the remaining 6,000 are white elephants. Total state sector output is growing by only 2–3 per cent (against 70–80 per cent output growth from joint ventures and the private sector), and at least 50 per cent of the state companies businesses are operating at a loss; many are probably technically insolvent. Many owe large sums to each other; most are critically short of working capital. See Table 2.1 for a history of the evolution of SOE reform.

As part of the 1998 state reforms, Premier Zhu identified 512 state-owned enterprises (SOEs) as being potentially world class. The rest will pass into local or private ownership or close (bankruptcy) but this may take a long time. Some quite ingenious debt-for-equity swaps are being arranged for those with positive cash flows and modern management.

One of Britain's ministries (DfID), in yet another triumph of hope over experience, has volunteered (1999) to sort out two of these SOEs, at Britain's expense, to show China how to do it. Cognoscenti in both countries are observing this experiment with some amusement. Time may prove the DfID right and it should be seen as part of China's wider plan to retrain SOE managers in best modern practices, preferably at other people's expense. Some of the leading business schools, e.g. Peking University, have special MBA programmes for SOE managers. In September 1996, Rolls-Royce led a consortium of British businesses to create the China-Britain Industrial Consortium (CBIC). Three years on this has developed five training programmes and is looking for new members with the enticement of expanding their *guànxì* with SOEs (*China-Britain Trade Review*, August 1999, p. 17). The five are:

- Annual prestige seminar on e.g. change management.
- Three-week course in UK divided equally between Cranfield School of Management, the City of London and visiting consortium companies.
- MBA and similar scholarships.
- Three- to six-month placements in UK companies for middle managers.
- Experts from consortium members act as week-long consultants on specific problems in SOEs.

Needless to say, the PRC government would like to see this scheme expanded.

China's social security system (if there is one) is simply not able to cope with large numbers of unemployed. In 1994 and again in 1999, reformers backed away from full-scale closure of ailing state enterprises for this reason. There remain, the State Statistical Bureau believes, 80–100 million workers in the state sector who are surplus to requirements, i.e. out of

Table 2.1 SOE reform

1983	SOEs begin to be taxed instead of turning over profits (*lì gai shui*); bank lending to SOEs begins to replace allocations from budget.
1984	Manager responsibility system (*chang zhang fu zhe zhi*) and 'above-price' pricing and production autonomy introduced
1988	SOE contract responsibility system begins (performance contract); on the basis of negotiated multiyear contracts, managers' rights of control and obligations to the state defined.
1991	Delegation of direct foreign trade rights to some SOEs; encouragement of enterprise groups and corporatisation, whereby the state's ownership rights take the form of shares managed by state asset administration bureau and state investment companies and the firm has management autonomy. Establishment of the Shanghai and Shenzhen stock exchanges.
1992	New operating mechanism and autonomous rights to SOEs give SOE managers autonomy to 'use and dispose of the property entrusted to them by the state for management and business purpose'; phasing out of production targets and price controls.
1993	Decision on establishing modern enterprise system.
1996	Programme of transforming 100 enterprises into fully autonomous corporations announced; smaller enterprises to be encouraged to merger.
1997–1998	Experimentation with different forms of ownership, including joint-stock shareholding, is declared to be compatible with socialism.

Source: Sachs and Woo (1997)

work. Jobs need to be created at least at the rate of 18 million a year. The search for a solution continues.

The problem of reforming the agricultural sector The agricultural sector, as mentioned, remains dominant in China, and the Chinese economy stands or falls on agricultural prosperity. The agricultural sector remains responsible for nearly 40 per cent of total output. The current crisis in the agricultural sector affects more than just grain and rice crops. The textile industry is facing a crisis of almost equal magnitude. China relies on domestically produced cotton, but land under cultivation for cotton declined from 6.5 million hectares in 1991 to 5 million in 1994 and boll weevil infestation reduced yields in 1994 and 1995. Part of the reform of the agricultural sector involves reducing the economy's dependence on it.

The problem of reducing regional disparities This is part of the developing wealth disparity issue. The economic boom in China has been largely centred on two regions, the mouth of the Pearl River and the Chang Jiang river delta around Shanghai. More generally, the whole of the coastal belt, which just about includes Beijing, has prospered when the inland regions have stagnated. As mentioned above, rural inflation is rising faster than urban inflation, and this is particularly true in the north and west, less affected by the boom. Despite steady migration to the cities, rural unemployment is rising faster than urban unemployment. But it is the standard of living which makes the greatest difference; in 1996, average urban per capita income increased by 8 per cent to about 3,800 yuan. In rural areas, per capita income increased only to 1,400 yuan.

The Chinese government is alive to these disparities and has made expanding the scale of economic reform a major priority. Regional disparities are already leading to, in the words of one Chinese newspaper, 'warlordism, banditry, clan feuds, uprisings, farmers demonstrations and protests'. Even allowing for exaggeration, these images strike fear into the hearts of many Chinese, especially those who remember past times of chaos. However, the investment required to realise this expansion is huge, many times greater than that which has already been provided. The Chinese economy, and foreign investment and participation, will have to increase by an order of magnitude.

Chinese attitudes to the West

In 1988 a television series called *River Elegy* was shown on Chinese national television. Widely perceived as an attack on China's ancient culture and history, *River Elegy* used a series of images to contrast China's past and its future. The past was shown in brown earth tones, using images of the Huang He (Yellow River), the Great Wall and so on; the future was shown in blue, using images of the open Pacific Ocean, representing freedom and contact with the outside world. The film's message was that China could only progress by jettisoning its own past and merging its future with that of the wider world.

Needless to say, the film generated a ferocious backlash, and several politicians made their careers by criticising it. A decade on, the proponents of closer relations with the West and those who favour an arm's length distance are sometimes known as the Blues and the Browns. The two factions are sometimes defined as modernisers and conservatives, but this is too simple. The Blues, generally speaking, are those who believe that China's future lies in opening up to the outside world, taking a step away from its purely Chinese heritage, culture, history and so on and deliberately becoming more like the West. The Browns are those who believe that

China's heritage must be maintained, as it is the country's primary source of strength, and that China must be strong but independent.

In these two factions, one can see much of the Chinese ambivalence about the West. In the attitudes of the Blues one can see much of the same sense of inferiority to the West, and the desire to reduce that inferiority by imitating the West and becoming more like it, that one saw in the Guomindang and the liberal reformers of the early twentieth century. In the views of the Browns we can see the remembrance of things past, the Opium Wars, warlordism, the Japanese invasion, and the fear that what happened once can happen again.

These are extreme positions; a little Blue and a little Brown can be found in most Chinese. Most people are at once looking forward to the future and apprehensive about what it will bring.

Why all this matters

We come back to the question posed at the beginning of the chapter. What does the business person of today need to know about China? Will an understanding of culture and history be of any assistance when doing business? Will a knowledge of the works of Confucius, or Mao's *Little Red Book*, be useful when negotiating a joint venture?

The answer, as with most knowledge, is that it depends on how it is used. Culture is not an exact science; it is a set of frameworks, which are often intuitive and emotional, within which people operate. As we discuss in the next chapter, we are affected by culture without being aware of it. Our attitudes to hierarchy, the way we make decisions (including purchasing decisions), our attitudes to others, ethics and personal tastes are all to some extent shaped by our inheritance.

This does not mean that culture is a predictor. Within the parameters of a given culture, vast allowances must be made for variations in the behaviour of individuals. With 1.2 billion people in the PRC and another 55 million overseas Chinese, the variations are very numerous indeed.

A study of culture as an environmental factor makes sound economic sense. Some firms seem to approach the world as if all humanity was universally the same. That is soon modified. The next level of simplification is racial, or national, stereotypes. Politically correct commentators are appalled by this but, for most international travellers, they are useful first approximations. The Chinese use them when they meet people from other parts of China. Marketers the world over are trying to get through these superficialities to understand the real people behind them.

Western and Chinese business people routinely misunderstand each other. In these circumstances one can retreat to fixed positions or try to empathise with the other person's frame of mind. Of course the other person may be trying to rob you, but that cannot be assumed of everyone. More than anything this book is about comparing how Westerners and Chinese see the world so that robbers can be distinguished and friends can come to terms. It is about risk assessment. Understanding the underlying forces gives better preparation.

Finally, and perhaps most critical is the appreciation of the differences between other cultures and one's own. By looking at Chinese culture and asking how it differs from our own, we are forced to start looking at our own culture in more depth. Why do *we* think and behave as we do. Are there any lessons to be learned from this? We can, if we are careful, use China as a mirror; although, as Sir Percy Cradock says, we are looking through a glass darkly, we can nonetheless see something of our own reflection.

Notes

1   This chapter deals primarily with 'mainland China', that is to say, the territory of the People's Republic of China. The Chinese communities of East and Southeast Asia will be dealt with in similar fashion in Chapter 9.

2   W. F. Jenner (1989) *The Tyranny of History*, Cambridge: Cambridge University Press; Moise 1994.

3 The furniture of the mind

The average Chinese has long been and still is an animist, a Buddhist, a Confucianist and a Taoist with no sense of incongruity or inconsistency.
(Latourette 1934)

Introduction

A comprehensive coverage of the roots of contemporary Chinese business thinking would take a thousand scholars a thousand days. Here, we seek merely to open the door into a room, one that is full of furniture that the occupants of the room themselves have, for much of the time, long ceased to notice. The 'room', i.e. the Chinese mind, is dimly lit. When the Westerner enters it, some pieces seem the same as at home; some are strange, some are old, inherited from ancestors long dead, and some are new. Some may not be noticed in the half light and blundered into, perhaps causing damage.

The Western mind has its own furniture that we likewise rarely notice. The way we think is inherited from Greek, Jewish and Christian patterns of analysis two thousand years and more old. Whether Westerners go to church or synagogue today is no reflection of the influence on our thinking today. With more powerful means of mass communication and a missionary zeal for which there is no apparent explanation, patterns of Western thinking have been more exposed to the Chinese than theirs to us. The lighting, in this metaphor, is thus brighter for the Chinese entrant.

The first focus of this chapter is on philosophies and how they affect the psychology of today's business person. Whether the inheritor of the culture is in the PRC, Singapore or the USA matters about as much as whether the inheritor of European culture is in Europe, Argentina or Australia. Location does make a difference and younger generations feel, as they always have, that they are very different from their parents' age group. We have chosen Latourette's comment above (to which can now be added Communism) to start these notes precisely to illustrate that point. Why, if every generation is so different, do ways of thinking survive for centuries?

The line between philosophy and school of thought and religion is not as clear as in the West. Confucianism is not a religion in the sense of believing in supernatural powers or beings which should be obeyed. Buddhism is not strictly a religion either, but the ancestor cult may be. Frankly, their classification is immaterial; we are concerned with their impact on modern thinking. This leads to a review of values.

From philosophy and values, we go on to discuss strategy. Sunzi, or Sun Tzu as he is more familiarly known in the West, could be called the greatest strategist of all time. His book *The Art of War* has had a profound effect on military thinking, especially guerrilla warfare. (It seems likely that *The Art of War* is by more than one hand, and like many Chinese classics it was probably added to and amended over many years.) Today, the thirteen chapters provide guidance to business people and generals alike and are too well known to need more than the briefest of recaps here. Another famous text, *The Thirty-Six Strategems*, has also had much influence.

Philosophy

In broadly chronological order, let us look at:

- Ancestor cult
- Daoism (or Taoism)
- Confucianism
- Confucian disciples
- Legalism
- Buddhism
- Neo-Confucianism
- Christianity
- Communism

Chronology is not necessarily the most accurate way of looking at these concepts, since they moved in and out of fashion in no particular order. Confucius may have lived before and/or after the early Daoist philosophers but their thinking seems to have preceded his. Confucianism, however, did not dominate until Han times 300 years or so later, and was followed by Daoism's resurgence.

These schools have supplied much of the furniture of the Chinese mind, but as the pieces have passed from one generation to another so the distinctions have become blurred. In any case, they have much in common. It is curious that so much philosophy originated in a relatively brief period around 400 BC, right across the world from Greece to China. 'The Pre-Socratic Greeks (Thales and Anaximander of Miletus), Confucianism, Mohism, Upanisadic Hinduism, Jainism, Taoism, Buddhism, Zoroastrianism, and Biblical Judaism' all flowered at about the same time.[1] Daoism and Indian Yoga (Sufism) are not just contemporary but very similar. Whether some of these philosophies inspired each other, or they were inspired separately by some common source is not known.

Ancestor cult

This is both the oldest belief system and the core of Chinese religious observance. For perhaps 4,000 years, all classes of society from emperors to serfs, intelligentsia to peasants, have swept out tombs and left food, drink and lights for their fathers and forefathers, particularly at the Qing Ming Festival (5 April) which is dedicated to this purpose. The beliefs seem to be traceable to Shang times (16th–11th centuries BC). At that time, the worship of royal ancestors was central to maintenance of the dynasty. Certain ancestors were worshipped on certain days, and the pattern of associations of days and observances built up.

The same period seems to have seen the birth of many of the Chinese equivalent of Western superstitions concerning numbers (such as Friday the 13th) and practices (such as walking under ladders), though the origins of these may be far older. Whether such things are rational is beside the point; they deeply affect doing business in greater China today. Eight and scarlet are still 'lucky'. There are right times to do things, such as start a business, or the right way for buildings to face. Fortune telling is strong, just as the West has an undiminished appetite for astrology. *Feng shui* is taken seriously by many. Popular beliefs of whatever type often exercise more influence over popular culture than does formal religion.

Daoism (c. 500 BC)

Dào ('Tao' in older texts) is usually translated as 'the way', although there are many other connotations as well. Daoism is not a religion as such (though there are religious movements based on Daoist principles) but suggests a way of thinking that will bring harmony and wisdom through respecting 'the all-pervading, self existent, eternal cosmic unity from which all created things emanate and to which they all return'.[2] The instigator was Laozi (Lao = 'old', zi = 'master'; older Western texts refer to him as Lao Tzu), who is supposedly the author of the immortal classic the *Daodejing* (in fact, modern scholarship has cast doubt on whether Laozi existed at all); in fact, modern scholarship has cast doubt on whether he ever existed at all. The title *Daodejing* was applied to the work subsequently; the title has been translated as 'the classic book of integrity and the way' (the middle word, *dé*, means integrity or virtue). It possibly began as a collection of oral stories developed over the great period for Chinese philosophy between 600 and 300 BC. Zhuangzi, the greatest of the Daoist writers whose existence can be verified, lived toward the end of that period.

We cannot overstress the importance of Daoist thinking in 'pairs of opposites'. On both sides of every argument, there must be right and wrong. Paradox and ambiguity flow directly from this concept of balance. So does 'and' thinking, as distinct from Western 'or' thinking (either A is right *or* the opposite of A). To a Daoist, the fact that A is right probably means the opposite of A is right too. And both are wrong. This kind of thinking has been referred to as 'the unity of opposites'.[3] The Chinese search for such solutions in negotiation baffles Westerners.

For those unfamiliar with the *Daodejing*, it is worth at least dipping into to get the flavour; it can be very enjoyable. Daoism has been accused of being at the root of fatalism in China. If what will be, will be, there is no need to do anything to prevent it. While people will rationalise in all kinds of ways, the charge is unfair. At the certainty of massive oversimplification, Daoism actually encourages people to do what they can do, but not then to do all they could but then worry about the results. This calm in the face of adversity may give the *appearance* of fatalism, but is an unfair reading of the situation. Of course it also leads many people too quickly to disengage and to assume that they have done what they can. Therein lies the danger.

We have looked here at Daoism before turning to Confucianism, whatever the precise chronology, because it provides many of the underpinnings of Chinese thinking which so differentiates it from Western thinking. Specifically, there are the concepts of balance and paradox: for example, 'Heavy is the root of light; calm is the ruler of haste'.[4] The *dào* is the 'non-being' (*wu*) within which any 'being' (*yu*) exists, and vice versa. The *dào* is the source of all being and non-being. The *dào* is, as, so to speak, the natural laws of the universe from which we spring, to which we return and with which we should be in harmony in the meantime. *Yáng* and *yìn* are essential Daoist concepts which we define later. They are not polar opposites so much as complementary halves of the same whole. Even, for example, the selection of a balanced meal uses these two powerful concepts. Food and drink are functional such as red wine (*yáng*) being perceived as good for the blood (which it probably is) whereas white wine (*yìn*) is more gentle and romantic (no comment). Thus choosing the dinner wine can have unintended overtones.

Confucianism (551 – 479 BC)

This period when philosophy flowered was also marked by continuous warfare around much of the globe, notably the period of Warring States in China (475–221 BC). Perhaps this was responsible for the intellectual search for a route to harmony. Certainly Laozi regarded war as a last resort: 'the killing of masses of human beings, we bewail with sorrow and grief; victory in battle we commemorate with mourning ritual'. Interstate rivalry changed the selection of senior advisers on the basis solely of hereditary principles to the most (intellectually) competent albeit from within the *shih* (gentleman) class. As a result there was considerable social and intellectual movement. It was also a time of rich cultural flowering, when the Hundred Schools of philosophy debated amongst each other. Only a few of these, including Daoism, survived; others like the Mohists were later suppressed, and of some, such as the Agriculturalists and the Story Tellers, only their name survives; we have no clue as to what their beliefs were.

While Confucius, a member of the *shih* class and a senior civil servant, was certainly affected by the war-filled times in which he lived, his philosophy did not become official orthodoxy for China until about 300 years later, during the Han dynasty. The following traditional Chinese story is used to introduce a discussion of Confucian social philosophy, which is central to efforts to explain and predict Chinese social interaction.[5]

The protagonist, Hsueh Jen-kuei, is an accomplished soldier who left his pregnant wife eighteen years before to fight a distant campaign for the emperor. Returning home, he notices a young man shooting wild geese with great skill. Provoked, he challenges the youth to a test of marksmanship. The rival readily accepts, whereupon Hsueh immediately puts an arrow through his heart, saying 'a soldier like me could not let another live if he was a superior in marksmanship with the weapons in which I excel'.

Of course, it turns out the youth is Hsueh's son whom he had never seen. The remorse of the father is tempered by the fact that the son has violated two cultural imperatives. First, he did not recognise his father: so strong are the bonds of family and the imperatives of filial piety that a son should know his father regardless of any factors which may disguise his identity. Second, the son has committed the cardinal sin in the Chinese tradition: he has challenged his father and thereby affronted social order. In the words of a Chinese proverb, 'In a family of a thousand, only one is the master'. A threat to the family is a threat to the body politic and a violation of heaven's mandate. It must therefore be ruthlessly put down.

Confucianism has been guiding the behaviour of people of all classes since the Han dynasty, irrespective of the criticisms. Under Mao,

Confucianism was officially out of favour even though Confucian thought patterns were too well entrenched to be much affected (and he himself was imbued with them). In 1985, though, a special institute was founded in Beijing for the study of Confucian thought (Laaksonen 1988).

In the time of Confucius, the great problems were how to govern, how to maintain order in society and how to guarantee happiness and prosperity for the people (*plus ça change*). Confucius's solution was that both the rulers and the ruled should be educated. Governing is in the first place education and training, and the ruler should first educate himself and then govern with the help of 'virtues', meaning something close to the Daoist 'integrity' in that the word does not have quite the same connotations of morality that it has in the West.

In this sense, there are 'Five Constant Virtues': humanity, righteousness, propriety, wisdom and faithfulness. These virtues are expressed in 'Five Cardinal Relations': sovereign and subject, parent and child, elder and younger brothers, husband and wife, and friend and friend. Of these five relationships, the first two are the most important in Confucianism but the last virtue, faithfulness, is still seen as necessary, especially in business. Constancy is, as we will see, a key part of *guànxì* (relationships).

Confucius held that all men were alike in nature. He suggested that good and capable people should be appointed to official posts, a proposal that was contrary to the prevailing hereditary rule. Yet he also defended the hierarchy of the nobility. He advocated the elevation of good and capable people, but never opposed the hereditary system and advised people to accept their lot. Confucius saw a world in which harmony could best be achieved by everyone recognising his place in the world. Confucius thus legitimised the strong hierarchical order which dominated the family and the society of his time and throughout much of Chinese history. This is in interesting contrast to Western thinking where liberation of slaves, for example, is associated with the overthrow of the current governance.

Confucius distinguished two kinds of individuals: Jun Tsu (Gentleman, Prince, Great Man or Proper Man) and Xiao Ren (literally Petty Man or Small Man):

- Great Man, being universal in his outlook, is impartial; Petty Man, being partial, is not universal in outlook (Confucius, Book 2).
- He (Great Man) sets the good examples, then he invites others to follow it (Confucius, Book 2).
- Great Man cherishes excellence; Petty man, his own comfort. Great Man cherishes the rules and regulations; Petty Man, special favour (Confucius, Book 4).

- Great Man is conscious only of justice; Petty Man only of self-interest (Confucius, Book 4).

Leadership belonged to Great Man; he need not be of noble birth, but should have the Five Constant Virtues.

Confucius defined filial duty as:

> While his father lives, observe a man's purposes; when the father dies, observe his actions. If for three years (of mourning) a man does not change from the ways of his father, he may be called filial.
>
> (Confucius, Book 1)

Both the subject and filial relationships lead to a predominantly vertical structure of relationships. In modern business, a paternalistic management style is thought by some to be a direct consequence in both China and Japan.

According to Bond and Hwang 'the essential aspects of Confucianism in constructing a Chinese social psychology are the following: (a) man exists through, and is defined by, his relationships to others; (b) these relationships are structured hierarchically; (c) social order is ensured through each party's honouring the requirements in the role relationship'.[6] The Confucian scholar A.S. Cua defines Confucian philosophy as 'primarily a set of ethical ideas oriented towards practice', found on the threefold principles of benevolence, righteousness and propriety.[7] In essence, Confucianism sets out a framework for interpersonal relationships of all kinds.

Confucian disciples (Mozi, 5th century BC; Mencius, c. 371–289 BC; Xunzi, c. 298–238 BC)

Confucian thinking was the standard against which others pitted their wits. Mohism advocated universal love, which was an extension of the idea of humanity. Mozi, the movement's leading thinker, believed that people with 'virtue' and ability should be elevated and was opposed to inherited wealth or nobility.

Mencius developed a theory of government by benevolence believing that man was born with goodness. In his view, man possessed inherent qualities of benevolence, righteousness, propriety and wisdom which some people were able to preserve and others not. In Mencius's view, every sovereign was able to rule by a policy of benevolence and every citizen was able to accept it.

Xunzi thought that man was born inherently evil, but education can change man's nature. Further, he emphasised self-improvement and self-fulfilment. was one of the first thinkers after Confucius to focus on the importance of education as a means of developing oneself and reaching self-improvement and self-fulfilment. As he says, 'If an ethically superior person studies widely and daily engages in self-examination, his intellect will become enlightened and his conduct will be without fault' (quoted in Cua 1998). This view, that study can lead to self-improvement, remains current. The educationalist Clive Dimmock, reporting on surveys of attitudes among Hongkong high school students, noted that the prevalent belief was that by studying hard one could improve one's abilities. This was precisely the opposite of the view current among American students at the same time, where studying hard was seen as a way of compensating for *lack* of ability; if you had ability you did not need to study, and studying was unlikely to make you any better.[8]

Legalism (c. 220 BC)

Legalists believed, quite simply, in law and order. Moreover, Legalists believed that the law possessed a virtue that set it above any other human principle; everyone had to obey the law in every circumstance. This was law applied exactly, without exceptions. The Legalists believed that man is amoral and is guided purely by self-interest and the future, not by tradition. People must therefore be coerced by law into doing right. Otherwise, they had to be punished. Thus the Legalists are more or less opposite to the Confucians.

Han Feizi, the most prominent exponent of Legalism, suggested that one may as well coerce everyone, good and bad, to do right. Those few people (if any, in his view) who do right naturally should not object, since that is what they would do anyway. Han's views were adopted by the Qin emperor, Shi Huangdi, and Han himself became the first prime minister of a united China, with full authority to put his philosophy into action.

The Legalists felt that the power of laws should be combined with hierarchical power and the personal power of the ruler or emperor. The people were there for the benefit of the ruler, not vice versa. Precise and written laws should define the rights and obligations of individuals.

Apart from being a convenient doctrine for powerful leaders, this concept never gained much ground, and when the Qin dynasty were replaced by the Han dynasty, Confucian thinking became the norm and Legalism was consigned to the scrap heap. Some traces of Legalism can still be seen in Chinese thinking, particularly on the authority of the state over the individual, and certainly elements of Legalism can be found in some of Mao's writings. But these are influences, not whole systems.

Modern commerce, therefore, exists in an environment where legalism did *not* prevail over Confucian thinking.

Buddhism (c. 4th century AD)

By the third century AD, Confucianism was discarded by the then governing class, had run out of steam as an intellectual stimulus, just as the Han dynasty also began to fail. ~~People~~ Social elites were looking for something new and, as in most cases in China, this meant that they turned to the past to resurrect older, purer forms of thinking. Daoism enjoyed a resurgence. At the same time, Buddhism arrived from India.

Buddhism's official arrival dates to about 70 AD when the Han emperor Ming Ti had a dream of a golden flying deity but it did not become fully established for several more centuries. Why the Chinese were suddenly so open to a foreign religion is not very clear, but it may be that Buddhism and Daoism have enough shared ground to allow the Chinese to see it as meshing with previous belief systems. Certainly Chinese Buddhism quickly evolved away from many of its Indian roots. Although Indian classics like the *Awakening of Faith in Mahayana* were widely read and studied, within a few generations Chinese Buddhist scholars like Fazang and Linji were establishing 'Buddhism with Chinese characteristics'. Perhaps the most famous Chinese Buddhist school was that of Chan, which later took hold also in Japan (where it is known as Zen). The masters of one particular branch of Chan had some unusual ways of teaching. One used to belabour students with sticks during lessons; another would interrupt speakers by shouting at them, 'If you meet the Buddha on the road: kill him!' Needless to say, this was not mainstream, but it does illustrate one of the essences of Chan, namely stretching the mind to think the unthinkable.

By the sixth century the monasteries, largely thanks to imperial patronage, had obtained substantial economic power. Inevitably, excess power led to corruption, and in 845 the Tang emperor Wuzong began a persecution, destroying monasteries, works of art and scholarship. Over 250,000 monks and nuns returned to the laity. Later, the Cheng brothers and Zhu Xi built many elements of Buddhist thinking into their Neo-Confucian synthesis (see below). Today, Chinese Buddhism is so intertwined with Confucianism and Daoism that it is difficult now to tell the consequences of the three apart. Buddhism was largely suppressed after 1949 and many temples closed. In the 1990s they have reopened both as tourist centres and for their traditional purposes.

Neo-Confucianism

Neo-Confucianism appears in the period of imperial revival in the Sung and Tang dynasties. Like many reform movements in China, it sought to make China strong again by ridding the country of foreign and corrupt influences and adopting a purely Chinese philosophy. A group of scholars set out to resolve the apparent contradictions between Confucianism, Daoism and Buddhism and create a unified system of thought. Much of the early work was done by the brothers Cheng Hao and Cheng Yi; the exposition of the final product was the work of the most important late Chinese philosopher, Zhu Xi.

By building a single thought-system which took in all the different aspects of Chinese philosophy and thinking, the Neo-Confucians (the name is a later tag) set a framework for thinking in China. Highly conservative, looking back to the masters (Confucius, Laozi *et al.*), the Neo-Confucians reinforced views on education, self-development and interpersonal relations along largely Confucian lines. This system has persisted until this day.

Christianity (1583 AD)

Exactly when Christianity arrived in China is not known, but there was a Nestorian Christian community in the west of China from at least the 8th century, and in 1289–90 a Chinese Christian called Rabban Sauma visited England and France as an envoy of one of the Mongol rulers. He must have caused a sensation.

Franciscan missionaries followed (or maybe preceded) Marco Polo into China; an archbishopric of Beijing was set up, but converts never numbered more than a few hundred. Matteo Ricci pioneered a Jesuit presence in 1583, even though the Ming emperors had closed China to foreigners. He was well trained in language and Confucian thinking by Chinese in Europe. With modern echoes, the Jesuits' market entry strategy was to make themselves valuable to the Ming emperors through technology transfer (including cannon manufacture) and thus earn import rights for Christianity. Ricci determined that the ancestor cult and Confucianism were 'social' rites, and could thus be incorporated within Christianity, just as Saturnalia had become Christmas.

Initially the strategy worked well, and by the end of the Ming dynasty a substantial foothold, and converts, had been achieved in Beijing and some cities further south. In the 18th century, however, other Catholic orders, perhaps jealous of the Jesuits' Chinese exclusivity, challenged Ricci's acceptance of ancestor cult and Confucianism. One thing led to another, the missionaries were forced to leave and Christians were persecuted.

As the Qing dynasty weakened in the nineteenth century, fresh waves of missionaries of all denominations appeared. Undoubtedly heroic, they made various contributions to health and education at local levels and achieved many converts. Nevertheless the impact on China, and Chinese thinking, overall was minimal, apart from the unintended disaster of the Taiping Rebellion (1853–60) (see Chapter 2). This counterfeit Christianity (intellectual property rights have always been a problem) must have damaged the real thing. During the conservative Boxer Rebellion in 1900, many missionaries were killed by the rebels. Today there are perhaps two million Christians in China; they have little or no influence, certainly less than the three million Moslems.

Communism (c. 1920s)

The history of Communism in China has been well covered elsewhere and does not need repetition here. As a *philosophy*, Communism never really put down roots in China. Mao ruled in much the same way that the emperors had, and so did Deng. Today it operates as ruling *Party*, which is a good enough reason to join, but Communist ideology has adjusted to market pragmatism. The cynical might think that acceptance of the ideology was convenient for providing a rationale for revolution and to get support from Russia. That would be unfair. Mao and his contemporaries had a genuine desire to reform China, and to distribute wealth from the rich and give it to the poor. Corruption and the abuse of power in the thirty years either side of 1900 had advanced to the point where some puritanical doctrine was essential to clean the stables. Confucianism, which respected inherited order, was banned; yet many of the precepts of the two systems, such as the idea that government is for the benefit of the people, coincide, and Confucian ideas continued to infuse practice. Mao's doctrines on education and (early) concepts of government owe more to Confucius than to Marx.

However disastrous it proved and however badly history now judges it, the Cultural Revolution was, at least in part, an attempt to bring the furniture of Communism permanently into the Chinese mind alongside, or in place of, earlier philosophies. Mao noted that, whilst the means of production, both industrial, commercial and agricultural, had wholly been transformed from private family ownership to state ownership, the same old civil servants still seemed to be running the place. The Big Idea was to unleash young idealists, brandishing his thoughts in *Little Red Books* in order to democratise authority. Government would be by the masses, for the masses.

With hindsight, it is hard to conceive a more crass notion. Barring one, perhaps: after the Japanese, Civil and Korean wars, Mao told the Chinese to restock the population, resulting in the overpopulation that now causes China, and the rest of the world, so many worries. Anyway, nothing brings Communism down faster than implementing it.

While Communism, a Western creed in any case, has been rejected, Maoism is still there. Walk in any park and witness the respect accorded to his poetry and literature. We are too close to events to be sure, but we would not be surprised if 'Maozi' was read alongside Zhuangzi a thousand years from now.

Eight key concepts in Chinese thinking

Dào 道   The Way.

Dé 德   Virtue. A key Daoist concept which guides people to correct behaviour and away from narrow self-interest.

Lì   Rituals or rites. Sets out the correct form of behaviour in a given situation so as to preserve harmony and face.

Miànzi   Face, including one's self-respect and public dignity. Preserving *miànzi* is a key goal in most interpersonal relations. Having a 'thick face' means that one is impervious to face issues, i.e. thick-skinned in English, probably because public respect is already eroded.

Rén 仁   Literally 'benevolence'; but in fact covers the traditional ethical code of how one should treat other people. Not to be confused with the same (pinyin but not Chinese) word for a person.

Yì 义   Rightness or righteousness; the knowledge of what is correct in any given situation.

Yin-yáng   The two halves of a whole, often in reference to *dào*. Treated as complementary, rather than polar opposites, *yáng* and *yìn* describe two halves of the same whole; they are, so to speak, the sunny and shady sides of the same mountain, but one needs to be careful with analogies. *yáng* which also means the sun, is associated with positiveness and masculinity; *yìn* (the moon) is negative and feminine.

Zhì   Knowing or knowledge but procedural rather than factual. In other words, knowing *how*, not knowing *what*.

Values

A discussion of values in Chinese society deserves a book in its own right. Here we focus on a few of the most important, including:

- age, hierarchy and authority which are strongly linked
- wealth
- face
- cultural dimensions

Despite the caution introduced with the Latourette quote at the beginning of this chapter, one must recognise that younger managers do not necessarily share the values of their elders. As is also true in Japan, Europe and elsewhere, the younger are more international, more prepared to experiment, more looking to have fun and less dedicated to family, or any other, ties.

Age, hierarchy and authority

Respect for tradition, ancestors and age, stemming from Confucius, were among the main values of people in old China. The respect for age was manifested especially in family life which had a profound effect upon other parts of social life. The hierarchical relations of a Chinese family were determined by age. The names of sisters and brothers follow the age-order of the family members. For example, an older brother is addressed as 'older brother' (*gege*) and a younger sister likewise (*meimei*). Only parents call their children by their given names.

Similarly, industrial workers in old China did not typically question higher authority or seek authority themselves, thus reinforcing the subordinates' subservience and dependence on superiors. Authority in industry and business was viewed as an absolute right of owners and the managers in control. Superior–subordinate relationships were typically personal, subjective and viewed as father–son or master–servant relationships. No two persons were equal in relation to each other. An older person had more authority than a younger one, and a man had more than a woman.

The Qin dynasty (221–207 BC) held the family responsible for the public acts of its members as part of their social pressure on each individual, inculcating obedience to the government and to the social order through the family. This still operates. The one-child rule, for example, is enforced more through family and local community pressures than any legal system.

Wealth

The need for self-sufficiency traditionally bred a savings mentality. Money should be hoarded: if times were good now, they were likely to be bad later. The culture required even the rich to pretend to be poor. *Inside* the PRC, the first-class cabin is likely to contain only the occasional Western business person. But there is paradox here. Whether it was Shanghai in the 1930s or Hongkong more recently, the opposite view was that money attracts money. It should be flaunted. *Outside* the PRC, first-class air travel is taken by some who cannot afford it but must be seen to do it. Here is another warning: do not be taken in by appearances. Old money is more likely to be hidden, new money more likely to be flashed. That does not make one, necessarily, better than the other (nor is it so different from New York, San Francisco, Paris or London).

Face *(miànzi)*

The pervasive Chinese concept of gaining, giving or losing 'face' focuses on questions of prestige and dignity, reflects surprising vulnerability in self-esteem. The Chinese are acutely sensitive to the regard in which they are held by others or the light in which they appear. Causing someone to lose face can have severe consequences: at the very least, co-operation will cease and retaliation may ensue.

Losing and saving face are well understood in the West. Less so is the concept of giving face, that is, doing something to enhance someone else's reputation or prestige. The heavy use of shame as a social control mechanism from the time of early childhood tends to cause feelings of dependency and anxieties about self-esteem, which produce self-consciousness about most social relationships. As a result, a great deal can be gained by helping the Chinese to win face and a great deal will be lost by any affront or slight, no matter how unintended, especially for older and/or more senior people.

The Chinese concept of sincerity is the opposite of the Anglo-American, in that the Chinese believe that they can manifest sincerity only by adhering carefully to prescribed etiquette, whereas Westerners believe that etiquette obscures truth.[9] In a sense the Chinese are saying, 'I will show my sincerity in my relations with you by going to the trouble to be so absolutely correct toward you that you will be untroubled about any matters of face.' Again, the form of the interchange is as important as the content, as is laid down by *lì*.

Giving face is also closely connected with *guànxì* (see Chapter 4). We are more likely, obviously enough, to establish good relationships with those who always give us face, and vice versa. That accumulates. If *guànxì* already exists, then giving face increases the opportunity for rewards. Flattery, in short, will get you anywhere.

Cultural dimensions

Geert Hofstede has referred to culture as the software of the mind.[10] In research, which is very widely cited on differences between Eastern and Western business cultures, Hofstede uses four dimensions from Western research and found that a fifth was required when the work was re-run in Hongkong. They are: power distance (hierarchic respect), individualism vs collectivism, assertiveness, uncertainty avoidance and, later, long termism. Since he was measuring IBM managers, the PRC was not included and it is dangerous to make inferences from Singapore, Hongkong and Taiwan. Nevertheless, it is reasonable that the overseas Chinese rated as highly hierarchic and low on individualism, and middle of the road on assertiveness/masculinity. Taiwan felt much more threatened by uncertainty than Hongkong, and Singapore was most confident of all. The PRC *was* included on the long-term orientation scale, and rated highest of all.

For many people familiar with both China and the overseas Chinese, however, Hofstede's conclusions do not match their own experience. The Hofstede research is not reliable in an oriental context because it falls into the either/or trap. Hofstede is a prisoner of his own (Dutch) culture and, frankly, this type of research is hocus-pocus. The Chinese are not *either* individualist *or* collective but both at the same time. In 1992, Li Huaizu and his colleagues provided what we feel is a more insightful and elegant perspective on Chinese tradition and Western decision-making theory. The authors identify five groups of differences between Chinese tradition and features of Western decision theory: motivation and consequence, unity and diversity, circle and sequence, harmony and self-interest, and certainty and uncertainty. Other writers have commented on a number of elements from Chinese culture that impact on decision-making, including face, the individual–collective dichotomy, hierarchy, equality, self and social role, and personal modesty.

Motivation and consequence

According to Western theory, the manager assembles the possible outcomes from alternative actions, judges the probability of each outcome and then chooses the action most likely to have favourable consequences. In contrast, the Confucianist evaluates the motives and intention of the manager, taking ethical, or moral, principles as the criteria. The consequences examined are those that arose in the past, facts about past decisions and not estimates about the future. In other words, if the principles worked before, continue with them and do not speculate about the future.

Examples illustrating this are found in classic Chinese doctrines such as 'The gentleman makes much of ethics; the villain of gains and losses' and 'The person who worries about outcomes is no gentleman.' Thus while governments go in for elaborate economic (i.e. Western philosophy) planning, Chinese businesses tend not to have any *financial* plans at all. They do, however, think strategically (see below).

In the 1920s, Li Zongwu's *The Theory of Thickness and Blackness* became an overnight sensation in China. Li argued that successful decision-makers in China are not those who adhere to the Confucian ideals and aim to preserve face and maintain good relationships. Instead, they are those who possess the qualities 'thickness' or 'thick face' (that is, they do not care what others think of them) and 'blackness' or 'black-heartedness' (that is, those who are able to act in their own self-interest without guilt). In traditional style, Li illustrated his work with examples from the Three Kingdoms period. But then, no one would assume that all Chinese act in a purely Confucian (or Daoist, or whatever) spirit all the time.

Unity and diversity

Chinese tradition emphasises synthesis and unitary principle, from which problem-solving attributes are deduced, while the Western approach is to focus on the specific characteristics of the problem whilst permitting a variety of objectives. An example of this thinking is found in the ancient Chinese classic, the *Yijing* (The Book of Changes) which deals with knowledge of the universe as a whole. Minor principles can be deduced from a few major ones, instead of working Western-style from the observation of reality. Having said that, Chinese thinking, obviously, includes the observation of reality as well.

Circle and sequence

Chinese think of nature in terms of closed, spiral or circular systems of interrelated elements, whereas Western decision theory is sequential (for example with linear, exponential, or repeated patterns such as economic cycles). In traditional Chinese thinking, consequence is from many interrelated factors. A circular network is used to highlight the effects as a whole. The more linear Western approach can be presented as a sequence of decisions, such as a 'decision tree', each analysing the problem more narrowly.

Harmony and self-interest

When determining the optimal decision, Chinese tradition is to emphasise harmony and the group, but Western decision theory presumes that the decision-maker will optimise self-interest (maximise subjective expected utility). There are many Chinese sayings which reinforce the idea that a person who stands out from the group will be criticised and may be prevented from reaching his/her goal: 'The tree growing high above the others will be blown down by the wind', and 'The gun fires at the first bird in the flock.' Similarly, the Confucian doctrine of the mean is, 'Take the mean of the two, remain neutral without bias' and the Daoist doctrine is, 'Strive for no fault rather than merit, retreat for the purpose of advancing.' Of course, business people, in search of first-mover advantage, will quite often seek to be first. A Chinese business person may well be embarrassed by being innovative when a similar partner in the West would be proud of it. Being first in China has profound cultural and social difficulties. Imitation, however, gives face.

Certainty and uncertainty

Chinese tradition is oriented towards certainty, not the evaluation of uncertainty that is emphasised in Western decision theory. In their struggle for existence against numerous dangers and disasters, the Chinese felt that the future was very hard to face. As luck and misfortune came from the supernatural, divination was appropriate for decisions. The Chinese value past experiences more highly, depending on these for future action; again, note the importance of history and historical thinking. Past experiences are the guarantee and premise for success (just as they are for many Wall Street analysts, come to that). This view is reflected in sayings like, 'The old finger is hottest', and 'One will pay for it if one does not follow an old man's words.'

Strategy

'Strategy', as most business school students learn at some point, means almost anything anyone wants it to mean. In chess, it refers to broad principles of attack and defence, to parts of the board on which attack will be focused; it does *not* mean the identification of a series of moves that anticipate competitive reaction. Even chess-playing computers can only look a few moves deep. Any decent strategy expects the unexpected.

In business (schools), the word is confused with planning and with marketing. In China, the idea that one can lay out strategic moves, step by step, in some pre-planned sequence is even more unlikely than elsewhere. One is not even a player surveying the chessboard, just one of the pawns. But that does not mean that Chinese businesses do not think strategically. Quite the reverse. For reasons of space, we will touch here on just two aspects: strategy as warfare, and cleverness or trickery.

Business strategy as warfare

As mentioned above, the period of Warring States (475–221 BC) provided plenty of material for strategist theorists, chief amongst whom was Sunzi. As the people who led the army during war and the government administration during peace were frequently the same people or drawn from the same circle, the same strategic management principles were applied in peace and war. According to Sunzi, the supreme aim of war was 'not to win one hundred victories in one hundred battles' but to 'subdue the enemy without fighting'. In competition either in politics or business, strategy should be aimed at disposing one's resources in such an overwhelming fashion that the outcome of the contest is determined before it gets started.

According to Sunzi:[11]

> Strategy is the great work of the organisation.
> In situations of life or death, it is the Tao of survival or extinction.
> Its study cannot be neglected.
>
> Therefore calculate a plan with Five Working Fundamentals,
> And examine the condition of each.
> The first is Tao.
> The second is Nature.
> The third is Situation.
> The fourth is Leadership.
> The fifth is Art.

Or according to another translation, the government, the environment, the terrain, the command and the doctrine.[12] In modern marketing terms, the equivalent would be:

- what kind of business are we/should we be in?
- analysis of the competitive environment
- competitive positioning
- motivational factors
- implementation.

In short, Sunzi describes, in subtle language, the modern marketing plan.

Strategists study these five factors to assess chances of success and calculate their strengths and weaknesses *vis-à-vis* that of their opponents. Deception, speed and concentration of forces are the rules of war. Norman Dixon, whose hilarious account of military disasters *On the Psychology of Military Incompetence* is a must-read, summarises the same principles into focus of firepower (small time and place) and the quality of information, which probably extends to disinformation – a Chinese speciality.[13]

Of the various military metaphors, guerrilla warfare is the most appealing both because marketers usually have too few resources for the task and because it is not just Army A versus Army B: the surrounding population (i.e., end consumers) are usually decisive. Guerrilla warfare, if successful, proceeds through three phases: invisibility, evasion and concentration. In the first, the guerrillas maintain the lowest possible profile and set up their infrastructure and relationships with the surrounding population. In the second, battles/skirmishes are fought only to increase resources at the enemy's expense. The third stage is akin to classic warfare.

Whether it is in the small wins early or the pitched battles later, all writers point to the importance of focusing energy onto the point of contact so that, in that place and at that time, the enemy is outnumbered, encircled and suppressed. Failing that, at least ensure your positioning occupies 'the high ground' whatever that may be in consumer terms. It may well be as simple as a higher price. As far as Mao was concerned, only now could resources be spent, only now could losses be justified by gains. Mao's formula for deciding on attack is reproduced here:

> We should in general secure at least two of the following conditions before we can consider the situation as being favourable to us and unfavourable to the enemy and before we can go over to the counter-offensive. These conditions are:
>
> i.   The population actively supports the Red Army.
> ii.   The terrain is favourable for operations.
> iii. All the main forces of the Red Army are concentrated.
> iv.   The enemy's weak spots have been located.
> v.   The enemy has been reduced to a tired and demoralised state.
> vi.   The enemy has been induced to make mistakes.

He was also fond of saying that his main two mistakes were over-estimating and under-estimating the enemy. That this recent Chinese history echoes Sunzi, is no surprise. Mao was a scholar. He was not just a master general but a master guerrilla and, in another time, would have been a master marketer or business executive. Brand names and business reputations in China live as long, perhaps longer, than anywhere else. In this long-term game, the Chinese players will have learned from these histories and the application of military game-playing to business is both a major and conscious part of their planning.

Damei embroidery machines

The North China Optical Instrument Factory is one of the largest in South Beijing, designed by the Russians during the 1950s entente cordiale. Part of the China North Industries Group (NORINCO), and therefore MOFTEC, so far as import and export are concerned but also part of the Chinese Light Industry Ministry, it manufactured aircraft control systems in the 1960s and 1970s. With the market reforms around 1980, their ministry asked them to transfer manufacturing to the consumer goods market.

By 1990 they had tried 100 different kinds of new products. There was no science or research. They were blessed with an able production staff, 2,000 strong, and 500 engineers. New ideas were discussed and the most likely ones made and sold. Quite often they just followed others. Computerised embroidery machines, branded Damei, which according to the writer's dictionary means 'achieving something beautiful', proved far the most successful.

The NCOIF market was mostly China (except Taiwan and Hongkong). They were keen on exports, through NORINCO, but not much had developed. They knew they had to take on world competition, largely Japanese and US manufacturers. Due to the size of the Chinese embroidery market, Damei was probably number 5 in global terms.

Industry statistics showed Damei as having about 50 per cent market share with about twenty firms in the market. They saw market share as an important performance indicator. Market research was 'parental rather than scientific' but they had a very large field sales force (120 people) which also conducted research.

Perhaps due to their military heritage, NCOIF executives found strategic thinking, e.g. Sunzi, useful. In particular they saw their township competitors as guerrilla fighters (You Ji Dui), being at an early stage, whereas Damei was a formal army (Zheng Gui Jun).

Guerrillas play a key role in the Chinese economy and NCOIF executives did not wish to look down on or disparage them.

The main formal marketing activity, both domestically and internationally, was trade fairs. The biggest was the China Textile Association Show which took place in Beijing and Shanghai in alternate years. Much attention was given to sales training. 'Customers don't buy eggs, buy chickens.' After-sales service was important and free parts were provided even where the customer was to blame, e.g. using unsuitable material. They have twenty representative offices in China and promise repairs within twenty-four hours as a embroidery machine breakdown brings the customer's, usually small, business to a standstill. No formal breakdown or other service statistics were collected though summer heat seemed to increase their number. The engineers, though, come from Beijing, the local staff of between three and five would not have the latest technical skills.

Trickery / cleverness

We have a semantic problem here: no-one, including the Chinese, likes a word like 'trickery', loaded as it is with negative connotations. At the same time cleverness (better) does not quite convey the legitimate role of disinformation. Context affects meaning: we like to be tricked by a magician at a party, but are angry if we are tricked out of our money by a fraudster. In this section, we refer to business practices which are legitimate but likely to mislead, and thereby outwit, other players. We are not talking about cheating.

We will call it 'cleverness' to avoid offence. The Chinese admiration for tolerance of cleverness in this sense (the monkey is quite a hero) is greater than that in the West. As ever, it is limited by relationships (you do not outwit your own father) and it is also reciprocal (the West is *expected* to be devious even when it is not). The cunning entrepreneur, the crafty businessman who is 'eight sides all wide and slippery', is an admired figure in many circles.

The monkey symbolises this cleverness and features as the hero in many Chinese stories. The view of cleverness or trickery is invariably one-sided. Here is a Chinese view of Western business people, written in a handbook for Chinese managers in 1990:

We have to know the tactics needed for the struggle, know the opponents and ourselves, and be able to see through their tricks. The foreign capitalists will always try to cheat money out of us by using every possible means including deception.

In China, as elsewhere, cock-up is far more frequent than conspiracy. The papers the other side left on the table when they took a quick break from the meeting may be valuable information, intentional disinformation or completely irrelevant and really left by mistake. The odds on the papers being a plant (especially if they are in English) are probably somewhat higher, but no more than that. This all contributes to the absolute rule for old China hands that no one source of information is reliable. When three independent sources provide the same information, one can begin to take it seriously.

The overseas Chinese

Most of this chapter will apply to the overseas Chinese communities, though with some exceptions. Most importantly, although most overseas Chinese communities had some Maoist sympathisers, especially in the 1950s and 1960s, Maoism was never put into practice in these countries and therefore this philosophy does not really figure strongly in their furniture of the mind. There has also been greater penetration of Western ideas in many cases; there are far larger numbers of Chinese Christians overseas than in China, for example. Finally, through education and the media, many overseas Chinese have accepted some Western modes of thinking along with their own Chinese modes. (This is one of the reasons why many mainland Chinese regard the overseas Chinese with some reserve.)

Be prepared for variations. Many overseas Chinese have become acculturated and even 'Westernised'. Others are strongly conservative in social and mental terms, and can be 'more Chinese than the Chinese'. See Chapter 9 for more on this phenomenon.

Conclusions

The purpose of this chapter has been to explore, and to some extent compare, mental furniture. No single individual, still less 1.2 billion people, thinks exactly like that, nor would anyone expect it. For the purpose of contrasting differences, we have tended to compare China with the West and ignored other parts of the world. Obviously, the closer the cultural and historical links – for example, with Japan, Korea and Vietnam – the more furniture is shared or similar; yet it does not do to ignore the great differences between modes of thinking in these countries as well.

Notes

1 Douglas Mair (1990) *The Scottish Contribution to Modern Economic Thought*, Aberdeen: Aberdeen University Press, 160.
2 Ibid.
3 Huang Quanyu *et al.* 1997.
4 Ibid: 91.
5 Bond 1986.
6 Ibid.
7 Cua 1998.
8 Clive Dimmock (1999) *Designing the Learning-Centred School*, London: Falmer, 2000.
9 See Pye 1992.
10 Hofstede 1991.
11 Wing 1988.
12 Chang 1976: 74.
13 Norman Dixon (1976) *On the Psychology of Military Incompetence*, London: Pimlico.

4 Relationships and regulations

The rules are fixed; the people are flexible.

(Chinese proverb)

We are not sure that this proverb is still entirely true. Rules only seem to be fixed for the moment; they may have been promulgated but overtaken before officials get around to implementing them. If anything, though, this makes the need for relationships all the greater. Foreign businesses in China need local partners in just the same way that they do in any world market. Relationships have to be cultivated with distributors, suppliers, customers, local government and administration, and the community in general.

The question of relationships is more important in China than in many other countries, however, for three reasons. First, government plays a much more direct role in the economy in China than it does in most Western countries or even in many developing economies. As we noted in Chapter 2, in China the economy is seen as being at the service of the state, and the state does not hesitate to intervene when it thinks the economy is going in undesirable directions. This applies to local as well as central government in the People's Republic of China, and to a greater or lesser degree it applies to every government in the region. Cultivating good relationships with government is therefore often a critical factor in assuring the success of a venture.

Second, there are sharply differing attitudes to law, particularly to its aims and purposes, in China than in the West. In the latter (for better or for worse), we tend to see the law as the essential set of rules of conduct governing our society, and also as our primary form of redress when things go wrong. Quite different traditions exist in China; here the 'rules of conduct' are the ethics and standards of behaviour required in a Confucian society. Social pressures rather than legal instruments are used to ensure compliance. Of course this does not mean that there are no laws in China; but the laws are used in different ways. As we discuss below, many of the issues which Westerners tend to think of as legal issues are better conceptualised in China as relationship issues.

Third, and related to the above, there is the fact that much of Chinese society – including its businesses – is organised on relationship principles. There are three key principles which can be added to the box in the last chapter:

* *Qíngmian*, or 'human feelings'; respect for the feelings of others is of great importance, particularly in relationship management.
* *Hé*, or 'harmony', a very powerful concept which stresses the smooth running of a group or a society. Harmony is seen as good, conflict as bad. *Hé* also means gentleness or friendliness.
* *Guànxì*, which is usually translated simply as 'relationships' or 'connections'. It is no exaggeration to say that relationships are the *modus operandi* of Chinese business. They are how things get done.

After looking more closely at this last concept, this chapter applies it in three contexts – government, legal/contractual and commercial – in all of which relationships are essential for doing business in China and around the region. They need to be considered and developed *simultaneously*. Some types of relationships will, in given circumstances, be more important than others; but over the long term, all three will be necessary and cannot be turned on and off like taps.

Guànxì

This complex concept carries expectations that, sometime, favours will be returned. Nevertheless it is not some form of bank account where net favour indebtedness can be measured. The whole system, *guànxìwang*, is a web of subtle, and not so subtle, obligations, not rights. *Guànxì* has both good and bad meanings. In this chapter we intend the good. (*Guànxì* and corruption will be discussed in the 'Ethical interlude' which follows this chapter.) Some business people, especially younger ones, dismiss *guànxì* as old fashioned and being replaced by modern Western methods. That is unwise; the two will co-exist. *Guànxì* is a comparatively new word, entering the vocabulary only in the twentieth century, but the practice goes back to antiquity. *Guàn*, from which it derives, means a customs house, gate or barrier. Thus, without *guànxì* the door to business is firmly barred.

Westerners have difficulty with the concept of obligations unmatched by rights. Conversely, the Chinese had no word for, and thus concept of, 'rights' until they had to import *chuan li*, via Japan, for Western translation purposes. *Guànxì* is rooted in Confucianism. Family and social context define the individual as distinct from the Western view in which the individual defines his context. 'In other words, self-individualisation is possible only through a process of engagement with others within the context of one's social roles and relationships … the self is always a relational self, a relational being'.[1] Mayfair Yang traces the influence of *guànxì* through all forms of social and commercial life in China.[2] Thus marketing in China, however much influenced by Western theory and practice, can be expected to depend on relationships.

The Chinese classify *guànxì* capital (*ziben*) according to its efficacy (*ling*). The key features are:

- Durability (*naiyong*), meaning unconditionality. Thus the more certain that support will be reciprocated, the longer it can be deferred.
- Hardness (*ying*) *guànxì* refers to the relative importance of the other party: the more senior the 'harder'.
- Connectivity (*lianhuo*) refers to the onward *guànxì* in relevant networks. However strong the relationship may be with a dead end, he is still a dead end.

The last idiom seems to be somewhere between consanguinity and the degree of obligation. The sub-components are 'endowed' (*tianzi*) by birth, whether immediate family (*zhizi qinshu*) or father's relations (*nanfang*). The weaker non-birth varieties are seen as personal savings (*jilei*) which may be pulled over (*laguolai*) for business. Feelings (*ganqing*) built up from shared experience accumulate: the longer, ideally since childhood, the better. Relationships formed within, are for the purpose of, business are the weakest and seen, to some extent, as instrumental (*liyong*), self-interest (*liyi*) and money (*jinjian*) *guànxì*.

The first of those is similar, perhaps, to trust and the last is similar to identity (of interest). This shared identification is sometimes called the *guànxì* base. Each of us is an amalgam of nature (genes) and nurture (experience) and this last idiom directly mirrors that with *tianzi* and *ganqing*. It is interesting, but not surprising, that expatriate Chinese are more likely to deal with other expatriates originating in the same part of China.

Guànxì is a mechanism for dealing with risk. The Chinese may be gamblers but, without *guànxì*, they prefer to miss the opportunity for gaining £1 million. On the other hand, they may prefer to risk losing £100 in order to build *guànxì* for the future. We should not risk what we cannot afford. This is why the Chinese build trust progressively by introducing more and more risk and seeing how it works out. They are looking backward, not forward.

These components need to be seen in a competitive environment in which they act at two levels: a strong enough relationship gains entry to the consideration set and then the relative *guànxì* affects the probability of doing business. The bigger the risk, the stronger the *guànxì* will need to be. For example, tendering for large contracts in China is rarely the free market auction Westerners expect. The supplier will be determined by *guànxì*; only the terms of that business are determined by the tenders.

We are not alone in seeing *guànxì* as an alternative to contract law; no less a figure than Singapore's Lee Kuan Yew has made the same observation. One could argue that it is also a great deal cheaper; but the US system, for example, and the Chinese system are not easily compared in financial terms. It is wrong to see China as backward in legal terms; they have had a better, or at least a different, system.[3]

Government

Since economic reform began in 1978, the government of China has consciously orchestrated legal and commercial changes so as to maximise *China's* economic interest, both domestically and globally. Relaxation of rules on foreign ownership and investment, reforming state ownership ('privatisation' is not accepted as a word) and liberalisation of the economy generally are only pragmatic tools. The government sees the free market as a means to its own ends, not as an ideological principle. The rules will change any time they think it suits them.

It is worth cautioning the reader again about the rate of change in China and particularly in government. New rules on foreign investment were announced in September 1999 (*China Daily*, 9 September 1999) and they will not yet be implemented, or they may have been superseded by the time this book reaches the bookshelves. Premier Zhu radically downsized central PRC ministries in the reforms of 1998; fifteen entire ministries ceased to exist. The Ministry of Education considered itself lucky not to be abolished or merged with the Ministry of Science (as in the UK). The total headcount was cut by 50 per cent to 447 employees. Thailand, for example, has nearly ten times that number in the equivalent ministry. In July 1999, Madam Chen, the PRC education minister, was highly amused by her British opposite number having no idea how many civil servants were on his payroll. Or maybe he was just too embarrassed to answer. In rather an enlightened manner, Premier Zhu arranged for free places at MBA schools for redundant civil servants.

The paragraphs that follow, therefore, are tinged with envy rather than criticism. The PRC bureaucratic process works remarkably well, from their point of view. They invented the concept of mandarins, after all, and had centuries of managing the country with very few, but highly intelligent, civil servants. Zhu cut the numbers rather than the work and left the demarcations between and within the new super-ministries unclear, so the frustrations noted below still apply.

Government in China has considerable powers. It can deny approval for proposed projects, and it can withdraw licences from existing ones. On a single day in 1996, the government of one eastern city withdrew licences for over a hundred joint ventures, for reasons ranging from disputes between partners to lack of profitability. Government also has great authority. As distinct from power, this means that government in China often gets its own way without having to invoke its formal powers, by 'suggesting' that companies or individuals should pursue a certain course of action. This is very much in line with the Chinese avoidance of confrontation and preference for arriving at mutually agreed solutions (even if in this case, one party tells the others what they are agreeing to).

It follows that if you have good relationships with the relevant branches of government, you are more likely to get what you need, be it permission to build, develop, sell goods, set up a factory, form a joint venture or what-ever. Good relations with government can make the wheels of bureaucracy turn faster, even allowing you to 'jump the queue' and get approval more quickly than you might expect. Poor relationships or none at all, conversely, can put ventures at risk. The most famous example of all is probably McDonald's in Beijing. Having been granted permission to estab-lish a restaurant in a prime location on the south side of Tiananmen Square (ironically enough, almost opposite Mao's mausoleum), a few months later the company discovered its permission had been revoked and the site had been given to a Hongkong-based developer. After three years of wrangling, McDonald's finally recovered the site.

Outside the PRC, governments are also interventionist to some extent. Democracies like Taiwan have more restrictions on the powers of government and more give and take between government and business. In Thailand and Indonesia, on the other hand, government is every bit as omnipresent as in China. (The governments of Taiwan, Indonesia, Thailand, Malaysia, Singapore and several other countries are described briefly in Chapter 9; the rest of this section looks specifically at the PRC.)

Bureaucracy

Sally Stewart suggested that:

> It would perhaps be sensible, when introducing a paper on so contro-
> versial and complex a subject as the loci of power in the People's
> Republic of China, to issue a disclaimer to the effect that anyone (the
> author included) who imagines that he comprehends all the complexi-
> ties of the situation is probably deluding himself. Nevertheless, it is
> important for all those engaged in business with the PRC to have some
> feel for the general nature of the decision-making process; even
> though the complexity and size of the organizational chain, and the
> intervention of influential personalities, lobbies or local authorities
> and the like, may lead to there being endless exceptions to the rule.[4]

Bureaucracy has been a feature of China for millennia. Under the Qin
and Han dynasties, strong centralised bureaucracies were developed first as
a counterweight to and later as a replacement for the land-owning nobility.
They became the elite of Chinese society. Selection was by examination,
after a course of study comprised mainly of studying the classics of literature. Bureaucrats were steeped in Confucian traditions and intensely loyal
to the state. The 1949 revolution brought some changes, mainly in the
nature of education and the way in which bureaucrats were selected; the
ideology changed, but the bureaucracy remained.

Any Western business going into China will encounter the bureaucracy,
probably sooner rather than later. Again, it is a mistake to think of the
bureaucracy as being homogeneous. Stewart lists ten branches of government that participated in 'a relatively low technology project'. This was not
unusual, though, as discussed below, bureaucracy is being cut down.
Westerners marvel at how decisions can ever be made through so many
authorities. Travellers' tales abound with decisions being made by silent
bureaucrats who seemed too lowly to take part in the proceedings, or who
never appeared at all. (In the 1970s, a joke business card circulated among
the Western community in Beijing. Printed in Chinese and English, it bore
no name or title, but simply the legend: THE RELEVANT OFFICIAL FROM
THE DEPARTMENT CONCERNED.)

Bureaucracy can intervene anywhere it wants but money is increasingly
a reason for doing so (China's economic benefit) and for not doing so (cost
to PRC government of getting involved). Decisions are intended to be
made by consensus and the extent of lateral communication can be
remarkable. Normally, the decision process begins with reports from subordinates, which are sent upwards to superiors; decisions then come

downwards from supervising authorities, after substantial consultation both up and down the hierarchy and across different functions and ministries. Individual responsibilities are not as clear as in the West but, since the goal is consensus, they should not need to be. There is much informal reporting and personal relationships play a key role.

Like civil servants the world over, initiative-taking is to be avoided. The aim is to reduce the in-tray by whatever means and react only when one has to.

Every department or agency has its own area of responsibility, but frequently these areas overlap; and, since every department also jealously guards its own privileges and responsibilities (just like in the West), disputes are frequent. One Western firm trying to set up a plant in Lanzhou ultimately gave up in frustration after securing approval from Beijing but then being persistently blocked by local government. *It is not enough to cultivate relationships with one level of government only*; you need to look at doing so on several levels.

This problem is further compounded by the fact that bureaucrats can hold many different positions simultaneously, including some in the private sector. Ian Rae recounts a meeting with a Chinese official at which the official handed out three business cards: according to one he was the deputy head of a government department, a second listed him as the vice-president of a construction company, while the third named him as consultant to an investment bank.[5] Such people are of course well-connected and make valuable contacts, but they do rather transcend Western thinking about the need for separation between business and government.

In Western perception, bureaucratic subordinates are seen as insecure and reluctant to make decisions. You can never go wrong or be criticised for doing nothing; you are only blamed when you demonstrate initiative. Thus even the most minor matters are referred up the chain of command, and the highest ranking bureaucrats are inundated with minutiae. This does happen, but it would be wrong to suggest it happens all the time. In fact, decisions get passed all around the organisation – up, down and sideways – but not for reasons of insecurity. Rather, the factor at work here is the Chinese dislike of confrontation. Any decision which could result in confrontation (with its possibility of loss of face) is bypassed; either it is handed on to someone else, or it simply ignored. When faced with a problem, Westerners typically feel the urge to resolve it; Easterners do not. Indeed, forcing a Chinese person to make a decision where consensus cannot be achieved may put the latter under real personal stress. (For example, Chinese managers can be very reluctant to fire workers.)

Bureaucrats, like Margaret Thatcher, prefer solutions to problems. And they mostly like the sort of solutions everyone else will like. Persisting in confrontation can delay the decision for ever as they do not like saying 'no' either.

One important point to recognise is that authority is used differently. In the West, a bureaucrat usually has the authority to say 'yes', whereas in China authority more usually extends only to saying 'no' if the interests of their part of government are threatened. In order to overcome this tendency, business people work out, in advance, the interests of each participating (and possibly competing) branch of government.

Our advice is to start with a map of the network (*guànxìwang*) involved. Then, for each network node, list the interests of those involved and see the situation from their point of view. Shape your plans with these interests and viewpoints in mind.

Beijing Air Catering Company, China's oldest foreign-funded joint venture, was set up in 1979 to provide in-flight meals for airlines flying out of Beijing International Airport. At the start, BACC serviced only three airlines, but a decade later this had grown to twenty clients. By then, its staff were preparing up to 12,000 meals a day on antiquated equipment with a theoretical capacity of 4,000. In 1987, the company decided to embark on a second stage of development. The Chinese investor, the Beijing Management Department of the Civil Aviation Administration of China (CAAC), and its foreign partner, the Hongkong Chinese Food Company, injected more capital to build a second production line which was supposed to be ready for the 11th Asian Games in Beijing in September 1990. Eighteen months after the games ended and despite more than 100 stamps of approval from various higher authorities, work had still not begun. Differences between the various government departments, including disputes over the complicated procedures required for the import of much-needed new equipment and other facilities, were the main reasons for the delay. The company was regulated not only by the Beijing Civil Aviation Administration but also by the Beijing Municipal Finance Department, Personnel Department and several others.

Better analysis of the *guànxìwang* would have avoided many of these problems.

One great advantage of Zhu's downsizing of ministries is that there are fewer relationships to build. Contacts are also more likely to stay in place; China does not share the Western fondness for incessant job rotation.

Branches of government

The legislature is the National People's Congress (NPC), whose responsibilities include approval of national economic plans, state budgets and state accounts. The Standing Committee of the NPC interprets the constitution and the laws, enacts decrees and has the power to annul or change the decisions of lower organs. The NPC used to be something of a rubber stamp body, but the representatives have recently begun flexing their muscles; the NPC as a body has not yet dared to veto measures approved by the State Council, but numbers of representatives voting against unpopular measures have begun to rise.

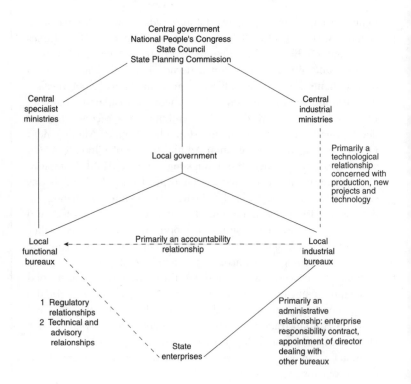

Figure 4.1 The higher administrative structure of state enterprises

Source: Child, J. (1996) *Management in China during the Age of Reform*, Cambridge University Press

In *theory*, the State Council, the executive body, which is chaired by Premier Zhu Rongji, is subordinate to the NPC. In practice, like any executive group and wide council, effective power rests with the Council. The premier, his vice-premiers and state councillors administer China through roughly one hundred organisations under State Council supervision.

The courts, of which the highest is the Supreme People's Court, settle civil disputes, including commercial cases, and punish criminals. More will be said on this later. There is no separation of powers between the executive and legislative branches, although there has been some discussion as to whether there should be (*Beijing Legal Daily*, 23 May 1994). Deng Xiaoping had said that China should not adopt a Western system 'of three governments', nor should it 'introduce the system of balance of three powers' (that is, the separation of the executive, the legislature and the judiciary).

Provincial and municipal governments mirror the structure of the central government. The chain of command among government units has, as noted above, given rise to a Byzantine system of multiple reporting. For example, a drug factory located in Shanghai might report to both the Shanghai Pharmaceuticals Bureau – a unit of the local government – and to the State Pharmaceutical Administration, part of the central government in Beijing. Various other agencies – the local labour bureau, the local environmental bureau, the local supplies bureau and so on – would have a say in certain activities of the factory. Also important to consider in the relationship matrix are the industry associations and commissions (known as 'mothers') that sit above the immediate partners, and other authorities such as taxation departments, who are known as 'mothers-in-law'.

Of course in China as well, government is not only active as a regulator; it is also an active player, owning and controlling many thousands of businesses. One result of the reform programme has been to relax control over individual businesses, either by assigning autonomy to their managers or by selling them altogether. But in some sectors and regions government is reluctant to let control go, and sometimes a relaxation of control by one level of government is replaced by another. Ian Rae comments that not only do regulations and their implementation differ from place to place, but many regulations are not actually written down.[6]

And, although government is less involved in running businesses, it is still very much involved in ownership; not only centrally, as in the case of the much discussed and much abused state enterprises, but also locally through forms such as township enterprises. As for these enterprises under collective ownership, there is no clear separation between state and private ownership, with a lot of hybrid forms in between.[7] Change is constant and ongoing, but does not always lead in the same direction; the government is quite capable of backtracking and reasserting control over sectors which are not performing as required.

Regulatory problems in China are almost a given. Regulations vary from province to province, but having the right Chinese partner can ensure that some regulatory problems simply vanish. Companies working with CITIC, for example, report that regulatory barriers are much lower than when working with smaller, regional businesses or institutions.

That kind of intervention can be very valuable because, to the outsider, Chinese business and economic regulation and planning can be confusing and bewildering, particularly when the effect of local government intervention is added to national law. Some superficially good projects might be vetoed by the Chinese local government because they do not fit with current economic planning; the reasons for the veto will make perfect sense to the Chinese authorities but may be completely mysterious to the Western firm that has been rejected.

In addition, the government of China is far from the monolith it is often portrayed as being, and some municipal and provincial authorities can be very strong-minded and take their own approaches to business. Shanghai has a reputation for being co-operative and helpful, Guangdong may be less helpful but is more easy-going, Beijing municipality tends to be bureaucratic and insist on the letter of the regulation being adhered to. However, there are plenty of exceptions in these three centres, and plenty of other variations in other provinces and cities. Much depends on the attitudes of local government, which can range from old-style Marxist (in parts of the west, for example) to go-ahead neo-capitalist (more common in the east and Manchuria).

The Communist Party

Little needs to be said about the Communist Party (CP) beyond the fact that it is still a powerful force in China, with more members today than it had at the height of the Cultural Revolution. It continues to operate as a parallel structure to the government, with considerable overlap; most bureaucrats are also Party members.

Formerly, the Party had an important role in the workplace, with enterprises managed by a triumvirate of the commercial manager, the senior trade union official and the senior Party official. The Party official was the top decision-maker. Since reform, the Party has begun scaling back its involvement; it is no longer mandatory for a Party cadre to be present in each workplace, though most state enterprises still have one, who is mainly in charge of ideology and some important personnel instead of business administration in the past. But the influence is still there.

Many join the Party less out of a sense of ideological commitment than out of a desire to gain access to privileges and take advantage of the networking opportunities. As networks go, the Party is an excellent one, with access to key players at every level of government and industry. Outsiders should consider these advantages as well; establishing contacts within the Party can mean opportunities for getting around some of the bureaucratic roadblocks.

Faced by a choice of hires, other things being equal, the Party member is probably the better bet because of the better *guànxì* he or she will bring.

The People's Liberation Army

The PLA is another *guànxìwang* peculiar to China. In fulfilling its primary function, national defence, it is subordinated to the CP, and the senior army commanders report ultimately to the Party Council. Unlike other countries, the government – the State Council in China – does not reign over the army. The PLA has a fairly free hand. Shortly after economic reform, the army was encouraged to become directly involved in commerce and establish joint ventures with foreign firms, partly to provide income to supplement the shrinking defence budget, but also to get access to better technology. Redundant defence factories were converted to consumer goods; distribution and trading companies were established like the giant Xinxing Group, which was owned by the PLA's logistics arm.

The PLA's goals are similar to those of the government, but they are pursued independently. Three times in the last fifty years (in Korea against the Americans, on the Yalu River against the Russians and in northern Vietnam against the Vietnamese), the PLA has fought a major foreign war against a better equipped and better trained army than itself, and has suffered terrible casualties. Further, the army sees itself as the guarantor of a strong China, and knows it can only carry out this task if it has the necessary technology and equipment. The driving force behind the army's involvement in commerce, therefore, is to make itself stronger and better able to discharge its primary function as the final guarantor of internal peace and stability in China.

There have long been rumbles of discontent about the PLA's commercial interests (and smuggling/corruption). As part of the 1998 state reforms, the PRC government divested them of their commercial ventures in return for a budget increase of 30 billion yuan. However, saying and doing are two different things. The PLA will have to operate remaining commercial functions under deeper cover but they probably remain a factor to consider when building distribution networks in China. The army has still considerable resources at its disposal, in terms of manpower, land

and buildings, and ability to influence the bureaucrats in the government. Also, an army is almost always a significant purchasing power.

Law

As one observer has commented, 'How Peking succeeds in spreading modern commercial and economic law will be instrumental in determining whether China can establish a stable base for continued economic development'.[8] Certainly China is under pressure to bring its commercial legal structure into line with that of the West, and all available evidence suggests it is genuinely trying to do so. How long it will take to succeed is another matter.

Traditionally in China, the law has generally been treated as flexible and subject to interpretation. In imperial times, magistrates were not simple judges, but feared officials with plenipotentiary powers who not only acted as judge, jury and executioner but also conducted investigations on an inquisitorial style (rather as in the modern Roman law system used in France, Spain and Italy). Magistrates had very wide discretionary powers within the broad frameworks provided by the law.

From 1949 until 1979, China had little commercial law and no legal provisions for foreign people to do business in China; during the Cultural Revolution, the law itself was effectively abandoned in many places. In 1977 there were virtually no practising lawyers, only three universities awarded law degrees and the Ministry of Justice (MOJ) had only just been re-established for a year after a twenty-year break. Since then, growth has been rapid. In 1986 the All China Association of Lawyers was founded, and by 1993 there were 50,000 lawyers and 4,100 law firms of which 200 were private partnership firms in China. Although sixty universities now offer law degrees, and there are claims that as many as 10,000 lawyers a year are graduating, China still remains short of lawyers with only about one in four commercial cases featuring lawyers on either side.

The relatively low profile of lawyers in commerce is probably explained by *guànxì* as we noted above. Chinese businesses rely on relationships rather than legal bonds. Increasing interaction with the West is bringing with it greater use of legal instruments, but only up to a point. However, with the migration to the cities, cowboy behaviour is growing. The PRC now recognises that it needs legal enforcement and that the traditional system is no longer enough.

Outside the PRC, more recognisably Western models of law exist. Taiwan, for example, has modelled its legal system on that of the USA, while Malaysia, Singapore and the Hongkong SAR continue to use the British legal system inherited from the colonial power. Legal training is more common, legal systems are more sophisticated, and there is a greater willingness to go to law. Nevertheless, within the Chinese business communities in these countries, mediation continues to play an important role. In this as in many other areas, the overseas Chinese still do business much like their mainland counterparts.

Commercial law

China's commercial legal framework is becoming increasingly complex, mirroring similar developments in the economy as a whole. In the 1970s, China's international business exchanges were relatively straightforward trade transactions regulated by comparatively simple sets of rules. By the end of the 1980s, foreign business people were involved in an ever-expanding variety of commercial transactions with China, including the establishment of joint ventures and wholly foreign-owned ventures, commercial and concessional lending, project financing, underwriting international issues of bonds and corporate shares[9] financing leasing, technology licensing, oil and gas exploration and development, processing and assembly, counter-trade, real estate development and other construction projects, hotel management and retailing.

Chinese law distinguishes between international commercial transactions and transactions between Chinese entities, which are covered by two different sets of legislation. Examples of this are China's contract laws, technology transfer laws and, until January 1994, the tax laws. Needless to say, this separation has been challenged in the World Trade Organisation, to which China is currently seeking membership. Because China wants to join the WTO, it can be assumed that the Chinese commercial legal system will fall into line with world standards in *legislative* terms. Law and practice are likely to diverge for some time.

As well as laws, there are national and local regulations. Conflicts between local, provincial and national regulations are not uncommon. In China as in the West, ignorance of these requirements does not constitute a defence.

Like many other countries, China also uses commercial law to create favourable investment climates in important regions and sectors. There are incentives to certain types of investment. In broad terms, projects that are export-oriented and introduce advanced technology, and also energy and transportation projects, can enjoy lower tax rates and preferential treatment when securing funding, employing staff and obtaining access to utilities.

Contracts

Contracts have a different place in Chinese negotiations. In the West, it is not unknown almost to begin with draft contracts and use them as working documents until agreement is reached. China is getting used to Western ways, but historically such a move would have seemed bad faith. The other countries in the region, with longer exposure to the West, tend to be more attuned to the needs of Western businesses.

Contracts should be drafted in Chinese as well as the language of the foreign investor, ensuring, of course, that they are identical in all material respects. Some China hands recommend having important documents translated twice by independent translators, and then comparing the two versions. Checking translations is vital to ensure that the wording of the contract is unambiguous. One European firm (which shall remain nameless) found itself committed to a technology transfer deal whereby the Chinese partner was not obligated to pay any royalties until they were capable of producing a 'first-class product'. Needless to say, they never did so; but they did manage to produce and sell profitably a great deal of 'second-class product' without paying a penny to the technology supplier. Another good example of 'eight sides all wide and slippery' – a Chinese phrase to describe a clever man.

Under Chinese law, contracts that must be approved by Chinese government authorities do not become legally binding upon signature, but only when the approval certificate is issued. MOFTEC (Ministry of Foreign Trade and Economic Corporation) or other relevant ministry and its subordinate provincial or municipal agencies are responsible for issuing approvals. The level of approval depends on the amount of investment involved and the nature of the project. More than one Western firm has been caught out this way.

Approval by the relevant ministry secures the operating licence but is not the end. Separate applications must be made to the tax authorities, foreign exchange authorities and customs administration and the consent and active support of local authorities must be obtained for a host of matters under local jurisdiction such as assuring the supply of utilities, materials and labour, the plans and costs for the construction of buildings and compliance with environmental regulations. Consultants advise that, when possible, these approvals and commitments should have been ensured before signing the contract; failing that, make the contract conditional on their satisfactory resolution.

Arbitration and mediation

In China, there is strong preference for the resolution of disputes through conciliation with litigation being the last resort. Mediation and arbitration are not the same thing. Mediation, seen in China as good, is the process of facilitating agreement between two parties. Arbitration, seen as a poor solution, is the process of finding some fair compromise. Most Westerners do not notice the difference, which is important in China. Not surprisingly, there are many mediators in China (about 10 million), but few arbitrators. The courts and tribunals encourage mediation between the parties even after litigation proceedings have commenced. As arbitration is so ingrained in Western business thinking, however, China is learning to accommodate it.

China has used mediation for centuries, and its methods stem from the teachings of Confucius. Essentially, mediation seeks to resolve disputes in a way acceptable to all parties, without loss of face; it is primarily a method for defusing or dispelling confrontations. Much mediation, of course, is on family and social issues, not commercial, and is also quite informal. The Chinese are encouraged to resolve their disputes on their own initiative through mediation committees in their neighbourhood or workplace. Mediators are chosen within the neighbourhood, and no formal training is required to qualify. Since 1983, eighty times more cases have been mediated than have been tried by China's courts. Some 60 per cent of cases that proceed to litigation are also mediated at some point.[10] Mediation was also not disrupted by the Cultural Revolution in the same manner as the legal system.

Arbitration is much more formal. Where both parties to a dispute are Chinese entities (for this purpose, joint ventures and WFOEs are Chinese entities), arbitration must take place within China. Where one of the parties is foreign, a foreign venue can now be selected. Sweden, for reasons going back to the eighteenth century, is a preferred international source of arbitrators. Two China giants had a victory in a London arbitration in summer 1999. China National Petroleum Corporation and China Petroleum Technology Development Corporation resisted claims of about $50 million lodged by their US opposite numbers. Costs went to the Chinese.

Commercial cases can be taken to court, but the record of legal enforcement in China is poor. The courts do not enforce judgements themselves; instead, this is a matter for the police, who quite often feel they have more important things to do. A foreign firm has a better chance of succeeding in enforcing an arbitration award within China, but the enforcement process can still be lengthy and difficult. Even worse is the record of enforcing foreign court judgements.

Intellectual property

As is well known, intellectual property is the largest legal minefield in commercial international relations with China, and is probably the most difficult legal issue to solve. Part of the problem is that there was no history of patents or copyright; what was in print was freely available. This does *not* mean, as some journalists have written, that the Chinese do not see anything wrong with piracy. Piracy is wrong, and it is illegal in China. However, enforcing anti-piracy laws is taxing the powers of the legal and enforcement systems to the limit.

In the mid-1990s, industry sources in Beijing claimed that software piracy in China was costing the USA (with Microsoft being one of the largest victims) $500m a year and that fifteen pirate CD plants were producing 50 million CDs a year (as opposed to 3 million produced by the legitimate plants).[11] In terms of sales, pirate CDs and cassettes had shares of 83 per cent and 44 per cent respectively. These figures have certainly risen since then. The authorities have scored some successes; in 1994, Disney won a historic case of copyright infringement in Beijing, and the same year there was a crackdown on pirated video games. A number of pirate CD makers were put out of action in 1996. But the pirates are like the Hydra; cut off one head, and more appear elsewhere.

China's legal protection of intellectual property rights is, in theory, now only slightly weaker than in other Asian countries. Two specialist courts in Shanghai hear intellectual property cases. In 1992, China signed a wide-ranging intellectual property rights agreement with the USA and a similar one with the European Union in order to facilitate its entry to the WTO. Under these agreements, China has joined the Berne and Geneva copyright conventions, passed a new patent law affording greater protection to chemical, drug and food makers, and revised its trademark law to cover service markets. But even with these new laws, foreign companies are not secure from infringements of intellectual property rights.

A few simple precautions can make it easier to locate violators and obtain compliance:

1   Prepare an intellectual property inventory.
2   Appoint an intellectual property manager responsible for keeping the inventory current and scouting the China market for infringements.
3   Register whatever you can wherever you can *in China*.
4   Conduct regular market surveys to determine if trademarks, patents or copyrights are being violated.
5   Sue even though you do not expect redress, because the authorities will not take the matter seriously until you have.

The problem of intellectual property infringement is by no means unique to China, and it can be argued that China is doing more than some countries to deal with it. Taiwan is also home to many software and music pirates (strangely, the US government gets far less exercised about these than it does about those in China), and Indonesia, Malaysia and Thailand all have their pirate kings. And never mentioned, of course, is the scale of routine, everyday software piracy that goes on in many homes and offices in the West.

Commercial relationships and *guànxì*

The opening section may have seemed intimidating but it is all quite normal. We all develop *guànxì*-type relations throughout our lives, and we all have our *guànxìwang* (network of relationships) with family, friends and so on. What is different in China is that this same pattern of relationships gets transferred into the business world, on a quite explicit and open basis. Business associates within a network are referred to as being *zi jia rén* (one's own family). In a Confucian society, *guànxì* represents a natural blurring of the line between the professional and the personal.

Guànxì is a powerful social force in all Chinese cultures. People's sense of themselves, their self-perception and their self-worth, is determined mostly by their relationships with others. It is important not to confuse *guànxì* with the 'groupist' traits noted in Japanese society. Chinese do not identify solely or even primarily with the group to which they belong; the self is and always has been a very important concept. The distinction is subtle but there is a difference between the individual defining the network (US) and the individual being defined by the network (China). The Chinese are both individualist *and* group oriented, and the relationships between group and individual are complex and deep-rooted. Thus personal (and business) relationships are always formed on two levels; with the person as an individual, and the person as a member of a reference group.

So important is *guànxì* that some observers (such as Seligman 1990) maintain that you cannot get anything done in China without it, even simple things like buying a train ticket. That is no longer true, but in a commercial sense at least, establishing *guànxì* with partners, suppliers and even customers is an essential pre-requisite. Virtually every major success story involving foreign companies in China involves the building of *guànxìwang* (networks of relationships) before proceeding with business. Companies like IBM China and Shanghai Volkswagen have devoted literally years to this process.

Getting on the inside has been, and remains, Asea Brown Boveri's (ABB) corporate strategy. The Swiss-Swedish power engineering giant is seeing its payoff. ABB is part of the consortium for the 1,980 MW Shajiao C coal-fired power station in the Pearl River delta and provided the steam turbine and plant in the $34.5 million Fushun power plant in China's north-eastern Liaoning province. ABB's business strategy aims for solid vertical penetration, each step increasing its understanding of, and interdependence with, the China market. Becoming an 'insider' required ABB to:

1   Enter first as a technology seller. China most wants foreign investment and technology.
2   Licensing and transfer of technology.
3   Build market understanding and sales through opening representative offices and entering pilot joint ventures.
4   Establish a network joint venture that will absorb the representative offices. ABB's conception of being an insider in China also envisages it setting up a training centre in Beijing and targeting R&D to China's needs.[12]

Guànxì takes time to develop. Relationships, once created, are hard to break; the obligations you accept when you enter into *guànxì* are not easily avoided. Most Chinese are therefore cautious and proceed gradually step by step. Beware the Chinese contact who says shortly after meeting, 'now we are friends': this is either insincere flattery or mischief. The first steps in relationship building, however small, are critical: as one Chinese friend says, 'a satisfied beginning is equal to half the success'.

On the whole, Westerners have tended to be suspicious of *guànxì*. We like to think that in our societies, everything is done openly and fairly and everyone has access to the same opportunities and the same information. Indeed, we tend to regard instances where people do favours for friends in business as bordering on corruption, if not actually stepping over the line. The equation of *guànxì* with corruption is common, as for example in the following guidebook for managers:

> With the right connections, there is a window of opportunity for coming in via a side entrance, a fast track which will allow you to open a business at a fraction of the prevailing costs and the minimum of frustration. All you need is cash and a good Chinese partner, with the right connections – who did they go to school with or did their father go to school with or serve in the army with? – and anything is possible.[13]

In China state employees earn very little and can exert a great deal of power over private concerns. Small salaries but large fringe benefits (such as housing) encourage them to stay in their posts but earn cash on the side. Despite several well-publicised anti-corruption drives, the situation looks set to continue. As one businessman remarked: 'Here you have all these very powerful state-run organisations looking for a way to make a bit of money. The official who has got the golden chop to give you that licence you need to operate your business is now ready to listen to your proposal. That's bribery, of course, but it's always been part of the system – Guànxì'.[14]

We review the dark side of *guànxì* just after this chapter.

The Para-Keets

The Para-Keets are a rock band based in Manchester, who have just discovered by happenstance that pirate tapes of their recent, moderately successful album are being sold in street markets in Shanghai and Beijing. The company making the tapes calls itself The New Shanghai Music Company. The covers are poorly reproduced, but the tapes themselves are of good quality.

The band's agent, manager and lead singer/songwriter have different ideas about what to do. The lead singer believes that 'imitation is the sincerest form of flattery', and has also pointed out that at least *someone* is selling the band's tapes in the Far East; her suggestion is to get in touch with the bootleggers and set up a legitimate deal. The agent was all in favour of instituting legal proceedings on the ground against the bootleggers. The manager was more hesitant, pointing out that very little was known about the bootleggers and that more research was going to be required before any final decision on action could be taken.

China recognises all international conventions on intellectual property, including the Zurich and Geneva agreements respecting music copyright. The Chinese government's stated policy is to match and accede to all international standards, recognising that trust is an important element in both joint ventures and international trade. Some large Western music companies such as Polygram did distribute to retailers in China. However, the store prices for their tapes and CDs were relatively high. Large numbers of tapes and CDs were also smuggled in from abroad, but by far the majority of tapes sold in China were produced locally, in violation of international copyright but not usually in violation of Chinese law.

No one knew the size of the bootleg industry in China because no one had yet properly surveyed it. Chinese tourists and travellers abroad, especially in Japan and southeast Asia, bought Western-produced tapes and brought them home quite legally, or even

continued

bought them in shops in China. These tapes were then used as recording masters and recording machines, set up in garages or studios, produced tapes. Some of these were illegal black market businesses, but some were perfectly legal operations. It is not therefore a simple matter of getting the police to close down a legitimate operation; a lawsuit, should such a thing be required, could be long and painful. Other options, such as mediation, could also be explored.

Conclusions

Government, the law and *guànxì* all interweave and are hard to separate. No one 'connection', however good, is adequate. In cultivating multiple connections, we have to remind ourselves that they are reciprocal: favours received are credits against future favours expected. Be cautious about the favours you accept.

To the Chinese and others in the Pacific Region, cultivating and using relationships is second nature, a natural part of the environment and doing business. Westerners, however, need to plan and track such networks consciously and with great care. We need to build our networks carefully and patiently.

Notes

1 Tao 1996: 16.
2 Yang 1994.
3 A great deal has been written about *guànxì* in Chinese culture. For more on this, consult G.K. Becker (ed.) (1996) *Ethics in Business and Society: Chinese and Western Perspectives.* Berlin: Springer; Eric W.K. Tsang (1998) 'Can *guànxì* be a source of sustained competitive advantage for doing business in China?' *Academy of Management Executive* 12(2), 64–73; David L. Wank (1996), 'The Institutional Process of Market Clientelism: *Guànxì* and Private Business in a South China City,' *The China Quarterly* 820–37. See also the bibliography at the end of this book.
4 Stewart 1990: 17.
5 Rae 1997.
6 Ibid.
7 This could be important, depending on where and in what sector the foreign firm wishes to do business. See the bibliography for books on this subject.
8 Goldstein, in S. Stewart and Ip Kam Tim (1994) 'Professional Business Services in the People's Republic of China', The University of Hongkong, unpublished monograph, November.

9 Foreign business people can participate in B-shares, H-shares and N-shares. China classified the investor types mainly by A-share, B-share, H-share and N-share. A-shares can be purchased and traded by domestic investors. B-shares are available exclusively to foreign investors and some authorised domestic securities firms. The B-shares market is separated from the A-share market, with SHSE B-shares denominated in US dollars and SZSE B-shares in Hongkong dollars. For each company, each A and B shareholder is entitled to the same rights and dividends. Not all firms are allowed to issue B-shares and it is required that B-shares comprise no more than 25 per cent of a PLC's tradable shares. Firms issuing B-shares are entitled to favourable tax treatment and more freedom to export and import goods. However, B-shares are generally sold at substantially lower costs than A-shares. China also created an additional class of stock to facilitate direct listing of Chinese companies on foreign stock exchanges, mainly including H-shares for Hongkong Stock Exchange and N-shares for New York Stock Exchange. H-shares and N-shares carry the same rights and obligations as the A-shares and B-shares, but they can not be traded on domestic stock exchanges.

10 *Dispute Resolution Journal*, June 1994.

11 *Financial Times*, 16 February 1994.

12 *Business China*, 3 May 1993.

13 Murray 1994.

14 Ibid.

An ethical interlude

Two main consumer rights are universal: the right not to buy again and the right to inform others about the product. Repurchase rates and word of mouth are powerful marketing forces which may apply in China with *relatively* more importance in the absence of other rights Westerners take for granted. This section pauses to reflect on the general question of 'rights' and the dark side of *guànxì*, namely corruption.

The interlude is arranged as follows:

- Centuries ago, both societies were more concerned with responsibilities than rights. Here we mean rights of all kinds, human as well as political and economic. The assertion of rights has grown faster in the West than in China. This, like democracy, has both advantages and disadvantages. We see no *higher authority* grounds for asserting one orthodoxy over another but do see *evolutionary* benefits in going with the flow. Each set of ethics simply reflects the way that culture polices its people. As global cultures fuse, we are evolving toward a universal view of rights and ethics.
- Business practices in the West are backed up by contract law and in China by *guànxì*. Legal processes carried to excess are as corrupt as *guànxì* carried to excess but the corruption lies in the excess, not in the product itself. Determining where healthy business practices degenerate into corruption depends on the culture concerned. Some Chinese practices would be corrupt in the USA but conversely, some US practices would be corrupt in China. The issue turns on whether they reduce the public good in that context, not whether they have intrinsic merit. This is, of course, the relativist position.

The development of rights and responsibilities

The need for harmony between rights and responsibilities has long been noted in East and West but they are not a zero sum game. Having fewer rights does not imply having more or less responsibilities; the concepts are linked but independent. From the earliest times, the individual's place in the community has been described by responsibilities, e.g. Confucius. The idea of rights is more recent; in the West it mostly hails from the Age of Enlightenment 300 years ago. You will not find much, if anything, about rights in the Christian Bible. The New Testament drills home the need to be responsible to God and then your neighbour. The Old Testament is even more obligation-heavy.

Probably Descartes, with his focus on identity, helped develop the idea that, if others have responsibility to me, then that gives me some rights, or at least expectations. If the husband should be faithful to his wife, then the wife may expect faithfulness. 'Rights', in the sense of human or consumer entitlement, were given eighteenth-century support as a matter of fairness. Given a choice between having rights or no rights, I would rather have rights. And, given that, why should I have them if others do not? There was a recognition of reciprocity. Slaves had no, or not many, rights and it was not until recently that the human race had a problem with that. 'Rights' etymologically come from the word 'straight', like the Greek ortho in orthodox. It is straight to recognise that others have similar rights to those one expects for oneself.

What is important here is that rights grew from responsibilities and the demands for rights have been increasing. How far should that go? The increase of one does not necessarily imply a decrease of the other but if everyone demands their rights and no-one exercises their responsibilities, society will fall apart. Eastern commentators like Singapore's Lee Kuan Yew have pointed to the moral degradation of the West meaning just that, responsibilities to others buried by demands for one's own rights. Human, and consumer, rights, are important but may not have much value unless others exercise their responsibilities. We have just seen the East Timorese express a democratic right to independence whilst the Indonesian authorities abrogated their responsibilities. The result was worse than chaos.

Second, for whatever reasons, the creation of rights from responsibilities happened far more slowly in China than in the West. That may be because, as we suggested in the last chapter, settled communities could manage well enough with reciprocal responsibilities and had no need of rights or contract law. Wang Gungwu, vice-chancellor of Hongkong University, once remarked that, 'The ancient Chinese only knew of duties but had no notion of rights.'[1] Whatever may be the position in PRC, it is clear that overseas Chinese have latterly adopted the notion of rights with enthusiasm.

Third, whilst the concepts of rights and responsibilities are universal, the particular selection of what they are varies from culture to culture and time to time. They are evolving. Today Britain attributes rights to animals too. As computers become more intelligent, we can expect computer rights at some point in the future. We see no evidence of any of this being God-given: our rights and responsibilities are what different societies decide them to be.

While Western media harp continually on human, or civil, rights, these are only part of a continuum of rights, including economic rights. The introduction of the free market in PRC has undoubtedly had a dramatic effect on the latter and some commentators suggest that PRC consumers are far more interested in economic than civil rights. We are now witnessing globalisation forcing cultures to accommodate each others' standards for rights and responsibilities. That does not make any one set either correct or as universal as some of our American friends seem to believe. It just means that a shrinking globe is forcing the world's cultures into a shared channel of evolution. The imposition of ethical standards by one culture on another is ethical fascism, in the original sense of 'fascism'. On the other hand, as we are going to have to live together, it would reduce conflict and misunderstanding if we allowed our standards to co-evolve. This in turn requires each culture to respect the de facto ethics of the other, at least in the sense of seeking to understand their philosophic and historic roots. Asserting one's own standards as universal is both arrogant and unhelpful. It used to be called colonialism.

Western linear thinkers are puzzled by the Chinese ability to hold onto a mass of apparently contrary philosophies at the same time – ancestor cult, Daoism, Confucianism, Legalism, Buddhism, Christianity and Communism to name but a few. The Westerner tends to *replace* one set of beliefs by the next whereas the Easterner tends to *add* them. This may be due to the Daoist tradition itself.

Be that as it may, in Confucianism the individual is defined by his relationships with others whereas in the West, our relationships are defined by our self-identity. This overstates the distinction in order to make the point. The virtuous person only assumes rights to the extent to which he gives them to others. Descartes' *cogito ergo sum*, I think therefore I am, owes nothing to anyone else. As we noted in the last chapter, the Chinese did not even have a word for 'rights' until recently: 'they borrowed from Japan a term, *chuan-li*, manufactured for translating Western political thought about a century ago'.[2]

Contract law versus *guànxì*

We suggested that the divergent cultures of the law in the US and *guànxì* in China arose from the essential difference between cowboy and farmer communities. *Guànxì*, personal connections, implies the reciprocal granting of favours but not in any tit-for-tat sense. These are not bank accounts. There is just a responsibility when a favour is accepted that one day, when it is needed, the favour will be returned. Contrary to some Westerners' beliefs, *guànxì* cannot be purchased. In that sense it is priceless and explains why in China one builds friendship before seeking to do business whereas in the US, the order is reversed. In the West we feel vaguely uncomfortable doing business with friends whereas in China, one would be uncomfortable if they were *not* friends.

So passing money in red envelopes may or may not be corrupt, but it is not *guànxì*. If you define doing business with friends as corrupt, then the 'corruption' arises from your perspective and definition, not from degrading business in a culture where such practices are the norm. Thus it is a question of context: ethical Chinese practices may be corrupt in the US and, now this is controversial, ethical US practices corrupt in China. Where *guànxì* is the norm, behaving in a non-*guànxì* way will degrade (corrupt) business. The importation of some Western business practices into China today is doing just that. The 1999 Disney negotiations between Shanghai and Hongkong, while probably fair competition in a US context, can be seen as corruptive in China.

In the largely settled, rural communities that made up China until very recently, relationships between individuals and between families were very long and *guànxì*, with endless chains of gift-giving, is the very foundation of their relationships. The main reason, in our view, for the importance of improving legal processes in China has less to do with importing Western business practices than with finding new enforcement rules where people are moving in huge numbers from one part of the country to another.

Corruption is, of course, a major issue in China. Since economic reform, it has become one of the biggest problems facing the Chinese economy and has deeply distressed many ordinary Chinese. It played no small part in the protests of 1989. It has also led to a growing number of officials receiving a bullet in the back of the head from the official executioner. The Chinese are fearful of it for the same reason that Germans fear inflation: they remember the damage it did in their past.

But this merely reinforces the point that *guànxì* and corruption are *not* the same thing, any more than drink is the same as drunkenness. One can enjoy the one and still avoid the other. One Chinese term for corruption, *zou houmen*, or 'going through the back door' can be applied to relatively innocuous practices such as the giving of a *hongbao*[3] a red envelope with a small amount of money. But in context it certainly is not. Gift giving has a long and honourable tradition in most parts of the world.

Christmas presents between business people are less prevalent in the

UK than they used to be but that probably has more to do with accountants than morality. Accountants plead morality just as the UK chancellor is sanctimonious when he raises duties on alcohol, cigarettes and petrol.

The line between corrupt and harmless practices is not easy to draw. The US Foreign Corrupt Practices Act specifically excludes 'grease payments' and tipping, i.e. money given to encourage officials to do what they should do anyway. Some governments regard those as necessary salary adjuncts, i.e. they save money for the taxpayer. Corruption involves paying someone to do what he should not do.

But it is not as simple as that either. A British chief financial officer of a pharmaceutical multinational in China was recently surprised to receive an envelope from the taxman with a substantial amount of cash. He was told it was a thank-you for handing over the PAYE collections from the payroll so promptly – clearly an unusual event. He decided it was wrong to rock the boat and credited the money in the company's books. He was not personally corrupt and it is not immediately obvious that the taxman was. But was he wise? What happens when the taxman needs a favour? This is not *guànxì*, which cannot be bought, but it may be starting a chain that should not be followed.

Many business people think that corruption is an acceptable and necessary part of doing business in China. Or at least getting started. It is all very well for IBM and Johnson and Johnson (or Janssen Xian) to act high and mighty but the newcomer without brand equity is under pressure to go through the back door if he cannot get through the front.

Bribery is expensive, tends rapidly to get more so, damages reputations, and leads to pseudo-*guànxì* with the wrong people. There is also the risk of substantial legal penalties in China and at home. Yet it is difficult to be too whiter-than-white about it. The entire alcoholic drinks distribution infrastructure in the US is built on illegal and corrupt, by any standards, relationships built during prohibition. And it has stood for over fifty years.

If marketers exercise their responsibilities, consumer rights will take care of themselves?

This chapter implies that rights are a recent, not wholly desirable, outgrowth from responsibilities. They are only as moral as the responsibilities that underpin them. We should worry more about responsibilities than rights: if marketers behave responsibly, consumer rights will take care of themselves. Furthermore, in China it is not enough to do the right things; they have to be done in the right way (*lì*). Bombing the Chinese embassy in Belgrade was clearly the wrong thing, but the American and British problems thereafter were compounded by a failure to observe the correct form.

A quick and apparently insincere apology made things worse. Genuine contrition required a proper investigation and explanation. Thus marketers should not only act responsibly but do so according to the conventions of the local market.

A small informal study in China recently indicated, as one might expect, that the Chinese have a very hazy view of both sides of this marketing coin. Consumers are quite happy knowingly to buy counterfeit goods on the grounds that they are similar but cheaper. They do not expect any consumer protection and, as yet, show little sign of wanting it. Retailers develop amnesia when faulty goods are returned. As marketing develops, so will both rights and responsibilities because reliable products and strong branding are in the commercial interests of both sides.

The idea that we should focus more on marketer responsibilities than consumer rights is perhaps more Chinese than American. Yet this is supported in the West by the declining profile given to consumerism since 1960–80. *Which?* magazine, the journal of the UK Consumers' Association, is struggling to keep afloat. One reason is probably the greater dominance of brands. With so much investment in these assets, their owners *have* to act responsibly and the need to protect consumer rights thereby diminishes.

Few China market entrants will be concerned with the theoretical and long-term implications of branding. They want to know whether to pay off Mr Li. All official advice will be to avoid doing so but ours is more complex. Whether everyone else is doing so is relevant but everyone else may not own up. Bribery (paying people to do what they should not do) is definitely a bad idea. Not only is it illegal; it damages the reputation of firms that do it. Grease payments are the problem.

Grease payments fall into two categories: tips and service payments where the amounts are minor compared to possible costs, and extortion. It has long been the custom, for example, to leave 100 yuan notes in envelopes under the plates of senior people invited for lunch and a business presentation. The money is ostensibly to pay for travel expenses. Clearly that $10, or so, is not going to make much difference to anyone. The practice is being replaced by small gifts like ties and pens and only the most petty minded would regard it as unethical.

Extortion, where quite a large sum is involved before something happens (unloading cargo for example), is another matter. Here it is tempting to regard the payer as the victim and the payee as corrupt but it is a brave, and probably foolish, foreigner who blows the whistle.

International business people have long got around the difficulty by hiring consultants at rather larger fees than they might otherwise expect so that they can take care of these matters. This 'monkey's paw' approach is less good in China than West Africa because of the negative effect it can have on long-term *guànxì*. This really is the issue. If the business is too small or too under-funded to survive without the grease payment *and* the longer term effects are not damaging to true *guànxì*, then it is an option we could not deny – especially if it is standard practice. On the other hand, there is little point in surviving if *guànxì* is harmed. Going out of business will just take a little longer and probably be more painful and expensive. Another solution needs to be found.

Finally, we must point out that foreign companies can, and should, help themselves through their trade associations. If an industry is being collectively held to ransom, then it is up to the industry *collectively* to do something about it. Differing national cultures may complicate matters. Americans worry that collective action is anti-competitive. Other countries are sometimes puzzled why the Anglo-Saxons make so much fuss about ethics. Until quite recently, bribes (and we are talking bribes not grease payments) were legitimate tax deductions in France and Germany. As a collective US/French/UK example, the drinks industry in China found itself paying escalating amounts of corkage to bartenders.[4] They all agreed to stop doing it. There is always a bit of cheating and disinformation on these occasions but, by and large, the ban held.

In this interlude we have reviewed the philosophy of rights and ethics and taken a relativist position. In other words, they reflect society norms and not some external absolutes. At the same time, as the world shrinks, they are co-evolving to a common, or more similar, future. After touching on consumer rights and marketer responsibilities, we moved to some pragmatic advice on bribery, extortion and grease payments. We have sought to be responsible but it is offered with no warranty: do not call us, call your lawyers.

Notes

1   Tao 1996: 11.
2   Hansen 1996: 107.
3   These are traditionally given out by more senior people at Chinese new year, by uncles to nephews, by bosses to subordinates and so on.
4   'Corkage' is a cash amount paid for every branded cork or bottle top returned by the retailer to the brand's local distributor.

Part II

5 Creating harmony

Alternative venture formats in PRC

The Way (tao) gives birth to the one.
One gives birth to two.
Two gives birth to three.
And three gives birth to the myriad things.
The myriad things bear *yìn* and embrace *yáng*.
By combining these forces, harmony is created.

Laozi

This chapter compares the different vehicles for foreigners to do business in the PRC. The technical details of company formation, governance and taxation are widely available from the international firms of lawyers; we are concerned with practicalities.

In the mid-1990s, the fashion was to decry joint ventures (JVs) and other forms of partnership, and to promote the wholly foreign-owned enterprises (WFOEs) as the new solution for China; by going it alone, you escape all the difficulties of working with partners. This is a delusion. All ventures, including WFOEs, rely on co-operation and collaboration with Chinese businesses and authorities. In China, we are always in partnerships so we need to recognise them and plan accordingly.

The chapter is structured to follow a path of increasing commitment:

- the distinction between production and distribution
- agencies and licensing
- joint ventures
- wholly foreign-owned enterprises
- identifying and negotiating with partners
- making the choice

The move towards WFOEs may been right but, as we will see, that depends whose figures you believe. China demands commitment so one may as well commit and get on with it. According to A.T. Kearney, of the multinationals operating in PRC in 1997, 62 per cent of their WFOEs were profitable but only 42 per cent of JVs were so. Twenty-two per cent had pulled out of JVs and, for 44 per cent of those, lack of profitability was the main reason.[1] On the other hand, John Child at Cambridge University estimates that in general, the success of wholly foreign-owned ventures is greatly overestimated, and that joint ventures are more likely to become profitable and to do so quickly.[2] The Economist Intelligence Unit also found that 47 per cent of joint ventures in China were profitable in two years or less; better figures than to be found anywhere else in the world. The Chinese themselves would not have been using joint ventures for decades if they did not work in this market. The empirical findings therefore are mixed.

The Chinese who, by and large, welcome inward investment with open pockets, have been progressively liberalising both production and distribution though they are rather more keen on the latter type of venture than the former. Factories export goods, bring in hard currency, and provide technology and skills transfer to Chinese workers and managers. Marketing or selling ventures threaten local industry and can have a perceived deleterious effect on Chinese culture and society. This is exactly the opposite of what many Western firms would ideally desire, which is access to the China market without the risk of having to establish operations there.

The distinction between production and distribution

In the West, setting up a factory automatically implies that one can distribute the goods in any way one chooses. That is not true in China, which has long encouraged production while discouraging foreign involvement in wholesale or retail distribution. A further distinction is made between local production and the import of finished goods where the restrictions on distribution are much tougher. Firms can get around that, to some extent, in much the same way that Ireland used to 'produce' bananas for the EU. Not noted for its tropical climate, the Dublin warehouses used to take care of final maturation and chemical finishing (no, do not ask – it was enough to gain the tax and duty advantages).

The consequence is that foreign firms need to consider each stage of the chain from raw materials to the end user – not just the production phase. All too many firms have invested much time and money in the factory, only to find distribution blocked. Distribution is the single biggest problem, along with staff, for the established firms and much of that is due to inadequate pre-planning. As we will later discuss, these have as much to do with the size of the country and its physical infrastructure as sales aspects.

A Western firm will not generally get distribution rights unless there is at least some technology transfer also involved. Alternatively, the firm may be required to set up a production facility which will export goods from China. With China's strong balance of payments, the old requirement for each firm to balance its hard currency transactions, while not dead, is much reduced. Even where there is no formal requirement, playing by this rule and offering some form of transfer can enhance chances of being accepted. The common result is a hybrid, where Western firms wishing to market in China also set up some sort of production facility, either licensing their own product entirely to the new venture or establishing a component or assembly plant.

Fosters, instead of exporting its beer into China, has formed joint ventures with breweries around the country to produce Fosters products in the country under licence and then sell it in the Chinese market. In other sectors, firms use a mix of imported and locally produced products; Shanghai Volkswagen's car assembly plants use both imported and locally produced components, with the proportion of the latter rising steadily.

Thus, obviously enough, there are three kinds of business:

1　Distribution only, which involve agencies and/or licensing. McCall Pattern Company set up a distribution network in partnership with the Beijing Garment Research Institute to sell its clothing patterns, which are printed in the USA and shipped to China. Most of the international pharmaceutical companies began as importers although local production is now opening fast. Of course, the local selling and physical distribution had to be handled by third parties.

2　Production only. A typical example is the joint venture between Ford, Shanghai Automotive Industry Corporation and Yao Hua Glass Works to make automotive components in China for the domestic industry. In this case, Ford aimed to get its foot in the door of the Chinese car market by setting up a low-cost production facility, in anticipation of being allowed to develop a full-scale vehicle assembly facility when the restrictions on foreign companies in this field were relaxed.

3　Combined production and distribution which may also be exporting to overseas markets. Marubeni computers, a major distributor for Apple, and China-based Legend Computers, makes IBM-compatible machines. By the terms of the venture, Marubeni has access to Legend's Beijing-area distribution network for imported Apple products and the two companies work together to expand distribution nationwide for both Apple and Legend/IBM machines. At the same time, Marubeni's East Asian networks are open for Legend to enter the export market. The two firms are also working together to develop, distribute and export Chinese-language software.

Agencies and licensing

The reader will be familiar with agency (importing) and licensing (local production by the third party licensee) arrangements which operate in China much like anywhere else. These classic ways to enter a new market minimise the demands on the exporter and use the existing resources and capabilities of the importer or agent or distributor or licensee. For this section, we will take all these terms as equivalent. The differences are more technical than real apart from licensing which involves the transfer of much more intellectual property.

If/when the licence expires or the arrangement terminates in some other way, the firm will have acquired an on-site competitor who can make the product cheaper (certainly) and better (possibly) than it can. There have also been quite a few cases of identical factories being opened just down the road and, coincidentally of course, producing identical goods.

Franchising, a form of licensing but with less basic brand risk, is also growing in popularity. It has the additional advantage of not requiring JV retail licences. Dairy Queen, the Hongkong clothing retailer Giordano, and 7–11 are commonly cited examples of success in the 1990s. For retailers and service industries, franchising offers less financial exposure similar to those above, but the control problems and the consequent impact on brand identity (always a problem for franchisors) need to be estimated.

China being as big as it is, the need to develop relationships and the future strategic extension of the agency or licensing arrangement into China, all suggest some form of local representation. A full-scale representative office is expensive but some sharing may be possible. For example, the British building materials sector have a joint office representing thirty companies, which was opened in Shanghai on 28 April 1999. More are expected to join though there is clearly a trade-off between a smaller share of costs and attentiveness to one's individual interests. Having no local office and changing the fireman who comes visiting every few months is such a bad idea that it would be better not to start. If the Chinese importer insists on buying the goods, then bank the cash by all means but do not consider market entry.

Joint ventures

The history of business in China suggests joint ventures have always been a standard format; certainly the *huaqiao* Chinese companies of East Asia use collaboration as an important strategic principle. The joint venture is a business vehicle well suited to the Chinese way of doing business, which stresses networks and collaboration. Unlike the West, where all business alliances have to be seen as temporary, Chinese joint ventures can last for generations. In *huaqiao* firms, joint business ventures often lead to personal ties between family-run firms, such as intermarriage between families. Large *huaqiao* firms in Hongkong, Singapore, Malaysia and the Philippines are frequently linked in this fashion.

Joint ventures are not an easy way to do business, and many in the West fail, often within the first year. Lack of trust is the prime cause of failure among joint ventures. And this is among companies within the same or very similar cultures; how much more difficult must the problem be when one firm is Western and one is Chinese?

In the past, at least, joint ventures have been the preferred option for Westerner companies seeking to do business in China, if only because the PRC government did not then allow WFOEs which were progressively introduced by region and sector. Joint ventures allow Western companies to lay off risk, to a certain extent. From the Chinese point of view, given the strong degrees of centralisation and state participation in the economy, joint ventures give the Chinese government and economic planners more control over economic development. By smoothing the path in some sectors and making life difficult in others, the government can channel foreign investment into the sectors, and regions, which it feels would benefit most from development.

From the Chinese point of view, JVs can be a way of recovering sunk costs. The newcomer is told how valuable are the assets, which the Chinese side will contribute in kind, whereas the foreign partner will be bringing cash. Herein lies the crux of the early negotiations of many JVs.

Often overlooked is the need of Chinese companies and the Chinese government to learn more about new technology in particular and Western ways of doing business in general. One example of this need in practice can be found in the telecommunications sector. In 1994, China began a programme of improving its national telephone network. The government could have simply offered contracts to tender; except that there was no one with the expertise to design a contract which could specify China's needs. Rather than risk getting the wrong systems, China chose to call for a number of joint ventures in research, development and production, which would allow local companies to learn about modern telecommunications and gain first-hand experience while at the same time providing a conduit for the government to make its wishes and needs known to the foreign partners.

Western companies also see joint ventures as a way of learning more about China. IBM took part in joint ventures for ten years before finally setting up a wholly-owned subsidiary, and still prefers the joint venture for big projects. There can also be other, more obscure reasons for setting up joint ventures. One example is the motivation of many of the Korean *chaebol* (large industrial groups) to set up joint ventures in China. While there are obvious profits to be made in China, the real reason seems to be that the *chaebol* can, through their China subsidiaries, invest in North Korea and thus bypass economic sanctions imposed in Seoul. Hyundai, Kia and Daewoo are very active in China, possibly for this very reason.

At time of writing, Chinese law distinguishes between three kinds of joint ventures: equity joint ventures, contractual joint ventures and oil exploration joint ventures. It also separates out FIEs from FEs (Foreign Investment Enterprises, which include Chinese, JV and WFOE firms, from Foreign Enterprises). The tax system favours the former but that assumes the firm is making enough to be taxed in the first place. These matters are covered by the guides produced by the major legal firms and, in any case, change from year to year.

Turning to practical problems, expectation is one of the most common stumbling blocks. The goal sets of the three parties, Western and Chinese businesses and the Chinese authorities, often have relatively little in common. In particular, Western firms may need to rethink their attitude to investment in joint ventures. The A.T. Kearney report noted that unsuccessful joint ventures were characterised by a lack of investment in key areas, especially in the critical area of human resources.

Some in the West treat China as a developing country in which second-rate or less than state-of-the-art products and technology can be dumped. In economic terms China may be developing, but in all other respects the Chinese consider the term insulting. They are quick to spot when they are being fobbed off with something that is second rate. Demands for leading-edge technology at second-hand prices (being a poor country entitles them to that too, or so it is sometimes claimed) leads to lively negotiations.

This happens outside the PRC as well. A high-profile joint venture agreement between British Aerospace and Taiwan Aerospace broke down in 1994 when the Taiwanese partner learned that BAe had no intention of transferring its top-line aircraft technology to Taiwan; and access to this technology was the Taiwanese firm's primary motive for getting involved with BAe in the first place. The whole affair was a very high-profile failure, embarrassing for both sides.

Another consultancy report by A.T. Kearney Inc., somewhat misleadingly titled 'Capturing the Southeast Asian Potential', suggests that in East Asia, WFOEs and foreign-company majority joint ventures are more likely to be profitable than 50–50 or minority joint ventures. The key phrase is 'more likely'. That does not mean minority JVs should be ruled out. They can, and do, work. The most important thing is to get the right fit between Chinese and Western partners, allowing both to reach all or most of their goals for establishing the venture in the first place. Slavish adherence to principles of how a joint venture ought ideally to be established can get in the way of this.

Wholly foreign owned enterprises

Most market entry is a matter of progressive commitment. As we show later, firms do not like to gamble so the key factor is balancing and containing risk. Accordingly, going straight into a WFOE, making a large investment in a market where the firm has no developed relationships or contacts, has high levels of regulation, poor infrastructure and rapid economic change, growth and uncertainty, carries a risk level which no sane banker should consider. However, for companies with the right experience and resources, WFOEs can and do work: good examples are 3M and Procter & Gamble.

As mentioned above, IBM China was established as a WFOE in 1992 only after IBM had been operating in China for more than ten years and had built up an impressive portfolio of contacts including former vice-premier Zou Jiahua. IBM China functions in every respect as a Chinese company; it pays taxes to Beijing, can hire Chinese employees directly, and can trade in local currency. Even now, however, IBM China prefers to set up joint ventures with Chinese partners for big projects.

Much of the point in a WFOE is making a fresh start and not getting tangled up in existing webs. Most WFOEs are greenfield operations, but some result from buying out existing partners and there are an increasing number of buyouts of going concerns (now that there are some Chinese going concerns to buy). Anyone feeling especially brave can buy a state-owned enterprise when they come up for auction. There may be bargains to be had.

Identifying and negotiating with partners

This section covers:

* the go-between

- what type of partner
- the time horizon
- negotiating

The go-between

One of the key aspects of relationship-building is the role of the *hongniang* (go-between, or literally, maid-servant). The *hongniang* has a long and honourable history in Chinese society both inside and outside China. Go-betweens are used for functions as diverse as village matchmakers and mediators who help settle legal cases. It is perfectly natural to use a go-between to help put together a business deal; and for the go-between to be a part of that deal and take a percentage from it. For foreign companies wishing to do business in China, the Chinese government has helpfully established a number of *hongniang* agencies, the largest of which are CICECC (Chinese Industrial and Commercial Economic Consulting Corporation) and the Shanghai Industry and Commerce Development Corporation. The Chinese government has also welcomed foreign consulting firms who come in to act in a *hongniang* role; Batey Burn is one of the best-known examples, but there are many others. Hongkong and other East Asian traders sometimes fill this role. In addition to these specialist consultants, Chinese banks and investment companies also sometimes act as go-betweens. CITIC, for example, will provide consultancy advice as well as investment for some projects.

Best of all, in our view, are retired government servants and executives who like to maintain their China contacts in return for comfortable air travel, hotels and a reasonable retainer. Edward Heath, the former British prime minister, was behind the creation of Batey Burn and has introduced innumerable companies. So have a few retired ambassadors. Conversely, we would keep well clear of the global consulting firms but that is a matter of taste. Their clients are presumably happy with them.

A go-between does not have to be used; Western companies are free to set up one-to-one relationships independently and many do. However, particularly for firms with relatively little experience of China, the practice has many advantages. Furthermore, the go-between should not just be used to make contacts but for strategic advice. For example, the next section deals with the type of partner needed. By the time the *hongniang* is briefed on the mission, he may as well contribute to re-defining it. Little more time is needed and, perhaps, much enlightenment.

We have not mentioned confidentiality because it is obvious that the *hongniang* must have no conflict of interest or competitive clients. One argument for the sole operator, as distinct from the large consultancy, is that he is more likely to stay free of *future* conflicts. Otherwise the learning the *hongniang* does on your account today may be credited to your competitor next month.

What type of partner

The Daoist way would be to look for complementarity rather than similarity. IBM went into business with a railway company to deliver its computers. A US East Coast flight simulator company went into business with a Chinese Provincial tobacco monopoly. Both succeeded. On the other hand, GrandMet's spirits company had no success from a JV with a Chinese spirits business. No doubt other factors were at play but the point remains.

The Economist Intelligence Unit (1996) defines three types of partner:

- The 'nuts and bolts partner'. This partner's primary function from your point of view is to help solve problems of access, to land, resources, labour, government, distribution or other factors. The usual quid pro quo is technology transfer or skills training. The EIU notes that these tend to be set up with a short-term focus, and problems can arise once the immediate problems have been solved. Nevertheless, this can be an ideal type of partner for a first-time entrant.
- The 'well-endowed godfather'. These are more powerful partners, and the EIU identifies them primarily as government authorities, such as the Ministry of Posts and Telecommunications or the China National Automotive Industrial Corporation. While slow and bureaucratic, these partners are also very powerful and have access to resources. Their primary contributions are during the start-up phase, and as powerful 'godfathers' who can help sort out problems down the road; they normally take minority stakes and have little direct involvement in day-to-day management.
- The 'four hands on the wheel partner'. This is a more strategic partnership in which the Chinese partner is interested not just in technology transfer but also in building its own strategic position. The EIU cite the example of the strategic partnership between Rohm & Haas and Beijing Eastern Chemical Works, which are expanding together to set up operations across China. Instead of setting up a lot of small joint ventures to get national coverage, the single joint venture is expanding and setting up sub-ventures. Not surprisingly, this type of partnership is believed to have a higher chance of survival.

Key factors to consider when choosing a partner in China

1 Technical expertise. What skills does the prospective partner have? Can the Western firm provide the missing skills, and at what cost?

2 Facilities. What facilities (production, distribution, etc.) does the prospective partner have or have access to? Will these need to be modernised or upgraded, and what will be the cost?

3 Location. Is the Chinese partner geographically well placed to exploit market opportunities? This is particularly important given the physical problems associated with distribution in China. Setting up an operation in Guangzhou to market in Sichuan is likely to involve a lot of extra time and expense.

4 Relationships. How good is the Chinese partner's *guànxì* with other firms in the supply chain, with customers, with government? This is the big one. If the *guànxì* is right the partner should be able to fix anything else. The main three components (durability, seniority and onward connectivity) need separate consideration. Will the Chinese partner's *guànxìwang* complement that of the Western partner?

5 Partner goals. What do partners want? Are they 'nuts and bolts' partners, or might there be true strategic vision in their thinking?

The time horizon

Relatively speaking, Chinese companies care for long-term relationship and interest, although they want even quicker (if that is possible) profits. Maximising the short- and long-terms simultaneously is good Daoist thinking. Western companies, on the other hand, usually want to keep their longer-term options open whilst they see how it goes. Most joint ventures in the West are for periods of six months to three years. It can be a considerable shock to realise that China expects commitment of fifteen or thirty years.

Western companies normally want quick profits too, but investment in China is usually regarded as a medium to long-term payback. Shanghai Volkswagen, established in 1985, repatriated profits for the first time in 1993. Chinese partners, on the other hand, usually want to see profits quickly in a joint venture, since they perceive the comparative advantage when joining hands with their Western partners. This disparity in expectation strains communication and a consensus over the highest NPV (net present value) corporate strategy and plan.

Negotiating

Much is made of the difficulties of negotiations in China. They can be long and frustrating, and there are plenty of tales of negotiations dragging on for months or even years. Others are amazed that all is concluded in a few weeks, but the home office should be prepared for the long haul. There are obvious cultural differences in approach to thinking and communicating, as we discussed in Chapter 3. Beyond that, negotiations mostly run into trouble here for the same reason that they run into trouble everywhere else; because the parties involved can't agree on what is best for both. The days when negotiations were bedevilled by political issues and cultural misunderstanding are largely over. The Chinese now understand the Western game, although the reverse is less true.

Chinese negotiating techniques can take some getting used to. A typical ruse is to conceal the identity of the most senior player. Westerners, on the other hand, typically exhibit the pecking order all too clearly. When Walls (Unilever's ice cream business) was negotiating a fire safety certificate for their new plant in Beijing, they worked very hard on satisfying the smart man in the suit only to find that the badly dressed, tramp-like figure sitting quietly at the end was in charge. (The owner of a Yorkshire brewery used to play the same game with unsuspecting sales reps. He would stand with a broom in the yard and accept tips for looking after their cars. Then reception would call him to the meeting and he would dish out the same level of respect he had received in the yard.)

A more typical manoeuvre is to keep the boss entirely out of sight. This slows things down quite a bit, as regular reports are made, and prevents the Westerners seeing any body language. Fortunately, the Chinese increasingly see time as money, and game playing for the sake of it is probably diminishing.

What does not change is the Daoist advice to see the problem and potential solutions from both points of view. Defending a position politely, firmly and consistently may seem boring to you but will impress those who are comparing their notes with those of several hours, days or months ago. Creative new arguments may free the log jam but they may also provide a whole new area for exploration and reconciliation – especially if the language is complex or subtle.

Negotiations in China are at once both formal and personal. Due recognition must be given to protocol, procedure and precedence. Be prepared to make informal small talk before and after each negotiating session; never rush. If you are getting along well, negotiations will also be accompanied by drinks, dinners and even banquets. Gifts may also be exchanged; Mayfair Yang's book probably remains the best guide to etiquette on these occasions.[3]

Key points for negotiators in China

1   Joint ventures, even when all partners appear willing, can take up to two years to negotiate.

2   It may be good manners to talk around a subject rather than address it directly, though Chinese negotiators are becoming less sensitive and more direct. Look for opportunities for empathy.

3   Conventional wisdom is never to show anger but always be polite, softly spoken and gentle. Probably right but we have seen, very occasionally, anger used to good effect both between and with Chinese negotiators.

4   Silence is considered a valuable negotiating tool.

5   Words and gestures may have hidden meanings and, especially in the early stages, many devices are used to test sincerity and commitment.

6   Use your opponents' strengths, jiu-jitsu-like, rather than taking undue advantage of their weaknesses; they will remember and resent it. That may seem a bit gnomic but what we mean is that your arguments should give face.

7   The time component, or pace, of negotiation is actively managed. For example, they will be conscious of when you have to leave and of the pressure from the home office to get a deal.

8   Knowing where the exits are. Leaving the prospective partner an exit demonstrates trust and increases the probability of good will. If he takes it, then all the better to find out sooner. Leaving oneself an exit is more tricky (shows lack of commitment), not least because your partner should have left one for you. That does **not** mean he wants you to use it.

Research and a tight definition of strategy and goals are an essential part of preparation for doing business in China. All the warnings about negotiating in China can add to the usual fever of speculation until the Western team get spooked by a dinner cancellation which is no more than they said it was. Holding onto a clear agenda and being unfazed by any side issues, still less the possible motivations for them, works wonders. If it is boring for you to say the same thing, in the same words for the umpteenth time, think how much more boring it is for them to write it down. As a general rule of thumb, distrust and paranoia are usually reciprocal unless you are up against a truly professional team. If you judge that you are, ring your *hong-niang* for someone to bolster the skills of your team.

Chinatex

China National Textiles Import and Export Corporation, once the largest textiles exporter in the country, is expanding into manufacturing and diversifying operations in an effort to fight back against fierce competition on the world market. The company has plans to build five factories – four for textile production and an elevator plant – and is about to begin the search for one or more joint venture partners.

Established in 1951, Chinatex was until economic reform the main state agency for the import and export of textiles. The company handled finished cloths only, not raw materials or garments. At present it employs more than 50,000 people, with 20 subsidiaries and a large number of branch offices in China and 37 enterprises and representative offices overseas. With customers in 150 countries, Chinatex counts itself as China's second largest exporter. Total income for 1995 was just over $5 billion. Exports accounted for $1.94 billion of this total.

Beginning in 1990, Chinatex found its market position becoming much more vulnerable. High cotton prices, falling production in Chinese textile plants, stiffening world competition, the introduction of quotas in the key American market, and delayed or reduced export tax refunds from the Chinese government all cut into the company's position. In response, Chinatex is transforming itself from a trading company into a diversified manufacturing and trading organisation. Expansion upstream into manufacturing is one arm of this strategy; expansion sideways into other product fields is another. The ultimate aim is to make Chinatex into an industrial giant in its own right, selling its own brand names through its existing distribution channels around the world.

With five new projects on the drawing board, Chinatex is now looking for foreign partners. It needs a number of things:

1   Capital investment. The sum it has earmarked is insufficient to get all five plants into operation on schedule.

continued

2 Technology. In textiles, the best equipment comes from Germany, Switzerland, Japan and the US, from manufacturers such as Toyoda, Murata, Pratt and Trutzchler, though Chinese firms do make lower cost, less reliable alternatives. The same is true of the elevator plant. Chinatex wants the best technology, but cannot afford this on its own.

3 Expertise. Similarly, Chinatex is having trouble locating Chinese staff with sufficient expertise in modern manufacturing. It needs to find sources of learning among more technically advanced Western firms.

Making the choice

Each strategic option carries its own levels of risk and reward. The usual evolution is to use organisational learning in such a way that risk is reduced at the same time commitment is increased. In the Chinese context, *guànxì* is part of that because *guànxì* is the traditional way to manage and reduce risk. Thus firms like IBM began with agency arrangements, then JVs, then a WFOE and now a complex mix of both to cope with their R&D, production and distribution interests.

In making the choice it is worth analysing risk more closely into investment, presence and control risk components. Table 5.1 shows the approximate levels of risk of each type, based on the experiences of past ventures in China.

Investment risk is how likely you are to lose it multiplied by the amount at stake; in other words, if it all goes sour, how badly will you be hurt? Agencies, where the Western partner puts in little if any money, obviously have a much lower risk level than WFOEs, where the Western firm puts up

Table 5.1 An analysis of commercial investment risk in China

Type of venture	Type of risk		
	Investment	Presence	Control
Agency	Low	High	High
JV	High/Moderate	Low/Moderate	Moderate
WFOE	High	Low	Low

all the capital and take all the risks. Joint venture risk levels in this category vary, depending on exposure and situation, but at least the Western firm has the (sometimes dubious) comfort of knowing that the Chinese partners are also risking their investment. If they contributed dud assets in the first place, or have a matching plant up the road, the comfort will not last long.

Presence risk refers to the rewards which may accrue from a physical presence in China, or the penalties which may be associated with absence. The risk really refers to lack of presence. Being there may hurt but not being there may hurt more. As noted in earlier chapters, the Chinese, especially the Chinese government, value commitment from Western firms and tend to reward it eventually. Companies that show they are prepared to 'stick with' China (IBM and Volkswagen are two prominent examples) tend to have higher levels of success when negotiating new ventures and securing permission to expand. WFOEs and high profile joint ventures are a way of demonstrating commitment. Agency relationships may give brands some profile in the Chinese market, but their lack of commitment could tell against future expansion. Presence risk has to be assessed against the firm's own future plans for China and the region. It may be that a loss-making initial investment can be the key to unlocking further, highly profitable investments.

Control risk refers to the ability of the firm to control its operations and products in the Chinese market. WFOEs obviously offer far higher levels of control risk than agency relationships because so many more things can go wrong, and each from a higher base. In JVs the risk varies, as different partners will agree different levels of control but the worst case scenario is one where the foreigner has, de facto, to pick up all the risk without having enough managerial control to spot and prevent the leakages. This, in essence, is why WFOEs have become favoured.

Control will never be absolute, however, as even directly owned WFOEs always have a 'hidden partner' in the form of the Chinese government which can and does interfere in the workings of business.

We have focused on risk even though most feasibility studies focus on profits and cash flows. Firms should surely continue with upsides and their usual forecasting methods but China requires a good hard look at the gloom. Even for the best managed companies the short term is probably only a 50–50 bet. Unless one is sure one can beat those odds, e.g. one has something China really wants, China is simply not a worthwhile short-term bet at all.

On a long-term view, however, the picture improves. If one has to be there one day, now is cheaper than later. The only good time to do it is when the firm can afford it; not when the accountants fantasise about an optimal net present value. *Guànxì* will gradually take care of risk if it is properly and patiently managed. So quantify the range of likely NPVs and the three risk components for all three types of entry. Have everyone take part even though you will never silence those who will later claim prophetic powers.

Xian Janssen (Johnson and Johnson) launched their JV in October 1985, when WFOEs in that sector and region were not available. It went into operation in May 1991. Those five and a half years spanned the Tiananmen incident and you can imagine how much nay-saying went on in the home office. Today it is a huge success, with market leadership and competitors trailing far behind. We can count the cost but it is still too soon to count the profits.

The overseas Chinese

Even though most overseas Chinese communities operate in considerably freer market conditions than in the PRC, the joint venture remains a favoured device in Taiwan, Indonesia, Malaysia and other countries in the region, especially in manufacturing and distribution. Why? Because joint ventures can provide local knowledge and access to key players in vital networks. *Guànxì*, as we have said before, is possibly even stronger in the rest of East Asia than in China. Joint ventures allow a firm to tap into someone else's *guànxìwang* without having to go through the arduous process of building their own.

This chapter has shown an obvious predisposition to the joint venture. Yes, they can be tricky to manage; but whoever said management was supposed to be easy. Yes, they can be risky; yet at the same time, the right JV with the right partner is actually a terrific means of laying off other forms of political and economic risk. Don't believe all the statistics you read, and don't automatically discount the JV as an option, no matter what country you are working in.

Notes

1   *The China Business Handbook* 1999, p. 72.
2   John Child, in *Financial Times Mastering Management Review*, 1999.
3   Yang 1994.

6   The marketing mix

The plan of Heaven is more certain than the plans of men.

(Chinese proverb)

Discussing the current situation with professors of marketing in September 1999, they failed to identify any area of marketing where China differs from the West. Chinese MBA schools use standard (mostly US) marketing textbooks – some translated and some not. They teach in Chinese, of course, and are desperate for local case studies. Tales from Harvard Business School are about as familiar to their students as the Arabian Nights. You may think this renders the next two chapters, on the tools and process of marketing, unnecessary. Or you may think that Chinese marketing academics live in ivory towers just like their Western colleagues. Either way the differences, while reducing, do in fact remain and we also need some understanding of where marketing, over a remarkably short space of time, has come from.

The lot of the international brand marketer became more difficult as the 1990s wore on. The fizz left the market, the inflation which took care of pricing errors departed, and the consumer love affair with international brands is diminished, if not over. Few ad or market research agencies are making money. This gloom will not last for ever and may seem quite dated if you come across this book in a few years' time. So we have retained some observations from a few years ago for perspective (note the dates) but focused on the deeper aspects of marketing in PRC which we do not expect to change rapidly.

This chapter is structured as follows:

*   looking back
*   marketing strategy
*   products, branding and packaging
*   pricing

- promotions and advertising
- place, channels and distribution

Of these, the last is probably the most difficult and is likely to remain so. The picture in other parts of greater China, and Chinese Asia come to that, will obviously vary according to local circumstances, notably the strength of the economy, but lies along the spectrum between PRC and typical international factors. Accordingly, our purposes are served in these two chapters by concentrating on the PRC and leaving the reader to adapt this account to the local scene either within or outside the PRC.

Looking back

Under the centrally planning economic system before the Chinese reform, the marketing mix[1] was not an issue for businesses in the People's Republic of China. Product line and design decisions were made centrally; any changes began on the production line, with little reference to customers or consumers. With the major economic goals focused on boosting output, production was guaranteed to be bought by government buyers. The system was known as *tong gou, tong xiao* (unified purchase, unified sale). Producers found this a 'relaxing' time: industrial businesses focused on making their quotas and on celebrating their successes. As in the old USSR, the heroes of labour were those who beat their quotas. More commercially aware managers, however, became anxious about overstocks and realised that the recorded income posted by their businesses was artificial.

Advertising and promotions were considered unnecessary during the early years of Communist rule, and were totally banned during the Cultural Revolution of 1966–76, when they were labelled a tool of 'bourgeois capitalism'. Pricing levels were determined by centrally controlled pricing bureaux, and were invariably subsidised by government. As all output was predetermined, producers generally had no input as to the distribution for their products. Distribution channels were unduly long, and in some instances moved through three levels of wholesaling on their way to the retailer.

After economic reforms began in 1979, advertising was reinstated as a legitimate business tool. Enterprises now advertise in all the classic media and a few besides. In the first decade, the advertising industry grew from just ten people in 1979 to 11,100 agencies with total employment of 128,000 in 1989. These agencies were controlled by the state with responsibility in advertising planning, creative execution and media planning. During this time, the media developed their own in-house services, both creative and production, directly for advertisers. Larger advertisers created their own in-house advertising departments for creative and, more rarely, for production. Private domestic agencies had gained perhaps 10 per cent of the total advertising market by 1993. That year seems to have marked something of a turning point; the number of private agencies tripled or quintupled (depending on which set of figures you use), and advertising expenditure reached US$16 million.

Almost all other major multinational agencies that have set up in China have done so primarily to service multinational clients. At the end of 1993 there were more than forty international firms with offices in China, with Beijing having the largest number, followed by Guangdong Province and Shanghai. There were also two joint venture advertising offices in Dalian, Liaoning Province, as well as two in Tianjin, one in Hainan Province and one in Xian, Shaanxi Province.

Chinese advertising agencies, struggling with competition both from media, advertisers' in-house departments and the multinationals, cried 'unfair'. Some order needed to be brought, and the government introduced a set of Interim Regulations on Advertising Agency System. In essence this introduced traditional Western practice, limiting print and broadcast media to display and turning the rest over to agencies. Commission rates were set at 15 per cent. There is some interpretation on issues such as who does 'production', and it is likely that some agencies will rebate some part of the commission. Furthermore, Western ventures (JVs and WFOEs) were required to pay higher media prices. While this remains true in theory, free market negotiations and de-regulation, for WTO compliance, have removed most of the sting.

Today, most of the ad agencies established in the 1990s have gone bust. While many thousand still exist on paper, only a handful do serious amounts of business.

When selling products in China, JVs and WFOEs are subject to the same distribution restrictions that apply to state-owned enterprises. Thus, products subject to planned distribution could sell only to designated entities, which then resold them through the channels to end users. However, the ongoing liberalisation and decentralisation of distribution practices has increased the flexibility of foreign-invested enterprises when choosing distributors. For products that do not fall under the mandate of a monopoly distributor (i.e. a Chinese import–export company that has sole authority for distributing a product, such as Sinochem for potash fertiliser), manufacturers can now use whichever distributor they prefer. Producers can choose to sell to only one particular distributor, although in some cases local regulations may force a producer into certain channels of distribution, or the distribution channel may already have been written into the JV investment contract. In 1993, the market situation was sufficiently chaotic to allow producers to sell the same goods to different dealers at varying prices. Evolving market mechanisms are bringing distribution in line with normal practices, albeit subject to infrastructure problems. Unilever, for example has successfully (1999) secured distribution rights for the products its subsidiaries make in China and other foreign firms are sure to follow.

Marketing strategy

Chinese marketers need no introduction to the writings of Sunzi. On the other hand, they are likely to be graduates of one of China's fifty-six business schools and trying to write plans according to textbooks which do not mention him. Strategic thinking is even more important in China where there are, by and large, more options and less resources. Furthermore, we are not dealing with big, conventional warfare issues. Very few Western companies, Procter & Gamble possibly being an exception, are in that position. The Western brand, and we refer equally to industrial and services marketing here, is at the beginning of a long guerrilla campaign. Focus is crucial and that means sacrifice.

Segmentation is a good example. Kentucky Fried Chicken, whose appeal is universal in the US, targeted children in China. The product was not to conventional Chinese tastes, but they knew the 'little emperors' would be indulged. Much advertising in China focuses on children for one-child family reasons, but following the herd may or may not be a good strategy.

In the same way, guerrilla strategy (and Mao Zedong is a good guide here) dictates reining in one's territorial ambitions and selecting the smallest, most favourable ground (market) one can hold. Never mind where the brand 'should' be, where can it win? Inner Mongolia and Xinjiang are not, we admit, the most attractive options and, as with the Long March, the brand strategists need to consider where to go next. Nevertheless, winning beats losing. There is a temptation for Westerners to opt routinely and start in one of the big three centres (Shanghai, Beijing or Guangzhou) which are easily accessible rather than the hinterland where competition may be weaker. Once one gets on the ground, one can overlay the geographic strengths of each competitor on a map of China before choosing. The good news is that Chinese marketers have just as much trouble crossing provincial borders as do Westerners.

Most of the products we are concerned with will find themselves in an awkward gully. On one side will be the imported international brands with a higher reputation but tiny sales. On the other side will be the massive volumes of Chinese products but at prices our brand cannot touch. So the campaign has to be fought on two fronts: international brand equity and affordable pricing. Both are fragile. Pabst Blue Ribbon was long the leading Western-style beer, albeit brewed in China. That rested on the belief that it was also a major brand in the US. When the word got around that it was small in the US, sales tumbled. On the other hand, 555 remains the dominant cigarette brand, perhaps still bolstered by its legendary lead user (Mao), even though enough people must know by now that it has virtually disappeared elsewhere.

Leading marketing companies, having analysed the competitive environment and empathised with the end user's situation, write the brand's 'positioning' down in a short statement. By 'brand' we mean the thing being marketed, whatever the sector. Reputation is just as important in industrial marketing as branding for the consumer. A positioning statement is effective when it is focused and sacrifices all the easy compromises. It should identify immediate customer and end user and pick out the single reason why the brand is (a) different and (b) better from their point of view relevant to the most threatening key competitor. Not a woolly 'everyone' but the firm you would most like to take business from and least like to lose it to. A few other key strategies may need inclusion but a positioning statement should not exceed one page no matter how big the brand or market (China).

Products, branding and packaging

A *Harvard Business Review* article of 1994 describes *guo qing*, which means 'Chinese characteristics' (or perhaps more accurately 'Chinese circumstances') or the 'special situation in China', and advises that foreign companies need to adapt to it in order to reach Chinese consumers.[2] One can of course take this approach too far. IKEA has the standard international approach of opening a market with their usual range of products and only adapting when they have to. In the US, IKEA took many years before the eventual adaptions suited Americans and the stores began to make money. History is repeating itself. Chinese visitors thronged into the new (1999) IKEA stores in Beijing and Shanghai, but few bought. The furniture seemed too expensive. Being the professionals they are, no doubt IKEA will get it right, but our point is that adaption needs to be based on what is necessary in reality, not theory.

Some new products introduced from the West may well have perception problems in China. In the early 1990s one Beijing bath house was reputedly offering its clients Nescafé; not to drink, but to bathe in. More seriously, marketers introducing unfamiliar products have had success using methods such as personal demonstrations and sampling. Mary Kay Cosmetics and Avon have used these methods when introducing their health and beauty lines in Guangzhou and Shanghai, though they have had regulatory problems since. Colgate, Remy Martin and Orange Tang all used this method, as did Coca-Cola.

For consumer goods, therefore, a small sampling and/or demonstration promotion in a key entry market should be standard practice until it is shown to be unnecessary; that is, when more sophisticated techniques are more productive. For products like automobiles and farm machinery, a showroom is necessary. Before 1949, major international automobile companies all had showrooms in China, employing salespersons to persuade potential buyers to have a close look and take a drive. Now, cars and farm machinery are being displayed once again in showrooms. In the early 1990s, these showrooms are usually the offices of the agents who import the products, and they tend to lump many different products together. This is changing, but the long lines of car showrooms that grace the outskirts of most North American and European towns and cities have yet to appear. The Chinese government has an ambivalent attitude to the car. Auto production was at first encouraged and now discouraged. The lack of roads, pollution and traffic jams concentrate the mind. Beijing has reduced taxi fares (but banned the cheapest version) in an effort to curb ownership, jams and pollution. So far only the first shows any effect and long lines of empty cabs block the road.

But this is by the way. The importance of branding and packaging simply cannot be overstated. Packaging is one of the ways in which economic reform is slowly changing some aspects of Chinese culture. The universal big bag (*midai*) for carrying home the rice is replaced by packaged rice as supermarkets take over. Packaging's key role is communication; it is the carrier of the brand name and symbol. This is where Chinesing has to start. Specialist consultants are available to explain how Western brand names and packaging will be seen, said and understood – in all the major Chinese languages.

Orange Tang, which is advertised as a 'fresh-squeezed-orange-taste instant drink', has the Chinese name 'Gu Zhen' (fruit treasure). The mark and the package are both very appealing: the latter carries the wording 'Selected by NASA for U.S. Space Flights', and the advertising strap-line is, 'the drink in space time'. The Changsha Refrigerator Factory, which uses Italian technology in its manufacturing, adopted the brand name 'Zhongyi', which means both 'Sino-Italian' and 'satisfactory' or 'to one's liking'. Sometimes successful brand names can be construed from Chinese words which sound like the company's Western brand name; thus Gillette used the Chinese name 'Jili', which means 'lucky'.

Numbers are also important: for example, 8 is lucky and 9 is everlasting. Colours also have strong significance. The scarlet, imperial yellow and gold are now a cliché; you will see them most commonly on Chinese goods which are destined primarily for sale to the West. White is unlucky and should generally be avoided.

Unsurprisingly, in a culture where symbols are so powerful, brands need to develop a unique iconic symbol. Research in the West indicates that non-letter symbols (e.g. those for Apple or Shell) communicate more effectively than words or letters (BP or IBM). In Chinese culture, non-letter symbols can be even more powerful. Remy Martin's centaur ('man horse') has positive associations and has much to do with that brandy's dominant market share.

Some commentators have written off the Chinese attachment to brands as a passing phase, and have compared it to attachments to brands in other developing economies. The reasoning is that, once consumers reach a certain level of sophistication, they become more cynical about brands and less likely to remain loyal. This has happened to some extent in China. You no longer see the maker's brand name on the sleeves of suits. Certainly in the PRC, one reason for the importance of brands is the variability of quality. Returning a defective product or achieving some form of compensation for poor quality is difficult in China, and retailers rarely accept responsibility. The reassurance of a famous brand, whatever the price, is thus even more important. On the other hand, consumers now quite happily buy counterfeit brands. They are not fooled but just imagine that, if the counterfeiters have been to so much trouble, the quality is probably a reasonable match for much less money. Experience with rip-offs will reinstate the importance of genuine brands, in time, but without much help from the law.

It seems likely that brands will be *more* important in China than internationally over the long haul. Our reasons concern overseas Chinese behaviour, *guànxì* and the associated lack of consumer rights enforcement. Overseas Chinese consumers, who have been buying in sophisticated free markets for some time, still exhibit high levels of loyalty to brands. In an uncertain world, consumer–brand relationships should prove enduring once they settle down. One should not read too much into the teenager-like early process of infatuation and rejection. Brands will remain more expensive than local unbranded, or private label (which are actually retailer brands), or counterfeits. But they are also reassurance and reducers of risk. Economic factors play a part and the long-term strength of brands need a big enough middle class for whom the marginal extra cost is a small price to pay for these benefits.

Earlier we mentioned the old adage about how Westerners seek for the meaning of life while Chinese seek for a way to live. Brands convey status and achievement; their possession signals one's place within one's social group and community. The associative aspects of Chinese culture are significant. Individuality matters but so does the need to be seen to belong to a certain group. As people leave villages for the cities they need to find new ways to express that. Hongkong is a good example. Once a brand has the reputation of being powerful and 'good', people will wish to be associated with it.

Certainly branding is not limited to foreign products, and companies like Qingdao (beer), Forever (bicycles) and Legend (computers) already have strong brands in China. In 1997 the state announced a programme of support for seventeen domestically produced brands, including consultancy support and funding for advertising and marketing. It is probably only a matter of time, and getting the quality right, before Chinese brands start becoming major players in Western markets.

Product issues

- Start with the packaging. What does it communicate, not just in meaning but in price, quality and other associations? How does the brand name sound, indeed is it sayable, in all the main Chinese languages?
- As anywhere, forget the intentions and the rest of the world. How would/does the *Chinese* consumer use this product? What problem does it solve for her? How could it do that better, e.g. a smaller pack size? What is the primary competitive advantage from *her* point of view?
- Consider using demonstrations and personal selling when introducing new products not only as a good way of introducing the product to her but as crucial market research to check on the two points above.
- Then consider sampling on a wider scale. It is expensive but it does get the product into the hands of the end user.
- Finally, consider the long-term brand–consumer *guànxì*. What needs to be done to reinforce that, build confidence and reduce her risk?

Pricing

We have already referred to the need for sensitive pricing between imported and local products. Consumer readiness to pay import prices for locally manufactured goods has largely evaporated along with economic growth. The skimming route is certainly an option. McDonald's successfully entered at a premium of four to five times the costs of eating out, but we would look hard at that today (especially when, at the time of writing, the pressure on domestic prices is strongly downward). Careful judgement is needed; once the brand's novelty value wears off, or once other high-profile competitors enter the market, prices need to come down to support continued brand growth. McDonald's did just this, gradually reducing its premium, and the brand has grown well. Kentucky Fried Chicken, however, held on to its margin for too long following entry to Hongkong in the mid-1970s. The business dried up; at the same time there were disruptions at a higher level as the parent company in the USA was bought and sold a couple of times, and it was not until the early 1990s that KFC re-entered the market, on a small scale and well behind many of its fast food rivals. Today KFC, problem fixed, is widely prominent.

But what about brand loyalty? If the Chinese are so brand loyal, why does price matter? Well of course, the PRC consumer is *not* brand loyal for Western brands, at least, because there has not been enough time for *guànxì* to build up. We have only, so far, witnessed a process of brand curiosity. It is unwise to build a long-term pricing on the ebbs and flows of that. Get back to basics, establish where the true competitors are and what the end users benefits are. Skimming has the attraction, especially inflation, of shooting over the top and bringing the sights down until one scores. The main alternative is to shoot for the target in the first place.

No one should imagine that price is not an issue for Chinese consumers: the reverse is true. Studies in Hongkong and Singapore show that they tend to be much more canny and discriminatory shoppers than the average person in the West. But for most brands, price has a display as well as an economic role and that needs to be factored in.

Pricing issues

- Consider two entry strategy options: skimming and shooting straight for the target. If you enter too low, it may be tough to get back up.
- Be 'premium' by Chinese, not international, standards.
- Pricing should be determined by the brand's strategic positioning and consumer empathy.
- If sales fail to show up, or evaporate, you will be told that price is to blame. Do not panic: that is the easy rationalisation by inexperienced marketers. Look again.

Promotion and advertising

Advertising

We are fairly sure that advertising in China is more strongly correlated with sales than in, say, Britain but that does not mean that it is more effective. It is just that Chinese businesses are quicker to hand cash to their agencies when sales are rising and to take it away when they are falling. Most Chinese advertisers and their agencies have very little idea of what advertising does for them, which is refreshingly honest.

Partly as a result, a large cultural gap exists between Western clients and their multinational advertising agencies on the one side and their Chinese counterparts on the other. The Chinese view is that their ad agents, who have little expertise beyond media buying, do not deserve much remuneration and that attitude rules out the multinationals. Conversely the multinationals expect more expertise.

Chinese clients, in short, admire the quality of the foreign agencies' work but do not want to pay the bills. One research project among Fujian school children (1993) showed half of the most impressive television commercials to be from foreign agencies; in other words, ad for ad, the foreign ones are about ten times better. No doubt this reluctance to pay will change in time but, meanwhile, no-one is making much money except the media which have grown geometrically.

Given the importance of brands, advertising should play an important role in terms of both brand awareness and reinforcement. Some Western advertising campaigns have proved even more effective in Asia than in the West; Michael Jordan became a household name among children in Singapore.

Advertising in East Asia does have its pitfalls for the unwary, and most of them concern culture. Simple problems with translation are of course responsible for many of these – almost everyone has probably had a laugh by now at the expense of Coca-Cola, whose slogan 'Coke adds life' was translated in Taiwan as 'Coke will bring back your ancestors from the grave'.[3] The transmission of cultural values is often more difficult. Many 'sexist' ads on television and in newspapers are simply not acceptable in the Chinese cultures of East Asia, where a relatively high moral standard prevails. Ads which show children rebelling against their parents, are also unlikely to be well received. Finally, the problems are compounded by cultural diversity in those countries with indigenous as well as Chinese and/or Indian immigrant communities. But this chapter deals with the PRC.

Attitudes to advertising in China vary. Advertising, in China as elsewhere, is disliked as undermining national culture, lowering standards, increasing demand for the 'wrong' things, and intruding into the landscape and/or media. Foreign advertising can be particularly offensive when it oversteps the bounds of cultural sensibilities, awakening not-so-very-deeply buried Chinese memories of foreign domination. On the other hand, advertising makes economic sense and consumers enjoy advertising and find it useful.

Television is the main vehicle for advertising, with all the provinces, autonomous regions and municipalities and a great many large and medium-sized cities having their own television stations penetrating to every corner of the country. There are now 3,000 TV stations, we were told. Similarly, there are 1.07 TV sets per urban household, while the rural penetration rate is 37.5 per cent. The most powerful station is China Central Television (CCTV). Its programmes tend to be horribly dull by Western standards, but products advertised on its channels do tend to become household names. As a result, CCTV can charge between 10,000 and 25,000 yuan (9 yuan = $1) for a 30-second slot depending on the time. Advertisers queue up to pay 19,000 to 21,000 yuan for 15 seconds immediately after the main early evening news. It is still true (but not for much longer) that agencies have to send staff to queue for the release of the most popular spots, even though price was used to ration demand. There is a certain status arising from auction and more traditional techniques that the far more efficient technology cannot supply.

Newspapers now also play an important role. Until the 1980s, given that the lack of newsprint limited the size of newspapers (eight pages is the norm) and newspapers were controlled by the Communist Party, advertising was almost non-existent. Now there are no limits. At the top end of the range, the official mouthpiece, the *People's Daily*, charges between 40,000 and 100,000 yuan for a whole page, while the popular *China Youth News*, with a million circulation, charges between 40,000 to 70,000 yuan. On 15 January 1993, history was made when Shanghai's most popular daily newspaper, *Wenwei Pao*, sold its entire front page for a Xileng (refrigerator) advertisement costing 1 million yuan.

In 1999, media prices levelled out with the prospect of declines in 2000. Pricing is complicated by a brokerage system in which entrepreneurs corner a particular niche market and hold out for higher pricing. You can hold your nerve and hope for last-minute deals. Some of these arrangements are hedged by the original media owner being prepared to buy back unsold space. Another local peculiarity is that space booked may not run when expected or even at all. As a result, advertisers have to pay for tracking systems to monitor the resulting live advertising.

Posters are also important, though curbs on some of the biggest users, notably tobacco, have cooled the market. Much of the disposable income lies in densely packed urban areas. Messages do not need to be complex for famous brands, but they do need to stand out.

Guànxì brand–consumer principles apply. If one can afford it, advertising early, before the product is available, and long can pay off even though the short-term financials are unattractive. Normally, in Europe and in North America, advertising should follow distribution. In China, a number of Japanese brands, such as Sony, were advertised for some years before availability. With hindsight, this was a smart investment, especially as advertising rates were a great deal cheaper then.

Admittedly some time ago but it is still a good story, an advertising lecturer came to Shanghai with a television commercial he had designed for Ivory Soap. In it a Chinese family – father, mother and children – all go to the paddy field to transplant rice shoots. Later they emerge covered in soil and use Ivory Soap to clean up. This commercial was completely off the mark. For one thing, this particular task is now done by machine; more importantly, no one who is experienced in this work becomes so soiled. The image of dirtiness, which may be used with some appeal abroad, is simply insulting to the Chinese working consumer. Evidently the commercial was made with a minimum of research. 'Ivory – the soap that floats', is still the best approach in China.

One can get a good feel for the kinds of advertising currently used on Chinese television just from watching CCTV or another main channel. Spot the differences between East and West. Most Western ads are produced in China but against international strategies. Much of the Chinese advertising is imitative. Lager always seems to be promoted by clean-cut young Chinese men in a Western-style bar, while Chinese spirits use images of the Great Wall, people dancing in ethnic costume, and elderly men proclaiming how the product has helped them reach a wise old age.

We do not take up space with advertising regulations which, WTO-inspired no doubt, are being brought into line with the rest of the world. The guidelines in the box below are not intended to be taken too seriously. In advertising rules, but not government regulations, were made to be broken.

Some advertising do's and don'ts

- *Be careful with comparative advertising and exaggeration*; most of the problems with the censorship board have been in this area.
- *Translate outwards and then back* when approving advertising copy; have an independent translation of the translation made, and see if the original matches.
- *Where direct response is being used, understand the communication and distribution problems for the responder.* Be convenient for the buyer.

- Don't assume your agency knows and applies the regulations.
- Don't say your brand is the leader (especially if it is).
- Don't use models whose appeal is based on sex. (Of course Chinese companies do, but from a foreign advertiser it is all too easy to portray this as exploitation.) The regulations state that female models cannot expose their bodies between the shoulder and 15cm above the knee (Article 2.19) apart from swimsuits, and only then in relevant context.
- Don't put ads on the backs of envelopes.

New media

It is arguable that China has leapfrogged the conventional land-line telephone infrastructure and jumped straight to mobile (radio) communications. Notwithstanding the phone boxes appearing in the streets, first pagers and now mobile phones are everywhere. It seems likely that China, already a leader in pagers, will dominate mobile telephony quite soon. A fascination with gadgetry and technology, peer group competition, and the burning need to keep in touch all lead to the same outcome. You can expect your host to be waiting at the door because your driver will have made half a dozen calls as you stop-goed through the traffic.

But this is just the beginning. Internet usage is growing just as fast and for similar reasons. A big difference with the West, however, is that radio linkage is broad band and does not limit screens to occasional snapshots in the way that traditional land-lines do. Combine that with the boring and controlled traditional media and young, technical Chinese are spending far more time in front of their monitors than their TV screens. Advertising agencies, notably Ogilvy & Mather, are responding fast because this is the young, affluent, upwardly mobile market they are after.

Nudged perhaps by IBM, a client whose business has been rescued by supplying Internet services, Ogilvy & Mather have already notched up as much business in Internet advertising as they conduct through traditional media. This puts them in the world leadership class, as well as in China. No other market has come so far so quickly. It has profound indications not only for their parent group, WPP, but the ad agency business worldwide.

Golden Hall Sausages

The Jen Man Tang (Golden Hall) sausage company is based in Zhanjiang, about 230 miles southwest of Guangzhou. In 1994 they were the dominant brand in their own market, but had no sales at all in the much larger market of Guangzhou, which was dominated by two other brands, The Emperor and Kung Ki Leng. The company contacted an advertising agency, the Sun and Moon Spreading Co., to advise it on how to break into the Guangzhou market.

The sausage market is highly seasonal. Like many traditional foods, consumption is ruled by the calendar rather than the weather. It begins with the Zhongqiujie (Moon Festival) in late September or early October and ends with the Qingmingjie (Spring Festival) in April. Sausages are made of 100 per cent pork plus flavourings. A sausage may be a meal in its own right or may be chopped up into other dishes. As with other meat products, sausages are not cheap.

Golden Hall sausages were shorter and thinner than The Emperor, which had over half the current market share, and had a lower fat content. It was believed that a 'lean appeal' might be successful with consumers. However, there were also production problems; Golden Hall sausages were not always fresh when sold, and there were quality problems such as variable levels of fat.

Competing with The Emperor would be difficult, as the rival company was a big spender on advertising, and Golden Hall could not hope to spend on the same level in the early days. Clearly some other tactics were going to be needed for the launch and the promotional period immediately following. The first and foremost objective for Golden Hall was to build up some *guanhai* (Yue for *guànxì*) in the Guangzhou market.

Other promotions

We have referred to the importance of demonstrations and sampling above under product. POP displays and demonstrations are very effective in these stores, which are, or perhaps used to be, crowded at peak times. Department stores have been hardest hit by the economic downturn and many, Chinese and foreign, have closed their doors.

Customers rely on the retailer for advice when purchasing unfamiliar products, which provides opportunities for promotions. In 1999, for example, Asahi beer (Japan) launched a major offensive in Beijing where restaurant customers were rather forcibly offered two cans for the price of one. This was advice with a heavy A.

Service centres can be effective, perhaps because the whole notion of after-sales care is so unusual. Omega appointed a watch store as its service centre in Shanghai, Sanyo established its own service centre and Citizen has service centres in Beijing, Shanghai, Guangzhou and other cities. Ricoh recorded twenty-eight service centres and Shanghai Volkswagen (SVW) had thirty-two SVW authorised service stations across China.

The Chinese calendar with its cultural associations remains (though less so for young people) an important tool for promoting seasonal products and reflects attitudes with respect to the capricious climate. For instance, a Shanghai rubber shoe factory advertised in the 19 February 1986 issue of *Xin Min Evening News* with the single headline 'Today is Rain Water'. The message was sufficient to convince great numbers of readers to buy rubber rain shoes, even though there was no sign of water. In another promotion, McDonald's gave away 'lucky' red decorations; these can still be found in many homes. Those were early days, however, and the consumer is now far more marketing savvy; approaches will need to be more subtle.

Place, channels and distribution[4]

Poor infrastructure and distribution have discouraged more than one investor. Power Corp of Canada, which had planned a joint venture in pulp and paper, dropped it in 1994 because it could not be satisfied that the transport networks were good enough. There are ways around the problem, but they often require some creativity. Fosters, referred to above, in expanding its interests in China, has set up a whole network of joint ventures, first with producers in a number of regional centres, and second with the Hongkong conglomerate Wheelock, which has experience at transport and distribution in China. By establishing many regional centres rather than a few large breweries, Fosters has cut down on the distance its goods need to be shipped; and where shipping is required, Wheelock's expertise and contacts help cut down the problems.

Mary Kay Cosmetics in Shanghai used party plan selling to reach its potential customers, mostly young working women. As most people in Shanghai have fairly limited residential space, Mary Kay established its own premises and made meeting rooms available to its sales agents, who could invite potential customers to parties on the premises (where, of course, they could be exposed to other forms of point of sale promotion). They, and Amway and Avon, were surprised to be included in the 1998 ban on pyramid selling.[5] After 50 per cent losses, they renegotiated themselves into a new regulation which requires, inter alia, their sales people to pass an exam administered by the local authorities. Even so they are outside the normal retail regulations and operating in uncharted waters.

The general reluctance of the PRC to admit foreigners to the distribution sector, despite the anticipated WTO requirement to do so, is illustrated by this network selling affair. Each foreign firm really needs to investigate its specific channels to the ultimate users, both sales and logistics, with some care in the reasonable expectation that this will be a problem area.

Retailing has had a chequered history. The first retail joint venture was established in Shenzhen in 1991, and since then they have proliferated. Manufacturers are allowed their own stores or rent counters in department stores in the cities, ostensibly as 'windows' to get market information. Realisation is dawning that retailing should be left to specialist retailers. As a result, retail quality is rapidly improving. A walk through Beijing or Shanghai shows the smartening up of department stores with traditional Chinese goods but, more importantly for the future, Chinese versions of international goods made to improving standards. The prices of imported goods leave plenty of space. Department stores remain a major force in retailing, with 400 in Shanghai alone. As noted above, however, their strength is waning as consumers, like in the UK, turn to chain stores. Sincere, part of the Hongkong department store chain, closed after only two years. State-owned stores were down by 4.1 per cent in the year to October 1998, with privately owned stores up 25 per cent – 7 per cent up for the whole sector.

Chain stores (end 1997 figures) totalled 15,000, including supermarkets, in 1,000 chains, 30 per cent being foreign funded and mostly in Shenzhen and Shanghai. There seems little doubt that much of the renaissance in retailing in China has been led by overseas Chinese firms, even though the latter are sometimes operating as franchise holders for Western companies (7–11, whose Southeast Asian franchise is held by the Thai conglomerate CP, is a famous example).

The regulations have been a bit of a mess. When retailing was first officially opened up in 1992, it was restricted to eleven cities and JVs needed to have Chinese majorities. This was widely ignored. In 1997 MOFTEC announced that licences would be revoked or refused if the latter condition was not complied with, but the city limitation would be removed. By 1999, only 20 of the 300 foreign JVs had been approved and the other 280 risk closure. This may explain the attraction of franchising, which is not subject to this regulation.

Before the traumatic events earlier this century, China, even more than England, was a nation of shopkeepers. Under Maoism, small enterprises were largely swallowed up by the state. After reform, the *huaqiao* from

Singapore, Thailand, Malaysia and elsewhere moved into distribution and trade, often via family members still living in China. Wangfujang in Beijing was one of the first areas to be opened up to joint venture retailers and was largely developed by Hongkong money; it could be a shopping street anywhere in East Asia. Dazhalan, on the other hand, is in a historic quarter of the city and was developed using local money, and remains more distinctively north Chinese. Shanghai has also thrown open its doors to foreign retailers, including Isetan, Sogo and Yaohan of Japan and Taiwan's Sunrise.

The strategy of the Hongkong real estate companies, in particular, has primarily been to build large-scale commercial buildings for rental to international chain store groups. However, some real estate companies have also sought to have retailing included in their permitted scope of business. Whampoa operates twenty Park 'n' Shop outlets in Shenzhen.

There is also significant European (but not British) and American retailing presence. Some, such as clothing and fast food, lends itself to franchising as discussed in the last chapter. Metro (Germany), Makro and Royal Ahold (Netherlands), and Carrefour (France) are represented, the last with twelve stores in eight cities. Significantly, Wal-Mart has four retail and one wholesale stores. Tesco and Marks & Spencer opted out, but there is a B&Q (Kingfisher) store in Shanghai.

The physical problems of distribution are caused by an inadequate infrastructure. Fast as China's road network has grown over the past two decades, the number of vehicles has grown even faster; companies shipping by road will face increased costs and uncertain delivery times and outcomes. The rail network, largely geared to the defence of China from foreign invasion, is inadequate to the task of shipping goods. Water transport is usually efficient, and now accounts for about 20 per cent of all freight, but is slow and does not reach all areas. Air freight tends to be quicker but less efficient; companies wishing to ship directly between two minor centres will often be told, in effect, 'you can't get there from here'. Manufacturers can also expect to face problems in road travel and transport of goods across borders as a result of inter-provincial rivalries. Some provinces in the past have erected barriers at their borders, preventing or charging high fees for certain goods such as rice or cotton.

Everyone has their favourite story about air travel in China; here is one example. One Western firm anxious to ship a large package on a Saturday flight from Shanghai contacted the local air cargo firm earlier in the week and gave the dimensions of the package. Would

continued

there be room for it on the plane? No problem, they were told. Come Monday, the package had not been shipped. Contacting the air cargo company again, they were told that there had in fact been no space. When reminded that they had confirmed that there *was* space, the cargo company conceded that, yes, there was indeed space on the plane that went the day the inquiry was made. There was no space on the Saturday plane, which was smaller.

Distribution issues

- Although distribution has been greatly liberalised in the last few years and state-owned firms no longer play a major part, both sales channels remain under-developed.
- Inadequate infrastructure greatly complicates distribution problems, and will probably continue to do so for some time.
- Waste no time before working out paper solutions for your particular products in the territories you intend to cover. You may need, for example, a separate business with a different governance structure as well as approvals from authorities which may take a long time to arrive.
- Try to find local or foreign companies that have already set up successful distribution networks similar to what you need. Use *guànxì* to get close to them and perhaps set up joint ventures.
- Consider getting a nucleus of the future sales team to start calling key customers before you have products to sell. Train them in providing technical advice.
- No one can offer complete distribution networks for all of China, so beware of signing exclusive deals.
- Use different logistics solutions for different parts of China.

Conclusions

We have boxed some points for each of the 4 Ps of the marketing mix and will not repeat them here. We began by saying that marketing in China is becoming much like anywhere else but there are enough differences for the foreigner to need to take care – especially with distribution.

We have paid attention to the PRC and to consumer brands leaving the reader to adapt the implications for other Chinese markets and sectors. The principles really are the same:

- Of the 4 Ps, the product really does matter most.
- To gain trial, first impressions (packaging, demonstrations, sampling) are a crucial gate (*guàn*).
- Once through that gate, the goal is to build long-term end user–brand *guànxì*. For consumer goods that is the role of advertising but in business to business, industrial and services, this role falls to the customer-facing employees. Industrial business may not see themselves as branded but that is what they are: their reputation makes the difference between profit and not making it through the door.
- But more important than those communications is the satisfaction from the use of the product itself.
- Pricing must be seen, with the context of the brand–consumer relationship and competition, as fair.
- And finally the marketer has to think it all the way through, and see it through, to the end user.

The way a firm goes about marketing strategy is also the same for all sectors. Segmentation and geographical concentration to gain enough focus and leverage can win. Too many marketers try to do too much with too little. Defining the positioning in a crisp, half page, statement. That way everyone should be able to understand and be motivated by it.

The overseas Chinese

The main differences between selling into PRC consumer markets and those of Chinese communities elsewhere in East Asia lie in better distribution networks meaning easier access to the market, and in greater consumer sophistication. Thus, it may be easier to get your goods in front of the consumer, but it may be harder to persuade them to buy.

Overseas Chinese customers have, by and large, become accustomed to modern advertising and branding. More subtle approaches are needed, just as they are increasingly becoming needed in China too as the consumer wises up to Western marketing methods. Nonetheless, many Chinese cultural attributes mentioned above are important when it comes to marketing in overseas Chinese markets. Many of the same sensitivities to, for example, advertising apply, in some countries more so than in others. Marketers considering Taiwan, Thailand or Malaysia can certainly use this chapter as a starting point, before going on to research local regulations and market preferences.

Notes

1 The marketing mix is the classic 4 Ps of product (including branding and packaging), price, promotion and place (including channels and distribution).

2 Yan 1994.

3 Although Coke got it right in the PRC, with a name which sounds phonetically like Coca-Cola but means 'tasty and refreshing'. Better still was TNT, whose Chinese name Tian Di means 'heaven and earth'.

4 Parts of this section make use of the helpful update by Melony Sanders (*China-Britain Trade Review*, August 1999). See also *Supply Chain Management in China: Pitfalls & Opportunities to 2005*, Financial Times Business, 1999.

5 'Pyramid selling', which depends on piling inventory on lower levels of sales representative rather than selling to real customers, is illegal in many countries and should not be confused, but often is, with 'network marketing' where the product is sold by, but not to, part time commission agents exploiting their personal contacts. At first glance, network marketing would seem well suited to China and it will be interesting to see how the concept matures – assuming it is allowed to.

7 The marketing process

The general who wins a battle makes many calculations in his temple[1] before the battle is fought. The general who loses a battle makes but few calculations beforehand. Thus do many calculations lead to victory and few calculations to defeat: how much more no calculation at all.

(Sunzi)

The last chapter opened by suggesting that marketing in China was like marketing anywhere else and then used quite a few words to show that maybe it was not. This chapter deals with market research and other key information, and planning. The China differences are important but fewer, so we will be briefer.

Apart from focus, the other key to winning battles is having, and using, superior information. A plan built on poor information is as useless as perfect information which is not acted upon. So what is new? Forty years of practising and teaching marketing has convinced one author of this book (and the other is quite prepared to believe it) that every marketing plan ever written fails one or both of these tests.

This chapter begins by returning to the subject of market research, discussed briefly in Chapter 1. We then move on to look at other information and discuss a practical strategy for integrating information needs. There is a tendency, in writing about business in China, to note *guànxì* as some sort of local peculiarity, and then get back to business as usual. We think it needs to be made intrinsic to the whole planning process. We make suggestions how.

Market research in the PRC

It is easy, albeit expensive and time consuming, to obtain PRC market research; it is somewhat more difficult to determine whether it is reliable. Published sources of quantitative data include those from the State Statistical

Bureau, foreign research agencies, and collections such as *The China Business Handbook* from the media. This last group is the cheapest, and in some ways most convenient, but they are very general and recycle other sources so consistency is no confirmation.

After reviewing published sources we turn to bespoke quantitative and then qualitative research.

Published sources

Data in China are likely to be used to paint a picture rather than give precise information. An enormous system collects and analyses information for central planning purposes: the State Statistical Bureau alone has 60,000 employees. This information used to be difficult to get hold of because it was scattered among various agencies (including commissions, ministries, national corporations and industry councils), and the 'right' person to approach within any particular agency might be unidentifiable. A Westerner who approaches a ministry for help is likely to be referred to the foreign affairs department within the ministry. Industry-specific market analysis can be undertaken, but the results may be crude. It may take a few hours to examine an industry yearbook.

However, the situation is now much easier so far as access is concerned. The State Statistical Bureau and some ministries have set up information service centres and much of their data is accessible, on CD-ROM and increasingly on the Internet. At the time of writing, we would still recommend that trusted local intermediaries are first commissioned to obtain data from these sources. Unreliability means that independent verification and interpretation are needed and this is best done by people with experience. They need to know the purpose of the research and the level of accuracy required. Quite often, one only needs to know that the number is big enough.

Generic information about consumers and their behaviour is available from these sources. For example, China's high-potential consumer markets are concentrated along its east coast in three distinct areas. Getting at each cluster of consumers is, therefore, possible through geographical focus. These markets with their average per capita GDP and populations are Shanghai (US$2,778 14.6 million), Guangdong (US$1,250, 70.5 million), Beijing (US$1,759, 12.4 million) and Tianjin (US$1,568, 9.5 million) (1997 figures from *The China Business Handbook*, 1999). Although only 50 miles from Beijing, Tianjin is a very different market; in particular, prices are lower there than in the capital. Of other major centres Chongqing is often overlooked but is the largest city in China (US$533, 30.4 million); Wuhan is a crossroads, though not as influential as some firms thought when they began setting up shop there in the early 1990s. Still, it is likely to become important in future.

Table 7.1 shows the impressive rates of growth, albeit from a small base, and that there is not quite such a dramatic ebb and flow as the world believes.

Table 7.1 PRC economic growth

Year	GNP (100 million yuan)	Growth (%)	GDP (100 million yuan)	Growth (%)	GDP per head (yuan)	Growth (%)
1978	3624.1		3624.1		379	
1979	4038.2	11.4	4038.2	11.4	417	10.0
1980	4517.8	11.9	4517.8	11.9	460	10.3
1981	4860.3	7.6	4862.4	7.6	489	6.3
1982	5301.8	9.1	5294.7	9.1	525	7.4
1983	5957.4	12.4	5934.5	12.4	580	10.5
1984	7206.7	21.0	7171	21.0	692	19.3
1985	8989.1	24.7	8964.4	24.7	853	23.3
1986	10201.4	13.5	10202.2	13.5	956	12.1
1987	11954.5	17.2	11962.5	17.2	1104	15.5
1988	14922.3	24.8	14928.3	24.8	1355	22.7
1989	16917.8	13.4	16909.2	13.4	1512	11.6
1990	18598.4	9.9	18547.9	9.9	1634	8.1
1991	21662.5	16.5	21617.8	16.5	1879	15.0
1992	26651.9	23.0	26638.1	23.0	2287	21.7
1993	34560.5	29.7	34634.4	29.7	2939	28.5
1994	46670	35.0	46759.4	35.0	3923	33.5
1995	57494.9	23.2	58478.1	23.2	4854	23.7
1996	66850.5	16.3	67884.6	16.3	5576	14.9
1997	73452.5	9.9	74772.4	9.9	6079	9.0

Note: Real exchange rates have, of course, fluctuated although not by much. In 1999, 1 US$ = 8 yuan

Bespoke quantitative research

Obtaining research is easy primarily because of the number of Western and Chinese market research agencies. By 1994, there were over 100 agencies in the PRC, including state, private and joint venture agencies. The number today might be two or three times that. Needless to say, the quality of service provided by these agencies varies very widely. Surveys (questionnaires based on interviews) are much the most common format along with retail audits and media monitoring.

Survey Research Group (SRG) was probably the first major external agency to establish itself, in 1984. Run from Hongkong, they have offices in Shanghai, Beijing, Chengdu and other centres as well as their original joint venture in Guangzhou. More recently, they have now merged with a worldwide market research network. Their main clients are foreign, mostly US; global clients tend to feel more comfortable with global marketing services. These big companies expect modern marketing services (using the logic of 'you get what you pay for'), and also, being big, they prefer to put their faith in statistics rather than intuition. Chinese marketers, being mostly smaller, have fewer inhibitions; Chinese market research tends to be based on feedback from salesmen, test introductions and personal field experience. Incidentally, this is quite similar to Japanese experiential research preference.

SRG's Guangzhou offices told us that in-house customised (door-to-door) usage and attitude studies for consumer products were their main item, followed by focus groups, in-depth interviews, retail audits and media monitoring research. Media monitoring is also important in China, and tracks whether advertisements actually appeared when and where they should. SRG's business-to-business work consisted mainly of desk research, for reasons noted above, and professional in-depth interviews. Interesting too is these agencies' perception of their own role: SRG, like other researchers, see themselves as interpreters of consumer/customer preferences and behaviour for foreign businesses.

The methodologies these agencies use are standard and would be familiar to most Western market researchers. The results they achieve, however, can be confusing. One survey showed a substantial demand, amongst over 500 million smokers, for products to help them quit. This turned out to be nonsense. The respondents were being 'helpful'.

There are three main reasons for unreliability. First, there is the differing nature of Chinese consumer psychology. People's responses in China do not always fit into the neat pigeonholes that our market research methods would like them to; a research programme which gives a clear and sharp segmentation when applied to a US or European market may give a much more fuzzy picture when applied in China. Providing information is treated as being valuable. Not only do respondents expect payment, as is becoming increasing true elsewhere, but the mindset of respondents does not match those of the people setting the questions.

Second, there are regional differences. As noted earlier, China consists of, basically, as many markets as you would like it to. The good news is that this makes it easier to position market entry: one can make mistakes in market entry in one place, learn the lessons, and start with a fresh sheet somewhere else. The bad news is that every new market in another region of China needs a fresh start. Chapter 2 discussed some of the regional variations that can affect the nature of markets and consumers. Let us consider just one: language. When conducting surveys in Guangzhou or Fujian, should you do so in Mandarin on the grounds that you have already learned and used Mandarin in Beijing and Shanghai? Or should you adapt to the local language? Most people will speak Mandarin, but they may be less willing to express themselves fully and honestly than they would in their local tongue. Closer is better: we strongly suggest that the data gatherers operate in the appropriate local vernacular. Written questionnaires, of course, make this easier although even the written language is not universal.

SRG has nearly 200 full-time staff and an extensive field force. Their talent and professionalism are impressive and yet, even after many years, there is still a sense of fragility about the operation, reflecting the difficulties that the mass of Chinese people are having in coming to terms with a market economy. Like other Western associated MR specialists, the calibre of the senior people is high in technical terms and they are familiar with international professional standards. Many of them have been in business for more than ten years.

On 1 January 1994, Gallup Research opened for business in Beijing in what it claimed was the country's first nationally licensed market research joint venture. This ruffled the feathers of those agencies that had been operating nationally for some time. Gallup's sponsors included a former Politburo committee member and the former minister of state planning, who believes the company's research can help money-losing state companies find more profitable products. The US firm is partnered with a trading firm with strong ties to the foreign ministry.

Gallup has rejected direct co-operation with the State Statistical Bureau (because of possible interviewer bias) in favour of working through university statistics departments, and in the initial stage after its establishment, the firm recruited 46 professors in 23 target cities. Gallup then developing a sampling frame based on the household registration lists of neighbourhood committees in those 23 cities. The sampling frame was used for random selection of interviewees. Gallup's early customers reflect its strong links with US-based multinationals and trade agencies funded by the US government. Its first three projects were for the US Chocolate Association, the US Agricultural Trade Office in Beijing and the Washington State Apple Growers' Association.

The third problem is the layers of processing and sub-contracting the data may pass through. Each time it does so, some subtle spin may be applied. Inspection of the literature of Chinese agencies, for example Hengtong Marketing Consultant Corporation (one of the largest Chinese marketing research firms in Shanghai), reveals that many of the Western marketers and research agencies seem to be sub-contracting to them. Perhaps therein lies the explanation of how relatively small firms can offer such a wide range of services across such a large market. There is probably quite a lot of laundry exchange (firms working for each other). Given the difficulty of understanding the market in the first place, one should always check who is collecting the original data and how many hands/interpretations it then goes through. Research that gets the Chinese whispers treatment is likely to be both more expensive and less reliable.

Market researchers are rationalists and so are consumers *when they are reporting their behaviour*. Yet much of the time, consumer behaviour is *not* rational. Applying (Western) logic to Chinese consumer behaviour is especially dangerous. Yet that is exactly what a firm applying Western market research methodology in China is likely to do. If the report is not littered with contradictions, it has been oversimplified. (This is also true of books on China including this one.) A new factor is the state's requirement, introduced in 1999, to vet research before it is presented to clients.

In consequence, the marketer cannot just commission the research and then accept the glossy, or otherwise, report. The research process has to be checked all the way through to the ultimate respondents both when commissioning and afterwards.

The option of commissioning two identical surveys and comparing the answers may be no solution:

- It doubles the costs.
- The second firm may find the same mismatch of questions and answers that the first encountered.
- How will the differences be explained?

These problems are less severe with retail audits and media monitoring which are really only concerned with checking the system and are more factual as distinct from strategic.

That said, if the budget will stand it, there is benefit in using two research agencies in China: one Western-style and one Chinese. When they come up with conflicting results, picking through the various findings may increase the chance of getting close to the real picture. If there are no differences, we would suspect collusion or that the work was sub-contacted to a single firm.

The simplest quality control system is to collect similar data through one's own distribution channel (the sales force) and to compare the answers. This has the advantage of improving the market orientation and understanding of the sales force but is little help until the sales force is in place.

Qualitative research

In setting up focus groups, be aware that the Chinese are probably more visually and less aurally focused than Americans, and probably Westerners in general. Given the subtleties of spoken Chinese, this second result is not intuitively obvious even though the two-dimensional visual nature of Chinese written characters relative to the (topologically) one-dimensional Roman script makes the first suggestion predictable. The consequence is that Chinese consumers should *see* names and other marketing stimuli more than they should *hear* them. In other words, research, and focus groups in particular, should be sure to provide rather more visual stimuli than they might in the West.

Thus the process of converting the raw gathered data into the neat folders presented to management carries the severe risk that the insights will be lost. No psychologist hired to run a focus group has the experience of the brand that the marketer should have. There is a good chance that the psychologist will miss the significance of what was said.

Our advice is always to experience the research if one possibly can; and that goes double for China. Sit behind the one-way mirror in focus groups, accompany some of the field force door to door. Some Western market research companies find this rather odd. Lack of the local language is, of course, a barrier but you can gain plenty of experience using your other senses. In China, the experiential research mode is all the more important given the depths and subtleties of meaning. It is also what the Chinese (and Japanese), themselves do and it may reduce some prices if one is hiring specific services rather than entire (Western-style) packages.

In particular research should endeavour to bring cultural values, the usage occasion and the product *together* as realistically as possible. The less hypothetical or artificial the research situation for the consumer, the more reliable it is.

Other information

In principle, many other sources of information are available, including own staff, especially the field staff, customers, trade associations, journalists and competitors. Even if there was time to track all these down, one would have to know what one does not know and what is important. And one would need much more openness than one can expect in China. Nevertheless, the difficulties with market research prompt reconsideration of the sources of intelligence used before modern methods became available.

Essentially, we are talking about reducing all the flotsam floating around marketing decision-making to the few key issues (a) that will make a major difference and (b) where there is substantive uncertainty within the top marketing team. Once identified, the collective *guànxìwang* can be put to work to piece together some answers with or without formal market research.

In China all information needs triangulation before one can take it seriously, or so they say, i.e. three or more independent sources. On the other hand, it only needs to be near enough to make the decision. Too often in the West, information is disconnected from its use.

Planning

Plans are not important: planning is. It should involve rehearsing the future. One can practise as many times as one likes, at some cost to today, but tomorrow only comes once. Or if you prefer a different cliché, there is Gary Hamel: 'to get to the future first, a company must find the shortest path between today and tomorrow'.[2]

Planning is also learning: learning from the past, from other business units, functions and competitors and from seniors and juniors in the hierarchy. We need to understand *why* what works does work, so that we can extend the principles in new situations. Otherwise we can never distinguish context, or simply luck, from good marketing. Most plans are simply adaptations of those that went before. They are evolutionary, not revolutionary. What works is extended, what didn't is cut back. Darwin, in effect, is preferred to purely economic analysis. Just as well but this is no help to those preparing their first ever plan in China. Should they bring in experts, e.g. consultants, with previous experience of preparing marketing plans in China? Probably not but having someone on the inside team with previous experience obviously helps.

A plan is also the minutes of all the meetings, possibly over many months, that went into its preparation. Most Western firms, including those in China, spend far too long working a plan around the hierarchy.

They begin before they can tell how the last plan worked out and then finish after the new year has already started. They would be better off, now we have electronic communications, to work twice as hard over one quarter of the time.

While the whole state apparatus, including SOEs, is built around formal planning, the typical Chinese family business has no formal marketing plan at all, not even the big ones. We are not aware of formal research on the subject but the difference may not be so large. What they actually do evolves along Darwinian principles just as it does overseas. So long as the current approach is bringing in satisfactory amounts of cash, it continues. When a new strategy is required, either because cash flow is drying up or because the leader has greater ambitions, the top team will analyse and test alternatives.

The makers of Damei embroidery machines (see inset in Chapter 5) believed that Western MBA methods would help them find the ideal niche more quickly and easily than the trial and error of the past. We wish we shared their confidence. In fact, experimentation, trial and error are endemic to market development (Damei's makers had tried over 100 different products before hitting on one that worked). Procter & Gamble are no different in this respect. Where modern methods do help is in what Sunzi called the 'calculation'. From a range of possibilities, one can calculate which ideas can be tested on the smallest possible scale. One can calculate whether a full-scale model is feasible, e.g. the resources needed and the competitive response. And then when the experimental results are in, one can calculate which is, preferably singular (focus, sacrifice), the best to pursue. In short, well-managed businesses frequently fail small in order to win big. China has the great advantage of providing plenty of opportunities for failure. The question is whether one can learn enough, and survive long enough, to win big.

The reasons why Western companies think it important to write marketing plans down, and traditional Chinese businesses do not, include:

* managers change (average 16 months) five times faster than in family businesses;
* approvals are needed from different sites, perhaps cross border;
* the financial (budgetary) system is far more formalised and a main plan function is to get financial approval;
* lack of trust;
* intolerance for ambiguity.

Linear, Western logic has many advantages but it also drives out the opportunity for unusual solutions gradually to evolve. Explicit information sharing is given greater weight than implicit. Nonaka and Takeuchi have sought to show how Japanese are better than Americans in developing strategically new businesses because they are more patient with implicit information and codify it (make it explicit) more carefully.[3] Professor Max Boisot (1995), who started China's first MBA school in the 1980s, independently came to much the same conclusion.[4]

So where does this leave us in practical terms? We suggest a small cross-functional team is assembled both to plan and to implement the plan. Planning for other people is a waste of time. Notwithstanding our reservations about formality, bridging the East–West cultural gap is helped by the written word so long as the Western side does not give the plan itself too much authority. It is not a legal contract but merely an aide memoire on where the market learning has got to. Flexibility and the door to new learning must be left open.

A plan should be developed over three phases and then, if the calculations reveal that the objectives have not been met, it needs to recycle through all three until it does:

- strategy
- *guànxì*
- calculation

Bad, but frequent, practice is to do it the other way about. They start with the required bottom line, deduce what marketing expenditure will be authorised and then forecast the sales needed to balance the books. Since the end result looks much like the previous plan with the date changed, this tends to work quite well which in turn reinforces the behaviour until something goes wrong.

Good marketing practice, however, begins with the customers and what they do, or might, want in the context of the competitive environment and the company's own capabilities. We call this the E+3 Cs analysis (Environment, Customer, Competitors, own Company). From this, as we have noted above, emerges the brand's positioning statement (one page or less). A plan without this crisp positioning statement can be consigned to the waste paper basket. The positioning will include customer segmentation and geographic focus.

Having, so to speak established who the friends and foes are, why the friends will love the brand and how it will kill the foes, we can develop the specifics of building the brand–customer relationship which is the essence of marketing. Who exactly makes up the brand's *guànxìwang*? Draw the network and prioritise those who matter most. Draw the network of the key players and their relationships. Players form nodes and relationships lines. No relationship means no line.

Every brand has many relationships and it is just as important to prioritise time as money. What activities will most enhance those relationships? Why should they want to buy more, more often, and at higher prices?

Guànxì is at the heart of creating demand which is what marketing is all about. Supply, even in China, *should* be easier.

Finally, and only finally, we need to quantify everything thus far. If financial numbers can be assigned, well and good. Quite often, brand equity (the brand–customer *guànxì*) can only be estimated non-financially and even then the numbers are fuzzy. Concepts like awareness, perceived quality relative to the competition, satisfaction, trust and commitment are important but vague – especially in China where, as we have rehearsed above, market research data are less reliable. Nevertheless these calculations are worth making using estimates where hard research is not justified. The process of measurement brings focus.

Planning should be fun but it rarely is. It should be fun because it is the annual opportunity to learn, to be creative and to play with wild ideas. We only live once (although that is just a majority opinion) but we certainly have the opportunity to rehearse next year's life as often as we like.

Smirnoff in Shanghai

Smirnoff is the leading brand of International Distillers and Vintners (IDV), with worldwide sales in excess of 15 million cases. In 1995, the company's Chinese arm, IDVC, began to consider the launch of Smirnoff on the China market, and chose Shanghai as its point of entry.

The Chinese imported spirits market is dominated by brandy (mainly cognac). Since 1980, the market had grown in volume by about forty times. Local products are mostly white spirits, of which Mao Tai is most famous. Most are highly aromatic and heavily flavoured. They are also relatively cheap, considerably less so than imported cognac. The local makers are highly fragmented, however, with the top 17 names accounting for just 2 per cent of volume. There are around 40,000 distilleries in China; the largest name, Fen Jiu, sells some 17 million cases annually.

IDV's usual policy is to spend on advertising *behind* distribution, partly on the grounds that there is no point in inviting consumers to buy the brand if they cannot find it, but also to fund advertising out of sales revenue. However, such is the potential value of brand equity in this case that establishing a strong position is perceived as

continued

necessary to support distribution of a high-price product. The key task, then, is to develop a promotional strategy to support this goal.

Given IVDC's limited resources, the alternatives are seen as twofold:

Spend whatever can be afforded on a focused TV campaign and measure the results. This will mean spending ahead of profitability.

Build word of mouth through targeted on-premise promotions (one example might be JJs, then the most trendy and popular nightclub in Shanghai) and then build advertising behind distribution.

Conclusion

Victory in war requires intensive research of the rival. Entering an unfamiliar market and making big money needs good intelligence too. Market research contributes crucially to the foundation of corporate strategy and the detailed corporate plans. But because in China it is expensive and unreliable, it needs to be used more selectively and with quality controls. And with the highly dynamic environment and regional variety, it may soon be out-dated. However, we need plans, since planning is vitally important to learning about this particular world – China. The next challenge, to convert planning into action, is the reason why plans must be constructed by those who will have to execute them – which is why we can save money on consultants.

China has masses of statistics and available research, far more than any company can handle. Many of these are inconsistent and unreliable. This bothers Westerners more than it does Chinese, who usually look for pictures rather than precision. Fuzzy focus is quite good enough.

To navigate through all this, a Western firm will need to be tough-minded in distinguishing between what they must know and what may be nice to know but perhaps should be abandoned. Integrating research needs and the planning process, be it the one outlined above or some other, is critical to distinguishing between essential and inessential information. The process needs to be seen as a whole: planning supporting information and information supporting plans.

The overseas Chinese

As far as this chapter is concerned, differences between marketing to the overseas Chinese and to markets in the PRC are differences of degree, not of kind. As mentioned at the end of Chapter 6, overseas Chinese markets are more discriminating and less naive; but the mainland Chinese are catching up very fast. The approaches to marketing, planning and thinking outlined here should work as well in Taipei or Singapore as in Shanghai, always providing that the detailed planning and thinking are adapted to local market conditions. But that adaptation has to be made inside China too; see Chapter 2 on China's geographical and cultural diversity.

Notes

1 In Chinese ancient times, it was customary for a temple to be set apart for the use of a general for his research and planning of a battle. Further, according to Sunzi, a successful general must have the knowledge of his adversary and their behaviour.

2 Hamel, Gary and C K Prahalad (1994) *Competing for the Future*, Boston: Harvard Business School Press, p. 181.

3 Nonaka, Ikujiro and Hirotaka Takeuchi (1995) *The Knowledge-Creating Company*, Oxford University Press.

4 Boisot, Max (1995) *Information Space*, London: Routledge.

8 Rightness and correct form

The *yi* and *li* of organisation in China

> I knew I wanted the job [as CEO of Hongkong Telecom] but I had spent 23 years with Cathay Pacific. It took me two weeks to finally make the decision to leave, and it was agony. I lost over ten pounds in weight.
>
> (Linus Cheung, Hongkong businessman)

> I want to do something different besides working the earth all the time. If I cannot succeed with my own efforts, then I deserve my failure. But please first give me a chance.
>
> (Bian Chengyu, Sichuanese entrepreneur)

Walk into any successful Chinese company and one is struck by what seems to us a contrast: there are a lot of people having a lot of fun and the hierarchical authority is much more formal. The bowing is not just politeness. Of course, there are plenty of dismal factories too, with women in poor lighting crouched over machinery, but that is a relic of the nineteenth century we would all like to leave behind.

We know the differences between Chinese and Western human relations (HR) practices are real because those companies who have imported 'best practice' have seen it fail. By now we should have some answers. Organisation studies is one of the four business areas studied in China before the market reforms – the others being accounting/finance, information systems and economics. Yet when foreign firms are over the big hump of getting started, this is the area which always comes top of every problem list.

The first section of the chapter deals with hierarchy. Almost all organisations are hierarchic: the differences lie in the shape of those hierarchies (flat or columnar), and inter-functional and senior/junior relationships, i.e. how they work. Western companies are more likely to make decisions up and down the hierarchy whereas Chinese managers are more likely to wait to be told.

An even larger adjustment needs to be made when working with Chinese employees, who have different sets of work values and often quite different goals. Many Western companies are currently experiencing severe difficulties in recruiting and retaining staff in China. We suggest that some of their difficulties may stem from the fact that, with the best will in the world, many are still trying to manage in 'Western style'.

After hierarchy, we look at the question of specialisation – or the lack of it – and then decision-making and leadership. People management has much to do with coping with risk. The West uses controls, especially financial controls, to do that and China uses *guànxì*. No wonder Western accountants struggle in China. Both systems work in their own context but severe losses can, and do, occur when they collide. Finally, we will briefly review some basic HR bread and rations issues such as unions and the Party, pay, bonuses and training. Today, enough experience has built up for HR managers from both cultures to be thoroughly trained in the PRC context, e.g. using video materials.

Chinese organisations are strongly permeated by Confucian values which do not always match short-term business interests. Neo-Confucianism has been widely held, most notably by Singapore's Lee Kuan Yew, to be responsible for the commercial success of China and the 'four tigers' (if you remember them). This question should not distract us here but is at best an over-simplification. Neo-Confucianism (or 'confusianism') has proved hard to define except in reference to successful performance which is circular. There is enough in the writings of Chinese philosophers, like the Christian Bible, to justify any position.

Oled Shenkar sums up the key distinctive features which characterise Chinese organisations as follows,[1] noting that all have parallels in the *Analects* of Confucius:

* formalised, detailed rules are destructive to human relationships;
* flexibility and versatility are essential qualities for a leader;
* the leader must set and enforce standards of commitment and morality through personal example;
* economic incentives alone will not motivate subordinates;
* a leader must be courteous, friendly, helpful and sincere when dealing with subordinates (*rén*).

This being China, the opposites of at least the first three of those are also true. The Chinese have plenty of formal rules in business, success comes from determination (inflexibility) and Mao was not famous for his morality.

Successful management in China may depend on the ability to manage in 'Chinese style' and provide Chinese employees with the kind of organisation that suits their needs. However, this is not a one-way street. Many Chinese managers admire the way Western companies organise themselves and do business, and we may ultimately reach a synthesis of styles of management. But ultimately is a long way away.

Hierarchies

Most organisations are strongly hierarchical, when compared with their Western counterparts, in the sense that the channels of reporting and authority are more formal. An organisational chart of a typical Chinese business would be more concave, with a few strong leaders at the top, a few managers running around in the middle and the majority of employees at or near the bottom. The majority of Chinese businesses are led by a single dominant owner/manager/director.

But some of the difference is temporal rather than cultural. British businesses used to be like that before middle management expanded. In Chinese SOEs and British nationalised industries, their aimless bureaucracies took over the asylums. That is why, presumably, the British Department for International Development thinks it can transfer the skills of privatisation but there is not much evidence that China is ready for the leaner flatter organisations now thought to be best practice in the West. Directionally, yes, but now, possibly not.

There are no accurate figures available, but certainly the majority of overseas Chinese businesses are family affairs. Hongkong businesses are often very family-oriented; Li Ka-shing's family are prominent in Hutchison Whampoa, while Peter Wu 'inherited' the managing of Wheelock from his father-in-law, Sir Y. K. Pao. A dominant family member, usually the father, is head of the business, other family members occupy key posts, and employees lower down the organisational pyramid look to the father and the other members of the family for leadership. This pattern is also emerging on the mainland China with the booming of the private sector.

The Confucian ideal of the family is thus translated easily and naturally to business. One of the consequences is that decision-making and power are highly concentrated and the 'power distance' (the barrier sensed by those lower in the hierarchy between them and those who run the business) is significantly increased. Cross-cultural studies have shown that power distance is greater in China even than in Japan.

Even in non-family organisations, the same model tends to be employed. We have already noted that the Communist Party tried to remake society along Confucian lines by casting itself as the 'father' or 'head of the family' for all Chinese. In business terms, that became a little confused as the Party cadre member, who held the ultimate power, was not usually the general manager. Power gradually switched in most businesses away from the cadre but the Party should not be forgotten when considering organisational matters.

This history can be glibly recounted but it has had devastating effects on individual people. For example, Wu Zinan inherited a silk factory in Suzhou from his father in the late 1940s and ran the factory until 1956 when it was nationalised. The Party asked him to stay on as manager, which he did, believing genuinely in the Party and wanting to help improve the Chinese economy. During the Cultural Revolution he was sacked from his job and forced to clean the factory floors wearing a dunce's cap; his erstwhile employees were encouraged to mock and abuse him. In 1976 he was reinstated; today, well past retirement age, he is working to take his factory into the new age of the enterprise economy. He feels he cannot retire; there is simply no one else who understands how the factory works.

One consequence of this family-styled system tends to be that Chinese businesses can have short life spans. Wheelock is an exception to the rule that the business tends to die with the leader. In Hongkong, nearly as many businesses close as open each year. The majority of closures were not due to insolvency, but simply because the owner had died, or wished to retire, and did not have a successor. It is even similar to the SOEs in mainland China, whose rise and fall are closely tied to the fate of the head of the individual enterprises. A retirement of a strong man often causes a large decrease of profitability. If not worse, the Chinese tend to be at least as bad at succession planning as foreigners.

The three conclusions we draw are that the organisation should be seen as a family. In China, where business and private lives are not so clearly demarcated, this makes sense. Second, the formal structure is developing along the same lines as elsewhere but, for historical reasons, flattening the pyramids and empowerment are some way behind. Thirdly, respect for authority and power is much greater. Chinese managers have a greater need for approval both in the sense of getting permission or instruction and in the sense of positive reinforcement.

Lack of specialisation

It may seem odd in the light of the foregoing, but Chinese businesses have tended not to employ specialists. The hierarchies that exist focus on power, responsibility and salary; they are less likely to be task-related. In a Chinese steel mill, for example, individual employees are likely to be notionally capable (though not necessarily trained) to carry out a variety of tasks ranging from stoking a blast furnace to skimming slag to sweeping the floor. Traditionally, a work unit is given a production quota to fill; it is up to the members of the unit itself to decide who carries out which tasks.

This is changing as the enterprise culture begins to take hold, and some Chinese businesses are beginning to adopt Western-style practices of organisation and specialisation. The adaptation is particularly noticeable in JV businesses, and in those run by large organisations. The former PLA-run textile and shoe factories around Shenzhen, for example, are highly structured and employees have set tasks on assembly lines. So do the silk factories in Wuzi and many other traditional operations where Taylorism still reigns. But in many businesses, particularly state-owned enterprises, the old systems are still in place. People have a hierarchy within their work unit based on salary and position, not on task; the work unit in turn has a hierarchy within the business, based on the nature of its work and, very often, on its past success in filling production quotas.

Another noticeable feature is the lack of ancillary departments such as public relations, labour relations, marketing, finance or personnel management for those old-styled Chinese enterprises. These are usually considered part of the leader's job along with his/her personal staff. The glass ceiling is far less prevalent in China than Japan or the West. Surveys which have looked at specialisation have found that Chinese businesses have a much higher proportion of the total staff directly concerned with the production of the company's main product or service – probably 90 per cent of the total.

Decision-making and leadership

The typical (good) Chinese manager operates in a very hands-on style and is familiar with all aspects of the business. He or she delegates far less than his or her Western counterpart, spends less time in meetings, less time consulting and more time actually making decisions and implementing policy. Some recent surveys have suggested that Chinese managers believe that travelling and meetings are the least important aspects of their jobs; they would rather spend more time doing desk work, assessing and evaluating information and making decisions. It is interesting that only 31 per cent of the sample believed that scheduled meetings were an important activity and only 4 per cent believed that unscheduled meetings were important.

Decision-making in Chinese organisations tends to be autocratic. Decisions are usually made by one individual, the owner/manager/director, and in private. The results of the decision are then announced, usually without explanation. It is assumed to have been considered enough that the decision is made and to be understandable to these people under the influence of this decision.

However, there is likely to have been extensive consultation first. The good Chinese manager listens to the workers and takes their opinions into account, up to a point. There may also have been lateral discussions with ministries, local officials and the *guànxìwang*. Decision-making in China can be remarkably quick or remarkably slow. The quick ones are where experience provides the (apparent) solution. Nevertheless, there is not much democracy about all this; the leader makes the decisions and the employees are expected to carry them out exactly.

Challenging a decision once it has been made is often considered a serious offence; it causes the superior to lose face. At this stage, workers are expected to keep their views to themselves. There is a saying: 'Honour the hierarchy first, your vision of truth second.'

One consequence is that people lower down the hierarchy tend to be bad at taking responsibility. There is a great deal of buck-passing and procrastination in Chinese organisations: more even than in the West.

Management by relationships

Western companies use systems to control relationships. Chinese organisations use relationships to control systems. Western companies use a legalistic framework of procedures and controls to police relations. One must not exaggerate: both cultures operate both arrangements, but the balance differs. This legalistic and financial control framework is confusing for Chinese managers who feel mistrusted and do not know how they stand in relationship to the boss. It also tells them something very dangerous: if this is the Western game, let us find out how it works and beat the system. Of course, this confusion is also a function of novelty. Once these systems become commonplace and accepted, the problems should decrease.

Chinese managers believe that one of their key tasks is to maintain harmony within the organisation, both between people and between work units. This is particularly the case where Confucian values are strongly extant. When the workers create discord or challenge leaders' decisions, their actions create bad feeling and cause loss of face.

Leadership anywhere in the world operates on the basis of respect. One may not like, or even admire, the leader but if s/he has established a good track record and observes the main principles laid down by Sunzi, the troops will follow. The authors are divided on the subject of how much Confucius has to do with leadership, if anything.

Leaders are certainly expected to develop a relationship with their employees. This is formalised as *wu lun*, the relationship of unequal pairs; each employee should feel a personal connection with the employer or manager, and should feel to some degree dependent on that leader.

At the same time, management is not just about leadership. One can argue about which matters more, but persuading people to follow is just part of the story. A tactical plan needs to be drawn up, practical decisions need to be made, and resources need to be in place – and not diverted. Business schools do not teach much about leadership for the simple reason that they teach management. It will be interesting to watch the principles taught in China's MBA schools (from Western textbooks) collide with the practices in their workplaces. They are taught mechanical controls, but operate in a *guànxi* environment for handling risk. The vast majority of MBA places are part-time; the students are holding down middle management jobs. In our limited observation, the students do not much attempt to bridge the cultures; mentally, they keep them apart.

The relationship approach to risk management clearly works better in small family businesses than in multinationals though it has to be said that the mafia, with similar if criminal and fear-laden characteristics, seems to span continents without difficulty. But note the need, as with *guànxi*, for close, family-like, ties. Maintaining these relationships requires constant communication – hence the significance of the mobile phone.

Western firms do not need to, even if they could, abandon the control systems that have served them well elsewhere. On the other hand, in China they need to understand why their Chinese colleagues find them awkward, to say the least, and they also need to develop *guànxi* systems alongside.

The unions and the Party in the workplace

Under Mao, the trade unions and the Communist Party had significant presences in the workplace. All were centrally controlled, the Party from Beijing, the unions through ACFTU, the All-China Federation of Trade Unions, and the businesses through the various ministries. Both unions and Party were expected to take part in decision-making processes and to adopt leadership roles. In practice, the factory director, the union secretary and the Party secretary, or cadre, competed for dominance, and one became de facto factory leader.

In 1984 Deng moved to restrict the power of the Party. Day-to-day responsibility for the workplace was concentrated on the director; the Party secretary moved back to an 'oversight' role, concentrating on issues such as worker education. The power of the unions too has been curtailed. Managers are still obliged to consult with the unions on many issues, but are no longer as strictly bound by union decisions. The present trend is a move back towards the pyramidal hierarchy described above.

While the Party members at local level are by and large accepting of and even enthusiastic about this change, there are signs of increasing labour unrest. Western diplomatic observers estimate there were 250,000 labour disputes across China from 1991 to 1993, ranging from disagreements over pay, conditions and promotion to all-out strikes. There may have been as many as 100,000 similar disputes in 1994. Labour movements have played important roles in instances of unrest, including the Tiananmen Square incident in 1989.

The 'personnel problem' for Western companies in China

Polls of Western businesses asking respondents about the problems of operating in China usually show that recruiting and training managers and staff come at the top of the list. That this should be so is a little odd. After all, Western companies have been honing and refining their personnel management techniques for decades. Most have a senior HR person at director level, influencing policy and making certain that the company remains focused on its staff. Chinese companies, on the other hand, have no concept of personnel management; instead they have *rén shi quan* or personnel authority. The company personnel manager, if there is one at all, has responsibility for hiring and firing, promotion (or punishment) and salaries. The situation becomes odder still when one reflects on the fact that most Chinese managers approve of Western management styles and believe they are more suited to the needs of business than traditional Chinese authoritarian management.

Why then are Western companies failing to cope with the Chinese labour market? Some companies report annual labour turnover of as much as 80 per cent, and over 20 per cent is common. Various explanations have been put forth:

- by providing higher salaries, Western companies are encouraging Chinese managers to become more mobile;
- traditional Chinese values are breaking down and China is becoming a much more fluid society;
- Chinese employees may feel loyalty to Chinese organisations, but never to Western organisations.

There may be a little bit of truth to all these explanations, but none is complete in itself. Certainly there is no excuse for the hands in the air attitude adopted by some Western companies, which simply believe that high rates of turnover are a given factor in China.

The danger is that, sooner rather than later, wage inflation will reduce the cost differentials that make China such an attractive operating environment.

The company that succeeds then will be the company which can manage a stable, loyal, committed workforce.

The changing labour market in China

Generally speaking, a manager who has been educated within China commands the lowest salary premium. Chinese managers who have been educated in the West command higher salaries, while, in the PRC, expatriate managers are the best paid of all. Some Hongkong managers often demand more in terms of benefits, making them the most expensive to hire. The problem areas concern foreigners less than overseas Chinese who return. Foreigners are few and far between and can easily be seen as different. For language, cultural and adaptability reasons, however, multinationals are increasingly engaging Western-trained overseas Chinese. Some even have to learn Pudonghua.

There are mixed views about the effect in the workplace of having two managers on vastly different salary scales working together. One company confidently reported that its indigenous Chinese management approved of the higher salaries being paid to migrants from Hongkong because they were obviously worth more. The company claims to know this because it asked its Chinese managers what they thought.

Until the Asia crisis, wage inflation was a serious problem, with salaries rising 15–30 per cent per annum in Shanghai, for example. That appears to have calmed down, for the moment, but salaries are bound to keep escalating. Increasing salaries have accelerated worker, and especially managerial, mobility. There is a tendency for people to hop from one job to another as soon as they receive a better offer, and this is particularly prevalent with skilled workers and educated managers.

The wide gaps in salary need to be addressed. Ignored, they will fester. Zhu Rongji, on a visit to MIT, stated that the PRC would be happy to engage returning Chinese business academics on US salaries. For one reason or another not too many, if any, have taken him up on the offer. In the long run these differentials will have to be ironed out as between Chinese managers. Foreigners will always get a premium for dislocation just as some Asians, e.g. Japanese, get in Europe. The answer lies in training and development. The company needs to be able to show that people in the same jobs with the same skills get comparable rewards. Just being at the same job level is not enough.

Promotion equals status. Before economic liberalisation, workers were often restricted in their choice of employment. They therefore worked hard to work their way up the promotion ladder in their own organisation.

One of the consequences of a planned economy is that in many organisations the drive to meet production quotas takes precedence over health and safety issues. Certainly health and safety standards have suffered in China, and there have been a number of serious accidents in recent years. Problems with the workplace environment are behind many of China's 100,000 or so industrial disputes each year.

Recruitment and rewards

Dismissal of an employee in China may be difficult but it is not the problem: keeping people is. Western managers in assigning roles may well cause loss of face and where that happens the individual is likely to resign. The main skill therefore in recruiting, and letting go, is sensitive handling of matters of face.

Although as mentioned above, Chinese employees at all levels are eager to improve their own skills and make themselves more marketable, Chinese managers do not currently see personal career development in the same way that foreigners do. Westerners job hop too. Firm comparisons are not available and the diminished loyalty by firms to employees has been matched, not surprisingly, by the reciprocal. Younger managers look to the market rather than their pensions as security. Critics of young Chinese managers, however, suggest that they are doing themselves no favours by accepting the next higher paycheck that comes along rather than building a strong career (or CV/resumé, if you wish to be cynical). It is alleged that they do move from one job to another with any idea that in doing so they will increase personal satisfaction or achieve any personal goals beyond the making of money. The chance of a trip overseas is an important incentive for managers who have never been out of China, though one survey shows that managers who have been out of China once often do not want to go again. Been there, got the T-shirt.

The old SOE culture provided housing, education and health benefits to make up for low wages. However big the salary from the JV these benefits are hard to make up, especially in areas such as Shanghai where housing is now more expensive than in many countries in the West. A favoured solution is to leave one partner on the state payroll, with the benefits, whilst the other works for a JV or WFOE. Companies now commonly provide housing for employees, though more often as cash allowances. Employee healthcare and other benefits and bonuses can amount to 75–80 per cent on top of salary.

Benefits can have a direct impact on retention. IBM and Procter & Gamble both offer comprehensive benefits packages, and both have very low staff turnover rates. Ciba, Bell and Shanghai Volkswagen also (a) pay well, (b) offer internal chances for promotion and (c) offer good benefits packages, and have low turnover rates. Those with high turnover rates are usually smaller operations or representative offices, with limited offerings to employees.

Recruitment

At present, representative offices are required to hire from state-controlled personnel agencies. Joint ventures and WFOEs are free to recruit anywhere. In *theory*, the recruitment of new graduates can involve repayment of part of their university tuition costs. Recruitment restrictions are relaxing all the time, and China is moving steadily towards a free labour market.

Some commonly used channels for recruitment are:

* Key employees may be assigned to a joint venture or Chinese institution by FESCO, the Ministry of Labour, or by local government. This is becoming less common, and the government is steadily backing away from the labour market.
* Local Human Resources Exchange Centres (*Rencai Shichang*) hold databases and manage job fairs for management staff.
* Local Labour Bureaux (*Laowu Shichang*) provide a similar service for workers.
* Campus recruiting – to find the best educated young Chinese, increasingly, top multinational companies in China place emphasis on this channel.
* Media advertising, usually in newspapers (broadcast media and posters appear to have little effect).
* *Guànxì* – knowing someone who knows someone who is qualified for the job.

Employing friends and relatives is now considered nepotism, or at least unprofessional, in the West, but that was not always so. Families joined in groups and introduced new generations as they left school. There is much to be said for engaging families especially when trying to get as close as possible to the style of a Chinese family business. Warmth is good. One of the authors surprised a very successful young brand manager by asking if she had a sibling with similar talents and then engaging her (as it turned out) sight unseen.

Of course a bad family in key positions can wreak devastation so we are not suggesting this is any panacea. At the same time, we are suggesting that the *guànxìwang* culture exists and it should be made the most of.

Zeneca China

Zeneca has a pre-eminent position in the Chinese agrochemical market thanks to long-standing support for the market, employment of high-quality management and good relationships with the Ministry of Chemicals. Investment in local production was an essential feature of the company's strategy, but there were a number of other options:

- Should Zeneca concentrate on production and internal issues, and leave distribution to Chinese partners?
- Should they concentrate on the central belt around the Yellow and Yangtze rivers, or expand to cover all of China?
- What were the priorities for developing local managers beyond their previous roles in import support?
- Should marketing be in line with international patterns, or were domestic solutions needed?

In transforming itself from an importer to a domestic producer, Zeneca China had to undergo some important cultural shifts. Its high-quality products had an excellent reputation but were expensive. A critical element in its marketing strategy was direct promotions to districts and other local buyers, building good relations with them in the process. In terms of management, Zeneca China needed to bring its management up to the level of the rest of the group worldwide, while at the same time focusing their attention on growing the domestic market.

Training and development

There are marked differences in education among Chinese employees, depending on the region and also on the age group. Those who were at school during the Cultural Revolution received no education at all for several years. The generation which entered school after 1976, however, has been educated to a fairly high standard. Many more people in China speak English than in England although certificates of proficiency should not be taken at face value. In some JVs English may well have been adopted, by the seniors, as the working language but that is just being polite to the expatriate(s).

Technical training is usually of a very high standard, given the variable technology levels with many hundred technical training institutes around the country.

Management training is growing slowly. The China-Europe International Business School in Shanghai, following its predecessor in Beijing, is training Chinese managers to European MBA standards. The Academic Council has authorised fifty-six universities to offer MBA courses – not including CEIBS which, to everyone's discomfort remains outside the state system (1999). After about ten years, many of these are doing a fine job despite the dire shortage of MBA teachers. The authorities try to get around this with teacher training and exchanges (mostly with the US) and getting stronger schools to train the weaker.

We have mentioned the retraining of SOE managers earlier and most training, of course, takes place inhouse and on the job. We also mentioned the Rolls-Royce led China-Britain Industrial Consortium, which has an extensive package of courses and training for middle managers. JVs and WFOEs without the resources to conduct formal in-house training can use the networking through their chambers of commerce.

A long-term outlook on employment is needed. One speaker at the Economist Conference on management in Shanghai in the early 1990s recommended committing up to 15 per cent of earnings towards long-term growth. Signal to your employees that you are committed, he said, and you increase the chance they will commit themselves to you. Maybe not a lot, but it helps.

Why did Chinese managers not job hop before? Of course, Chinese managers and workers stayed put because they had to, by government order and because of social pressures. But the traditional Chinese organisation offers something else. As a community, with strong leadership and values, it can offer the worker or manager a home and a sense of belonging. A set of concentric relational circles could be drawn around the organisation and the employee's place in it. JVs and WFOEs, however much they develop their staff, have a real problem here. At the end of the day they are still foreign.

Obviously there have been changes over time. The values of young Chinese today are as different from those of the Cultural Revolution as those of the Cultural Revolution were from the 1930s. Doubtless Chinese, especially the young and educated members of society, are influenced by the West and see Western managers as role models. But the job seeking and holding patterns currently in evidence do not so much suggest Western influence as no influence at all. With the communal organisations and their Confucian influences disappearing, Chinese managers are finding that the new style organisations offer them no sense of values. *Chinese managers leave their jobs and go on to new jobs simply because there is nothing to hold them in place.*

Conclusion

Western companies in China can and should market themselves as employers using the techniques of the last two chapters. The concept of the 'employer brand' is gaining ground in the West and it makes just as much sense here. Status can be attached to working for a particular company.

As part of that, companies can actively manage employee expectations. Disappointments with salary increases, unrealistic expectations and general job dissatisfaction are all responsible for departures from jobs.

Non-financial incentives have an important role to play in employee retention. Although the present move is away from the iron rice bowl and full security, many employees value these things highly, particularly in the inflationary areas of Shanghai and the southeast. Benefits can be a powerful inducement to employee retention.

Perhaps what is developing in China now is a synthesis of both worlds, one which will hopefully combine the best of both. Most Chinese recognise that Western management systems have a lot to offer in terms of efficiency, use of technology, and development of creativity. Thus it is a mistake to see Chinese business culture as being opposed to any of these things. As noted above, there is no either/or in Chinese management; it is both structured and unstructured. Our own stereotypical view of the entrepreneur as a free-wheeling loner does not make much sense in China (one can question whether it makes sense in the West as well). China has entrepreneurs, but they work within concentric circles and networks of *guànxì*, not as lone wolves.

The overseas Chinese

As Chapter 9 points out, many overseas Chinese firms are actually a synthesis of value systems as they typically (especially the larger ones) employ a variety of different nationalities. That said, the prevalence of (especially) Confucian and Buddhist values elsewhere in East Asia means that employees and managers in these countries often share similar workplace values to their counterparts in China. In fact, countries like Thailand exhibit even more strongly an attachment to hierarchy and to personal relations in the workplace. Taiwan, too, is noted for strong bonds between employers and workers.

We would also draw the reader's attention once again to the problems noted above, of employing overseas Chinese managers in

continued

mainland firms. There is no doubt that these managers offer a firm many advantages. However, the pay differential and the more general problem of clashing cultures can lead to tensions. The same problems can be encountered when moving managers between regions inside China.

Note

1 Shenkar 1991.

9 Doing business with the sojourners

The overseas Chinese communities

In this penultimate chapter, we look beyond the boundaries of the old People's Republic of China at the Chinese diaspora, the Chinese community living overseas. 'Overseas' means outside of China, by the Chinese definition. Hongkong, Macao and Taiwan[1] are not overseas, but they have business cultures distinctly different from that of the PRC prior to the integration of Hongkong and Macao as Special Administrative Regions (SARs). So we will fudge borders a bit and include Hongkong, Macao and Taiwan in the following.

Understanding the overseas Chinese communities is important for two reasons. First, the overseas Chinese communities (especially Hongkong and Taiwan) can be useful routes of entry into the Chinese market. Hongkong intermediaries are often used by Western companies as *hongniang*, and Hongkong capitalists are major investors in China on their own account.

Second, the countries of East Asia where the Chinese community is a major business presence represent major markets in their own right. Singapore, Hongkong and Taiwan are Chinese societies, using any kind of measures. Overseas Chinese dominate the economies of Malaysia, Indonesia, Thailand and the Philippines. There are strong links between ways of doing business in these countries and ways of doing business in the PRC, and the concepts in this book are applicable to a greater or lesser degree all over East Asia. There are also many differences, however, and we shall be looking at variants in business practice and behaviour between China and the rest of East Asia.

The overseas Chinese

There are an estimated 60 million Chinese living outside the PRC. Eighty per cent of these live in East Asia, and about 6.5 million live in North America. The remainder, about 4.4 million, are scattered across South America, Europe, Africa and West Asia with sizeable communities in

Jamaica, East Africa and the Seychelles. The largest single overseas Chinese community is in Taiwan, 98 per cent of whose 20 million people are Chinese.

These figures are obviously quite small when compared with the population of the PRC. However, these communities exercise an economic power out of all proportion with their size. These 60 million people had in 1995 a gross domestic product in excess of $500 billion and current assets of $2 trillion; considerably more than the PRC and nearly two-thirds the level of Japan. The East Asian Chinese have been a powerful force in the regional economic revolution, and as such they are increasingly important players in the world economy.

Hongkong: back in the family

Ninety-nine per cent of the population of Hongkong are ethnic Chinese and Chinese values are prominent. Since 1997, China has once again taken control of Hongkong, acquired by the British during the Opium Wars. But although Hongkong is now technically part of China, to Chinese eyes, Hongkong Chinese are strongly imbued with Western culture, particularly consumerism. To more traditional older Chinese, Hongkong residents are accordingly somewhat suspect, while to some of the younger generation they are to be admired.

The future of the Hongkong Chinese community may depend on events not in Beijing but in Shanghai. The Chinese government has long believed that Shanghai ought to be the financial capital of the Far East, a position which it was well on its way to occupying before 1949. Hongkong, in the Chinese scheme of things, has an important but secondary role to play. To a certain extent the heavy investment activity by Hongkong businesses before 1997, especially in south China, can be seen as an attempt to buy position and control in advance of the Chinese takeover. In the event, fears have not been justified; China has not interfered to any real extent in the former colony's economy, and so far Shanghai has failed to pose a challenge as a rival financial centre.

Who are the overseas Chinese?

In China, expatriate Chinese are referred to as *huaqiao*. The name means 'overseas Chinese', but there is a connotation that the *huaqiao* are only overseas temporarily, and that they will one day come back to China. They are also sometimes known as 'sojourners'.

Huaqiao refers to both Chinese nationals and ethnic Chinese who are citizens of other countries. There are also a number of sub-categories:

- *huaren*, ethnic Chinese who live abroad;
- *huayi*, 'persons of Chinese origin';
- *Gangao tonbao*, Hongkong and Macao Chinese;
- *Taiwan tonbao*, Taiwan Chinese.

The Chinese do make considerable distinctions between these and other categories, and are acutely conscious of where the *huaqiao* come from and their backgrounds. The four sub-groups above can experience vastly different treatment, depending on where they are in the country. Some Hongkong Chinese report being treated coldly in the north (though Chinese nationals from Guangzhou say the same) while *huayi* from Canada and the United States are often warmly received as prodigals returning to the fold.

There are other divisions within the community which are not necessarily recognised in China. Political divisions were important throughout the post-1949 period, with some overseas Chinese supporting the Communists and others vehemently opposing them. Ethnic divisions, between north and south Chinese, occasionally appear but are less important as the majority of overseas Chinese families come from south Chinese backgrounds. The most important distinction concerns the degree of acculturation and integration; some overseas Chinese regard themselves as being citizens of their host country and have adopted much of that country's culture, while others emphatically regard themselves as Chinese.

Taiwan: dismantling the fortress

Taiwan is still officially part of China, although there is a trend towards independence, currently. Taiwanese businesses are still formally prohibited from investing in China, and the Taiwan-held islands off the coast of Fukien, within artillery range of the mainland, are still heavily garrisoned.

Taiwan has one of the best education systems in the world. The country spends 20 per cent of its GDP on education, and has more universities per capita than any other country. Taiwan has also pioneered the development of a privately funded corporate university sector, with higher education institutions funded by major corporations existing alongside the state schools. Both private and state universities are often free.

continued

Taiwan also has a strongly entrepreneurial culture. Both government and big business encourage the growth of small business, and people wanting to start their own companies are encouraged. Ninety-eight per cent of businesses in Taiwan have fewer than 50 employees: the Taiwanese themselves have a saying, 'Throw a stone out a window and you will probably hit a company president.'

The flip side of all this activity has been one of the most strongly protectionist economies in the world. Taiwan has made self-sufficiency its goal, but having achieved this, and as the military threat from the mainland recedes, the limits of growth are now being reached. Taiwan is beginning, slowly and cautiously, to dismantle some of the borders around its economy (the need to respond to the Asia crisis is now showing signs of speeding up this process). Taiwanese companies trading in China are not being prosecuted, although political relations with Beijing go up and down, depending on what local politicians are saying/not saying about declaring Taiwan to be a separate country.

Origins of the overseas communities

If one excludes the debatable case of native Americans, the earliest Chinese emigrants were possibly the groups who moved to Japan in the period before the Japanese Warring States and the closing of Japan's borders in the eleventh century AD. During this period, the Chinese had a powerful influence on emerging Japanese culture, bringing Buddhism and pictograms among other things to Japan. Japan served as a useful outlet for Chinese emigration for about a thousand years.

The modern period of Chinese emigration began in the seventeenth century, when the dislocations caused by the Manchu conquest and Tibetan invasions led to a wave of refugees from the fighting and economic dislocations. Many from the southern provinces fled into Southeast Asia, while the Sinification of Taiwan begins from about this time with refugees from Fukien absorbing the native Taiwanese. Many Chinese were also encouraged by the Spanish authorities in the Philippines to emigrate there, as there was a great need for labour.

Through the next two centuries, economic migrants and refugees from political strife continued to swell the numbers of the Chinese communities overseas, especially in Taiwan and Southeast Asia. From the early nineteenth century the British authorities began encouraging Chinese emigration to other parts of the British Empire; Singapore became a major transhipment point for Chinese labour going to the Malay tin mines or on to Burma and India. The Dutch also recruited Chinese labour in Indonesia.

The discovery of gold in North America coincided with a period of great civil unrest in South China. The first wave of immigrants arrived in San Francisco, shortly after the gold rush of 1849 began; a second wave began around 1858, spurred by the devastation of the Taiping Rebellion on the one hand and the discovery of further gold in British Columbia on the other. More Chinese labourers were hired to help build the western links of the trans-continental railways in the 1870s and 1880s. Tens of thousands of Chinese emigrated to these two centres, most of whom came from a small strip of Guangdong province between Hongkong and Guangzhou.

In the twentieth century, the foreign invasions and civil strife which have damaged China so badly have produced new crops of refugees. The era of the warlords produced new emigration to Southeast Asia (the United States and Canada were by this time restricting Chinese immigration). After 1949 there were large waves of immigration from mainland China to Hongkong and Taiwan, many of them middle-class refugees. The Chinese populations of Southeast Asia were further increased when a number of Guomindang army units which had fought in Burma refused to go back to China and dispersed through Burma, Thailand and Laos.

However, not all the migrants of this period were fleeing Communism. The Indonesian and Malayan communities had substantial groups supporting Mao and espousing Communism. This led to considerable tensions in Indonesia, while in Malaya the Communist insurgents active until about 1957 were mostly Chinese.

Controlled movements out of China began again in the late 1960s when the Chinese government began supporting the Non-Aligned Movement after the split with Russia. Chinese workers and technicians were exported for a variety of civil engineering projects in the Third World. The most famous of these was the TanZam railway project in East Africa, which was largely built by Chinese labour. After the conclusion of the project, some of the Chinese workers applied for and received permission to stay on in Africa. The movement of oversea labourers continues nowadays, especially in the Middle East. Since 1978, the Chinese government has been sending out small groups of people to gain education and work experience overseas, primarily in Europe and North America. However, this group has signed contracts with the government to go back to China after their study or training abroad.

Studying abroad is not necessarily supported by the Chinese government. On the contrary, it is quite popular to apply for foreign scholarships on campus. For example, one half of the 1997 chemistry class in Peking

University went abroad with financial support from foreign universities, particularly those in the United States. These people do not have a legal obligation to return to China, which bothers the government somewhat, as it constitutes a brain-drain, but the government hopes that they will return to the motherland, and some do.

Canada has long been popular due to a relatively looser immigration policy. A massive number of layoffs and the deflationary situation in China bring a great sense of uncertainty, but the desire to be rich is probably stronger than at any time before on the mainland. The tales of overseas self-made billionaires excites a number of native Chinese to move abroad, sometimes illegally. Large parts of Western Canada's real estate is now owned by Chinese people.

Singapore: the crossroads

Singapore, once a great trading crossroads and now a major financial and technological centre, is reaching its own crossroads. As in China, the patriarchal figure who dominates government and society, Lee Kuan Yew, exerts much influence on Singapore with his dream of a developed Western-styled economy under Neo-Confucianist values. His successor is successfully following Lee's belief and holding Lee's edifice together.

Seventy-eight per cent of the population of Singapore is Chinese, with the remainder being of Malay or Indian extraction. Ethnic Chinese dominate the economy and the government. In contrast to nearby Malaysia and Indonesia, where Chinese business activity is restricted, Singapore is one of the great achievements of Chinese capitalism.

Singapore is possibly the most modern city in Asia. Its high-tech achievements are formidable; cyberpunk author William Gibson recently called it 'the first city of the computer age'. Singaporean Chinese, however, for all their modern lifestyle, tend on the whole to be socially conservative. The drive against corruption, the strictly regulated society, the intense and complicated hierarchies might almost be a deliberate model of rule according to Confucian principles. Look closely, however, and you will find them driving over the causeway to scatter their wilder seeds in Johore. Strangely, Singapore has quite a low level of education spending as a proportion of GDP, much lower than Taiwan and lower even than many Western countries.

What sets the overseas Chinese communities apart?

The nature of their origins should give some clues about the nature of overseas Chinese communities today. Wherever they are, overseas Chinese communities have a number of distinguishing features.

Commonality of background

Except for students and experts, the vast majority of Chinese emigrants over the last several centuries have been refugees, fleeing either economic disaster or political persecution and war. Even those Chinese who were recruited as labourers, in Malaya, the Dutch East Indies (Indonesia), the Philippines or North America, suffered discrimination from locals who saw them as a threat to the local economy and jobs. There is a common heritage of hardship and alienation in the overseas Chinese communities, which is responsible for a number of further features such as the importance of community and identity.

Low profile

In Hongkong, Taiwan and Singapore the *huaqiao* form the majority of the population and control government and society as well as the economy. In other countries of East Asia, fear of persecution has in the past – sometimes the very recent past – led them to maintain a low profile. The first massacre of overseas Chinese took place in the Philippines in the late sixteenth century, when hundreds were massacred; 10,000 died in ethnic riots in Batavia (now Jakarta) in 1740. Mention has already been made of the deaths in Malaysia during the 1950s, and there were more deaths, perhaps several hundred in Indonesia around the time of the fall of Suharto. Even today a number of countries, principally Malaysia and Indonesia, have laws restricting Chinese participation in business; as a result Chinese businessmen tend to work behind the scenes, using local businesses as fronts. A low profile means a quiet life.

In North America discrimination mainly took the form of legal restrictions on work. In Canada, for example, local legislation in the early twentieth century prohibited farmers from hiring Chinese labour. However, most of these restrictions were repealed by the middle of the century and Chinese communities have gradually become more visible, moving out of their Chinatown ghettos in cities such as San Francisco, Los Angeles, Seattle, Vancouver and Victoria.

Curiously, lack of discrimination does not necessarily mean that

Chinese communities become more visible. Instead, it seems to lead them to becoming more deeply integrated into the local community. In North America and in Thailand and the Philippines the boundaries between the Chinese and local communities are becoming porous; in Thailand, local Chinese commonly ask to be called by the Thai versions of their names (although this is also a legal requirement). This is low profile of a different sort, achieved by blending into the local community. This blending does not, however, mean that Chinese identity is in any way lessened.

Malaysia: looking for a foundation

Malaysia was created by the British colonial authorities out of a collection of principalities and rajates on the Malay peninsula and in north Borneo. Malaysia has only been an independent country since 1957, and the cracks still sometimes show.

Badly affected by the Asian crisis, Malaysia still came through better than others. The Malaysian government is concerned not to race into growth but to embark on controlled stages. Foreign investment is invited but controlled, and great emphasis is placed on technology transfer and education for the workforce. Controlled growth led in turn to a controlled crash, and Malaysia's recovery is now well on its way.

The Malaysian government is dominated by *bumiputras*, or ethnic Malays, who like to preserve a fiction that they actually run the economy. In 1971 the government introduced laws restricting participation in business by Chinese, but in the last twenty years the share of the economy controlled by Malaysian Chinese has increased. Many companies are fronted by *bumiputras* but are actually controlled behind the scenes by Chinese entrepreneurs.

Malay and Chinese employees and managers do work together, however, which can cause problems, even more so when Malay Moslems, Indian Hindus and Chinese of various non-beliefs are mixed together in the same workplace. For example, while pork and beef are staples of the Malaysian Chinese diet, Hindus may not eat beef and Moslems may not use utensils which have touched pork, meaning it cannot be served in factory canteens, for example. These and a host of other small issues greatly complicate human resource management.

Thailand: integration and growth

Thailand is a Southeast Asian anomaly. Never formally occupied by any colonial power, Thailand is also the only major state in Southeast Asia apart from Burma to have been a unified nation for more than a thousand years. Like the Chinese, the Thais have a long cultural tradition of which they are very proud.

Thailand is a monarchy but is virtually ruled by the army, which again is almost a state within a state. Despite very high levels of corruption the Thai economy is prospering and Thai companies such as CP (Charoen Pokphand) are now reaching multinational status. The Thais also suffered in the Asian crisis, with large numbers of private banks becoming insolvent and pushing a fair number of Thai SMEs into bankruptcy. The bigger firms like CP seem to have weathered the storm, and Thailand is now recovering.

The Chinese population of Thailand is believed to be about 3.5 million, but it is difficult to tell because the Chinese population has become heavily assimilated into the Thai population. Many Thais, including the royal family, are proud of their Chinese ancestry. Many Chinese are equally happy to be taken for Thais, and some have adopted Thai versions of their names.

Best estimates are that Sino-Thai businessmen control about 55–50 per cent of capital in Thailand, with ethnic Thais and Indians controlling the rest. Most large companies, including CP, have strong Chinese backing and also invest heavily in China.

Chinese identity

Where the overseas Chinese have been discriminated against they have tended to fall back on themselves, reinforcing their identity as Chinese. Fourth and fifth generation Chinese in Southeast Asia and North America have grown up in their own isolated communities, speaking their own language, celebrating their own festivals and having only marginal contact with the host country.

Chinese identity can even transcend internal political divisions within the *huaqiao* community. In Indonesia, a Chinese-owned printing business did work for both the pro-Nationalist, pro-Taiwan section of the Chinese community and for the Indonesian Communist Party (PKI). The Indonesian government put pressure on the pro-Nationalists to transfer their printing business to an Indonesian firm. The indignant Nationalists promptly telephoned their enemies in the pro-Communist Chinese community, who in turn informed the government that if harassment of the Nationalists did not cease, the entire Chinese community in Indonesia would take sanctions against the government.

These sanctions can be very effective, given the massive Chinese control of capital and business noted before. In South Vietnam in 1967 a Chinese businessman was arrested and executed for profiteering. The entire Chinese community in Saigon, from bankers to porters and rickshaw drivers, struck; within days the South Vietnamese economy was paralysed. The government released several other Chinese who were due to stand trial and made no more arrests.

Indonesia: Java leads the way

Like Malaysia, Indonesia became independent after World War II, after a long and bitter unification struggle led mainly by radicals from Java against the Dutch colonial authorities and other ethnic groups such as the Moluccans. A strong government backed by the military took control in the 1960s and governed the country until 1998, when a combination of the Asia crisis and domestic unrest toppled the Suharto government. Elections have since been held, but at time of writing the political system remains highly unstable.

Until the Asia crisis began, Indonesia was the fastest growing nation in East Asia, and when the crisis hit it crashed further and with more devastating effects. Signs of turnaround are few and weak, and nothing much will happen until the governmental crisis is resolved.

There are 3.25 million ethnic Chinese in Indonesia, most of whom live on Java. They make up about 3 per cent of the total population. However, they exercise an influence over the economy out of all proportion to their numbers; it is estimated that they control 75–80 per cent of Indonesia's capital.

The Indonesian economy is usually divided into four main sectors: the state sector (the largest), the military sector, the private sector backed by Chinese capital, and the private sector backed by ethnic Indonesian capital. In fact, as in Malaysia, Indonesian businessmen are often fronts for Chinese capital, and the Chinese have heavily penetrated the state and military sectors as well.

The Indonesian Chinese community was heavily penetrated by Communist agents in the 1960s, and provided much backing for the Indonesian Communist Party in its abortive revolt against Sukarno.

Since then the entire Chinese community has been harassed and there have been pogroms and expulsions. However, their economic clout provides the Chinese community with protection against any serious threats to their existence. Under a system known as *cukong*, Chinese businessmen finance the Indonesian military to a considerable extent, in exchange for which the military (almost a state within a state in Indonesia) provides licences, credit monopolies and physical protection for Chinese businesses.

Family identity

The same isolation and need for self-sufficiency has led to an even greater emphasis on the family. Surveys of overseas Chinese communities have found that Confucian family values are far stronger than in mainland China. This is partially because in mainland China from the late 1950s to 1976 the Communist Party launched a sustained assault on the family, attempting to replace loyalty to the father with loyalty to the Party. Even without this, however, it seems logical for family values to be stronger in the overseas community.

The Confucian family model is well-suited to withstanding an adverse environment. Advocating strong leadership at the top and intense loyalty at the lower levels, the family model has served very well as a model for business; and it is largely through its business activities that the Chinese community has been able to survive. No accurate figures are available, but it is believed that something around 85 per cent of overseas Chinese around the world work for firms which are themselves Chinese-owned.

Entrepreneurial qualities

All the pressures described above have served to increase the development of entrepreneurship in the overseas community. To the overseas Chinese, wealth means security; there is anecdotal evidence that the economic leverage which they have gained over their host communities was gained with the idea of creating security. As far back as the 1860s the Singapore-Chinese tycoon Whampoa said:

When we are poor, they despise us to our faces. When we are rich, they despise us behind our backs: but to our faces, they bow.

Sociological and psychological studies of the overseas Chinese communities in comparison with China show these communities to be more flexible and with a higher tolerance of ambiguity than in China, meaning in effect that there are likely to be more people within the population interested in going into business for themselves. The hardships of migration have cultivated the values necessary for business success, such as thrift and pragmatism. The story of the Chinese in Canada shows how a kind of Darwinian selection was at work. Those Chinese who went off to work as labourers in the goldfields and on the railway ended up impoverished and many died. Those who stayed in Victoria or Vancouver and went into the business of supplying the workers up-country (fresh vegetables were particularly needed) ended up prosperous, and their sons and daughters who took over the businesses often became wealthy.

Old values in new nations

One of the peculiar aspects of the overseas Chinese communities, one which has hampered assimilation and increased discrimination, is the fact that the Chinese came from a culture with thousands of years of history and ideas behind them, into (in the nineteenth and twentieth centuries) new nations which had no such common history. Only Thailand, and perhaps Burma, can claim a history as a single nation and culture similar to China to some extent, and it is perhaps for this reason that the Chinese and Thais have assimilated so well. Vietnam, Malaysia and Indonesia are collections of old territories and principalities, and Vietnam and Indonesia in particular have significant internal ethnic and cultural divisions. Singapore and Hongkong are geographic anomalies, independent or quasi-independent through accidents of history; Indonesia and the Philippines are geographically scattered; and the Chinese going to Canada and the US became immigrants in a community of immigrants without a common culture. This has undoubtedly contributed to a heightened sense of Chinese identity and cultural values; the overseas Chinese have clung to their own cultural identity because there is often no acceptable alternative.

Feelings about the mother country

It is expected in mainland China that eventually the *huaqiao* will return home. Many of the *huaqiao* expect this as well. Yet, many of the overseas Chinese do not wish to return to China and have no intention of doing so; and there is some doubt as to whether Beijing really wants responsibility for another 55 million citizens (though perhaps if they brought their wealth with them, it might be another matter).

The overseas Chinese have complex feelings about China. Even those strongly loyal to the PRC government look forward to going home with reluctance, and even a short absence can cause confusion and disorientation. Ting Gong, a Chinese academic who spent four years overseas in the late 1980s, recorded his confusion at returning home to find everyone complaining about the corruption the new reforms had brought and trading enthusiastically on the grey market at one and the same time.

These ambivalent feelings are by no means restricted to the Chinese. Expatriates of every culture, including British and Americans, sit overseas and dream about an idealised version of their own culture while at the same time criticising the present state of affairs in their homelands. The Chinese are no different in this.

Australian correspondent Richard Hughes, who spent forty years in the Far East, provides a summary:

> For generations the *hua-chiao* have clung to their Chinese characteristics and traditions, united – whether impoverished or wealthy – in their blood loyalty to the great motherland and the Yellow Emperor and assured, in the face of persecution and segregation, of the transcendental superiority and inevitable resurgence of the Chinese race. Their way of life invites the discrimination of which they complain. Most of them in the past preferred stubbornly to retain the status of colonists, and this is one reason why many who now prudently wish to become absorbed as legal citizens still find the doors of assimilation and naturalisation closed to them.
>
> The giant Chinese umbilical cord links them strongly to the motherland – young and old, industrialists and coolies, bankers and smugglers, Communist terrorists and Rotarian merchants, millionaires and beggars. They may often be isolated among themselves by their native dialects, but they are united by their common written language. The elderly, amid alien temples, remember and celebrate Chinese festivals. At the local Chinese-language schools the young proclaim their Chinese uniqueness: '*Wo shih Kuo jen! Wo chu tsai Nanyang! Wo ai Chung Kuo!*' ('I am Chinese! I live in the Southern Ocean! I love China!') Yet the 'sojourners' do not want to go back home, except sometimes to die or be buried there. Nor does Peking want them to come home.
>
> Their talents, their hardships, their industry, their success, their closely knit sense of family and history, their basic insecurity, their gusto, their inward-looking warmness have given them the title 'the Jews of the Orient', and in a perverse world, the economic benefits which they have brought to and shared with the country of their adoption are denounced as 'alien exploitation'. Their racial unpopularity is

a direct reflection and measure of their success. And their putative threat to their local alien rulers is too often nourished by those rulers' stubborn refusal to encourage assimilation – indeed, their blind discouragement of assimilation.

It is curious to note that the *hua-chiao* brought with them, nurtured and still preserve traditional aspects of Chinese life and philosophy which, ironically, no longer exist in their motherland. In fact, under a new Chinese regime, whose unifying energy impresses most of them and whose pragmatic success impresses all, these anachronistic survivals have become downright offences against the mores of the new China. ... To a large extent the *hua-chiao* are devoted to an artificial and outdated image of China which has been facelifted, transformed and disfigured since the forefathers of the present generation of overseas Chinese left the motherland.[2]

Vietnam: pragmatism and *doi moi*

Vietnam is another nation fashioned by the colonial authorities, with the old kingdoms of Annam, Cochin and Tonking being welded into one by the French. There is still considerable ethnic diversity in Vietnam, and economic and cultural differences between north and south are strong.

Vietnam in the 1980s climbed out of the doldrums of the Communist era with a speed which makes one suspect that Communism never had very deep roots in the country in the first place. The Vietnamese, pragmatic as ever, are opening doors to the West. *Doi moi*, or reconstruction, backed by foreign capital, proceeded quickly in the 1990s, and for a time Vietnam was the hot new market. The Asia crisis has dampened prospects considerably, but Vietnam should pull through.

About 3 per cent of the population of Vietnam are of Chinese origin. Most are concentrated around Saigon/Ho Chi Minh City in the south. The Chinese were not welcome in the north for a number of years when Vietnam was allied with Moscow and the Chinese were backing the Khmer Rouge who killed hundreds of thousands of Vietnamese nationals in Cambodia. In the south, however, they filled their usual role as middlemen and traders.

The Chinese community in Saigon is very closely knit, dominated by a few important families who employ most of the rest in a variety of businesses. Extents of capital are unknown, but certainly before the unification of Vietnam the Chinese banks played a major role in financing the South Vietnamese state. It seems likely that *doi moi* will give them a chance to flourish once more.

Doing business with the overseas Chinese: similarities and differences with China

The same rules of conduct for doing business in China apply when doing business with the overseas Chinese. *Guànxì* is every bit as important as in China, and the *guànxìwang* or networks of contacts are often even more extensive. Negotiating styles are similar in most cultures. Businesses are organised in much the same way, with a strong hierarchy headed by a father figure (very often the actual head of the family).

From this position, however, it is important to recognise a number of differences. First, Chinese-owned businesses overseas frequently operate behind fronts. In Malaysia and Indonesia especially it is not unusual for an ethnic local businessman to nominally be in charge of an organisation, but for the real ownership, hidden behind several layers, to be in Chinese hands. In China, if you get to the top of an organisation, you may know who you are dealing with. In the diaspora you may have to look behind the scenes to find the real decision-makers.

Second, the preponderance of Chinese-run businesses overseas are family businesses. Most overseas Chinese businesses are small and tightly controlled by a small group who are related by blood or by marriage. Even some of the Hongkong-based *hongs* fall into this category; family ownership is a key factor in companies such as Hutchison Whampoa, Wheelock and Hopewell. There is no equivalent to the state-run or privatised ex-state run industry, for obvious reasons.

Third, overseas Chinese businesses often come from a more entrepreneurial background. Hongkong and Singapore businesses are as sophisticated as any in the world, and even in emerging economies such as Malaysia and Indonesia Chinese businessmen and women tend to have more knowledge and more fully developed skills. They combined high degrees of spatial awareness with a strongly developed drive to succeed – a powerful combination. When compared with their mainland China counterparts, overseas Chinese business leaders tend to be highly motivated and ruthless about dealing with competitors, particularly those outside their own *guànxìwang*; but even then, relationships are often stronger than competition. When cut-throat competition between two Chinese-owned wholesale businesses in Malaysia led to the ruin of one, the winner bought the defunct company, gave his rival a position of trust, and arranged a marriage between the two families.

Fourth, and related to the above, overseas Chinese businesses are more likely to pay attention to short-term factors. Because many of them operate in more uncertain environments (either because of political pressure and discrimination, or because the markets in which they work are more developed and move faster), they tend to think more about the short term than their mainland China counterparts. However, they still have long time horizons when compared to their Western and indigenous counterparts.

Fifth, overseas Chinese are probably more likely to be concerned with Confucian values, especially respect for tradition. As noted above, the overseas Chinese are far more concerned with traditions and respecting the past than are their mainland counterparts – 'more Chinese than the Chinese'. Often there is also a much stronger emphasis on face, even in the North American Chinese communities, which may be surprising (unless you accept that Westerners have their own concepts of face). In a way this is no surprise. British overseas expatriate communities also hold onto old ways longer than those in Britain. As stated earlier, there is a limit to the value of the Confucian model, but the power of the family and the close links between the family and the business are important to recognise.

Last, varying degrees of acculturation means that when dealing with overseas Chinese it is not enough to know about Chinese culture; one also needs to learn about the local cultures as well. Appearances are unreliable; an individual who appears to be strongly acculturated may still hold strong Chinese values, and vice versa. In American and Canadian Chinese communities it is not uncommon to run across 50-year-old heads of families and companies who are fond of the Rolling Stones, and young men and women who wear fashionable clothes and drive sports cars who are nonetheless devout Buddhists and observe all the festivals. It is difficult to learn about both cultures and try to understand where your partner/rival fits in between them, but it needs to be attempted nonetheless.

The Philippines: hope for the future?

Occupied for nearly three hundred years by the Spanish and then by the Americans and the Japanese, the Philippines became independent after World War II. Endemic corruption and mismanagement under Marcos nearly drove the islands to bankruptcy, and armed rebel movements threatened to tear the country apart. Guerrilla activity continues in the, ethnically different, southern islands. However, the democratic experiment under Aquino worked better than expected and the government now seems to enjoy the confidence of the army, the people, and the Western banks. Special enterprise zones, modelled on those in China, have been set up on the island of Luzon, and foreign investment was rising until the Asia crisis struck. The future is uncertain.

Only about 1 per cent of the population of the Philippines is identifiably Chinese, although Chinese immigration under Spanish rule means that many Filipino families can claim part Chinese ancestry. Corazon Aquino's family, for example, were originally immigrants from Fukien. Nevertheless, the ethnic Chinese are a powerful economic force, controlling 33 per cent of manufacturing and 40 per cent of trading firms in the country. It seems that the Filipino Chinese community may represent the country's best hope for the future.

Cambodia and Laos: lost lands

French Indochina split after the end of the colonial period into four states, the two Vietnams, Cambodia and Laos. The latter two were ancient kingdoms which had been economic backwaters before the French arrived and continued to be so after. Both might have carried on quietly had it not been for the war in Vietnam, which quickly spilled over into both Cambodia and Laos. Both Vietnamese Communist propaganda and American carpet-bombing had their effect. Revolutionary movements began in both countries. The Pathet Lao overthrew the Laotian monarchy without a major struggle, but the bloody war between the Khmer Rouge and the Sihanouk government and the massacres of the Year Zero killed nearly a third of Cambodia's population.

Laos today is slowly coming out of its economic isolation. Most of the capital funding Laos' recovery comes from Thailand, primarily from Chinese firms, and the 200,000 Chinese in Laos, who are concentrated around Vientiane, are also playing their part. Sino-Thai entrepreneurs dominate the tiny Laotian economy. The only other significant Chinese population in Laos is in the north, around Luang Prabang; descendants of Guomidang soldiers who did not

continued

return to China after World War II, they are involved in local trade, including drugs.

In Cambodia, despite PRC support for the Khmer Rouge, the Chinese population suffered badly during the Year Zero and tens of thousands were killed. There are believed to be about 100,000 ethnic Chinese in Cambodia today, and they do make up a significant proportion of the business community in Phnom Penh. However, even though the Khmer Rouge conflict seems finally to have dragged to a halt through mutual exhaustion of the parties, it seems unlikely that Cambodia will achieve a real economic revival in the near future, with or without Chinese help.

The overseas Chinese and China

We have discussed already the possibility of using overseas Chinese businesses as conduits into China itself. The above notes should suggest that this is not as easy as it sounds. True, most overseas businesses, especially in major centres such as Hongkong and Singapore, are more in tune with the needs of Western businesses; but at the same time relations between the overseas Chinese and their mainland counterparts are full of potential pitfalls.

Most overseas Chinese are ambivalent about the PRC. They respect Chinese culture and they are impressed by the achievements of the Chinese government, especially during the past two decades, but many of them have no wish to return to China. They are, for the most part, more comfortable in their present surroundings: even when those surroundings include a potentially hostile environment full of prejudice and restriction. At the same time, the mainland Chinese have equally ambivalent feelings about the *huaqiao*. Many Chinese feel, even if subconsciously, that the overseas Chinese have let the country down by leaving, and have in some way lost face. Many Chinese also, and much more openly, resent the returned 'sojourners' from Hongkong, Taiwan and Singapore who are taking senior positions with joint ventures and WFOEs and being paid far more than their domestic counterparts.

At the same time, the overseas Chinese have equally complex and ambivalent relations with their host countries. Relations can range from very good (Thailand and the Philippines where the *huaqiao* are mostly welcome and integrated with the local population) to ambivalent (the United States and Canada, where there is now little overt prejudice but where strong cultural differences remain) to poor (Malaysia, where

Chinese ethnics, who are Malaysian nationals, are legally restricted from entering business). Dealing with *huaqiao* businesses in these countries will not always win a Western company the favour of local governments. On the other hand, given the economic predominance of these businesses, how do you avoid them?

The Americas: survival and identity in the melting pot

The last significant overseas Chinese community is that in North America. There are about 5 million ethnic Chinese in the United States and another million in Canada. Most are concentrated in the major cities of the west coast. Another 500,000 Chinese are scattered around the Caribbean, with the largest concentration in Jamaica.

Ghettoised for several decades, the North American Chinese have been coming out into the wider community in the last forty years. In California, Hawai'i and British Columbia, Chinese entrepreneurs own considerable capital and have invested in a wide variety of sectors, with wholesale, transport and light manufacturing being the most common sectors. In the early 1990s there was a major flight of capital and in some instances persons from Hongkong to the west coast of North America, primarily Vancouver, where several billion dollars of Hongkong money has been invested in the local economy. The result has been to give Vancouver and the Canadian west coast an economic shot in the arm, with this area remaining buoyant even through the recession of the early 1990s.

Many Chinese in North America show signs of being strongly acculturated. However, many others retain strong ties with China and some are now going back; Canadian-Chinese entrepreneurs are prominent in Shenzhen and Shanghai.

Summary

The overseas Chinese are a powerful economic force, and can make good partners for Western businesses. More economically sophisticated and more strongly motivated, they have reached commanding positions in the economies of many countries, especially in East and Southeast Asia.

The *huaqiao* hold many of the same values as do Chinese in the PRC. However, there are also differences in outlook and attitude and it is important to recognise these. Overseas Chinese tend on the whole to be more strongly traditional and more family-oriented, while at the same time paradoxically being more susceptible to outside cultural influences. It is particularly important, if planning to use a *huaqiao* company as a *hongniang* or go-between with China, to recognise that the relations between the mainland and overseas Chinese are complex and ambivalent. Finally, it is important to recognise the extent to which local cultural influences may be at work, and conduct negotiations and handle business accordingly.

Note

1 So far as we are concerned, Taiwan is part of China but not part of the PRC. The skirmishing could continue for a long time but it seems unlikely that PRC will forcibly invade on the one side or that Taiwan will become a separate country on the other. The current ambiguity has a lot going for it.
2 Hughes 1972: 190–1.

10 Western and Chinese commercial thinking

A distinguished colleague told us, 'There's no need for books on doing business in particular regions such as China. After all, doing business in China is just the same as doing business anywhere else.' This being China that observation is both true and not true.

Doing Business in China was written because there *are* differences between China and the West, differences in history, philosophy, politics and society. And because business is essentially a social process, there are differences in ways of doing business as well. This has two consequences for Westerners: when in China they have to adjust their ways to fit the environment and in the rest of the world they can apply what they have learned from China. The Chinese are, naturally, learning reciprocally and we then have to factor in what we both have to learn from Japan and other parts of the world.

Furthermore, China is likely to dominate world trade in the new century so those of us who plan to be around for long will need to listen and learn.

If we took what our gallant colleague said at face value, we would only have to understand how to do business in London, Chicago or wherever we happen to be, since the rest of the world is, or perhaps should be, the same. We were struck by the recent comment of the manager of the Chicago Futures Market following the Barings disaster in Singapore. Prevention was simple, we were told: the rest of the world should just adopt Chicago's rule book. The very same arrogance ('we set the standards') caused the stagnation of China through the Ming and Qing dynasties.

Our aims were twofold: to understand consumers, customers, partners, governments and other players in China and, in the process, learn about their business methods and ways of thinking. One of the keys to success in global business lies in learning global lessons and then in applying them locally. The more we can identify with Chinese thinking, the more widely we can benefit from it. And, naturally, vice versa.

Because events in China are happening so rapidly, we know that any current facts are ephemeral, although we have tried to provide up-to-theminute information where possible. Instead, we have attempted to give you a framework for knowledge. We hope we have given readers enough understanding of the basic issues for you to go out and do research on your own, and have a context into which to fit the information you acquire.

After briefly summarising the book, we will draw out the underlying structure.

Summary of the book

The first visit

Acquiring detailed, up-to-date information about China is difficult and one should not try too hard. The pace of change in China means that books with immediate detail are quickly obsolete. There are, however, many directories and sources, which specialise in helping businesses make preliminary contacts in China.

The most important requirement is to set up meetings for that visit. Conventional wisdom is that no amount of reading and preparation for the first visit is too much. We doubt that: the real aim of pre-reading is to equip oneself *socially* to impress the people you will meet. *After* your first visit, research will make more sense, as you build up macro-level knowledge to complement your personal knowledge. Beforehand, and apart from background reading, e.g. history, you only really need this one and a good tourist guide like *Lonely Planet*.

There are a number of options for organising the first visit. The brave can do it solo. For others, escorted tours, organised visits and trade missions offer good introductions to the country and, depending on how efficient the organisers are, at least some of the key players in the markets you are considering.

Finding business partners is essentially a networking exercise. Do not rely on one point of entry to the network, no matter how trustworthy and well connected the person may be. Develop multiple sources of information and contacts. There probably is no one best way to find the right partner (would you advise your children on ways to find the best spouse?). A lot of it is about being in the right place and networking as much as possible. Try to find ways of identifying real people and separating them from the 'ghosts'.

Go-betweens are a good option; but then you have to find the right go-between. At least the list of potential candidates is more manageable, however, and selection should be easier. Using go-betweens saves time, uses existing networks, gives you any necessary language capability and usually some business consultancy advice is thrown in as well. Disadvantages may include longer lines of communication, with the potential for misunderstanding.

The decision to enter is not to be taken lightly. Making the decision should require several visits, a non-trivial expense for a small company.

Culture and environment

China is not a unitary whole but is a number of vastly different regions, each with its own sub-culture and its own language or dialect. It has a long and eventful history and a rich culture of which its citizens are justly proud. History and culture are very important to the Chinese. History in particular exercises a powerful influence over thinking and behaviour. Bitter past experience has taught the Chinese that not all foreigners can be trusted, and that even with the best of intentions, contact with foreigners can have negative consequences for China. One of the most important themes here is the need for stability and the dread of chaos, which underpins not only government policy but much everyday social intercourse. Reformers who want China to become more like the West are unlikely to make much headway while this attitude prevails.

The question of whether China will remain stable is one that commands much attention in the Western press and academic circles. Our assessment is that it probably will. So far, at least, Chinese management of the domestic economic and political situation has been steady. Whether it will continue to be so as China's economy emerges more fully onto the global scene is another matter. The rumbling with the USA, over trade, human rights and Taiwan, has continued for fifty years and, given that they are the ultimate competitors for economic supremacy, are quite likely to rumble for fifty more. This leaves an opportunity for Europe, and for the UK in particular, which should not be missed. We will find that our main competitors lie in the antipodes: Australia and New Zealand, whose products complement China's better than Britain's.

Strategy and philosophy

China is also rich in terms of philosophical traditions and modes of thinking. Many of these share common features. Respect for age and authority is commonly ascribed to Confucianism, but probably has its origins in the ancestor cult. Time in Chinese thinking is not linear but circular; the past is also the future. Daoism has provided (or recognised?) the thirst for harmony, for balance, for paradox which is both a perpetual delight and a frustration to Western minds. It is not possible to overstate the importance of 'and' versus 'or' thinking. It recurs, in various forms, throughout business in China, and the Orient as a whole.

Good marketing process is very often the avoidance of decisions. If you have to choose A or B, both are probably wrong. The search for consensus, for meeting all objectives, as distinct from choosing between them, gives oriental mental furniture a head start over Western logic.

Cultural values play a major role in business relationships. The most important of these are age, hierarchy and authority, which are strongly linked; face and the importance of self-esteem and dignity; and the balance between individual and group orientation. Past researchers have tried to determine whether the Chinese are individualist *or* group-oriented. In fact, they are both simultaneously.

Strategy, is the second most important marketing, or business, paradigm in China just as it is in the West. Sunzi directly inspired some of the greatest guerrilla generals of all time, notably Mao Zedong and Ho Chi Minh. Guerrilla warfare is central to most marketers: conventional warfare is merely the final stage relevant to the surviving few. Nowhere is this more relevant than in China.

The essential lessons of guerrilla war are:

- Avoid the competition so long as you can.
- Concentrate your resources geographically and in time. Then concentrate again. Ruthless focus.
- Never do the obvious/expected.
- Achieve local knockout and then expand incrementally.
- Cultivate allies (relationships), steal the competitor's resources, be generous to losers: this is for the long term.
- When you are sure to win, kill the competition.

Relationships

Guànxì, relationships or connections, is the key to business in China. *Business may flow out of friendship whereas, in the West, friendship may flow out of business.* To the Chinese and others in the Pacific Region, relationship building is second nature, a natural part of the environment and doing business. Westerners, however, need to plan and track such networks consciously and with great care.

Corruption is seen by some as an inevitable outgrowth of *guànxì*. Indeed, some use '*guànxì*' as a synonym for grease. That is wrong and complicates an already complex subject. True *guànxì* cannot be bought. Pseudo-*guànxì* may be essential for survival but it can also erode future prospects.

Most advice is to avoid all forms of questionable payment. In the words of Ian Rae, 'once you start, they'll never let you go'. We have no doubt whatever that bribery (paying officials to do what they should not) should be avoided, albeit avoided with dignity on both sides. Grease payments and other borderline activities are more difficult especially if it makes the difference between survival or not. Those brands with high brand equity are more able, and have more need, to set standards.

We commend the 'sunlight test' to distinguish the legitimate from the illegitimate, i.e. if it becomes public knowledge, will you be damaged? There is much to be said for co-operative policing with one's competitors – assuming, of course, that they can be trusted either!

Establishing ventures

There are various options for entering the China market, including agencies, JVs and wholly owned foreign enterprises. For long the most popular was the JV partly because WFOEs were not permitted in that sector/region.

Establishing and managing a JV is always difficult; either or both partners may lack a clear agenda and/or trust. A *hongniang*, or go-between, can help partners come together. The importance of this role is misunderstood by Westerners just as the need for management consultants is misunderstood by Chinese. In practice, such misunderstandings may cancel out: some intermediaries may be seen as *hongniang* by Chinese and as consultants by their Western clients.

JVs in China are not for those who only think short term; negotiations can take years, and the Chinese expect that commitment will be long term.

Intellectual property remains a hot topic despite the progress the PRC government has made. International law is being applied, but enforcement remains very difficult and piracy is still a cause for concern. General advice is to use a multiple strategy when confronted with piracy; legal suits are necessary to persuade government officials that it is serious. Then, via *guànxìwang*, seek official backing.

Government, the law and *guànxì* all interweave and are hard to separate. No one 'connection', however good, is adequate. In cultivating multiple connections, remember that they are reciprocal: favours received are credits against future favours expected. It is not a bank account but expectations for the future are created. It is easy to get overloaded, in which case doubts and distrust will creep in.

Marketing mix

Brands are very important in China, and early leader advantage has more going for it than in other markets. Early sampling and 'name' recognition are important. 'Name' means branding: symbols, colours and numbers all mean more than Roman letters.

Price skimming is a general strategy worth considering, though it is possible to overdo it; several recent skimmers have had trouble as consumers considered the product overvalued. Chinese consumers are now better informed and less infatuated by the 'foreign-ness' of brands. Today one should aim to overshoot the right price by only a very small margin.

Representative offices are a must for all but the smallest traders with China. Medium-sized firms should consider sharing with Western non-competitors. Expect to give distribution issues more priority relative to developed countries.

The full range of marketing tools is available. The less conventional may be better value, depending on the situation. E-commerce is faltering at present due to distribution and payments difficulties but as a medium for communication it is moving fast.

Marketing process

Marketing process includes at least analysis, planning, implementation, measurement, both market research and internal. Some see it as including the development and motivation of managers and the host of other operational matters that bring satisfaction to customers and consumers. For this book we limited ourselves to information and planning.

China has more statistics than any company can handle. Unfortunately, they are unreliable. This bothers Westerners more than the Chinese who are looking for pictures not precision. Fuzzy focus is quite good enough. To pilot through, a Western firm will need to be tough-minded about what they must know and what may be nice to know but perhaps should be abandoned. Integrating research needs and the planning process is critical to selecting, and then acting on, crucial competitive information.

Plans are not important: planning is. It is rehearsing the future. One can practise as many times as one likes but tomorrow only comes once. The classic 4 Ps marketing plan format should be replaced by the strategy/*guànxì*/calculation sequence for China. It is not that one should adopt the Chinese format: such a thing never existed. The point is that planning, being a rehearsal or modelling of the future, should represent the Chinese market in a Chinese way. The essence of marketing is that it is outside-in learning. Absorb the context.

Management issues

Chapter 8 was partly devoted to a comparison and contrast between Chinese and Western business organisation. Chinese businesses are more formal than their Western counterparts, with decision-making concentrated at the top; in consequence, if you want anything done by a Chinese business, you usually have to go to the top.

One consequence, as most Western companies have already learned to their cost, is high staff turnover. Smaller, leaner, flatter organisations are less likely to engender staff and managerial loyalty, and staff tend to move on as soon as they get a better offer. We looked at how Western companies, by managing in a more 'Chinese way' can improve retention and keep costs down.

Chinese businesses overseas

The 60 million Chinese living in the overseas communities represent a powerful economic force, and literally dominate the economies of many countries outside China. Overseas Chinese can be good partners for Western businesses. However, there are perceptible differences between the overseas Chinese and their mainland counterparts, and we stressed that adjustments needed to be made when dealing with overseas Chinese in different countries.

Many overseas Chinese have ambivalent attitudes to China, and vice versa. Thus, there can be problems in using overseas Chinese as intermediaries to do business in mainland China. This does not mean it cannot be done, but Westerners need to be aware of these possibly complex relationships before setting out to build a partnership involving both overseas and mainland Chinese.

Doing business in China: the Five Pillars

There is no one 'model' for doing business in greater China. Conditions vary too much; any model would have to be so hedged about with conditions as to be uninformative or useless. Better to summarise the course in a Confucian fashion by presenting 'Five Pillars', or recommendations, as a framework for anyone doing business in the area. They are presented from a variety of angles, and their relative importance will depend upon the situation.

We see the structure arranged as four pillars surrounding the first and most important: *guànxì*.

The first pillar: Guànxì

Guànxì is the single most important concept when dealing with China and the Chinese in any social context, not just in business. The Chinese measure their own social position in part by the extent of their *guànxìwang*, or network of contacts. They use these contacts, sometimes almost exclusively, to do business.

It may be possible to do business in China without developing a network of relationships. However, we do not know of any examples where companies or individuals have ultimately been successful, and the recent history of Western businesses in China is full of examples of companies who have neglected *guànxì* to their cost.

Westerners often do business with people they do not know; sometimes with people we never see. This is much harder in China, and much less likely to bring success. We believe that in order to do business with a Chinese, you must first get to know him or her. You should ideally have been recommended to him or her by a reliable third party. Contacts breed contacts. It is the first stage, getting the first contacts and getting inside the magic circle, that is hardest; once in, it is possible to exploit contacts, and the contacts of contacts, and thus widen one's own *guànxìwang*.

At a more fundamental level, *guànxì* is a relationship way of seeing marketing. It puts the customer first. There is no need to recap this here but if the logical consequences are followed through, notably in planning, some of the predictable hazards, notably with joint ventures and distribution, may be safely negotiated.

The other four pillars all reflect the central importance of *guànxì*.

The second pillar: continuity

W.F. Jenner has written that China is influenced by two things: the 'history of tyranny' and the 'tyranny of history'.[1] Taoist and Confucian influences are still prominent. *Guànxì* itself is a concept rooted deep in China's past.

Any reasonably well-educated Chinese knows his or her own country's history well, and can quote incidents from it. All are strongly aware of the events of the recent past, and of the odds that such events could be repeated in the near future. Thus while most of China's people are strongly aware of and proud of their cultural traditions, they are also trying hard to escape the cycle of boom and crash that has torn the country to pieces three times and left 200 million dead in the last 150 years.

Sometimes overseas Chinese, many of whom have not lived through these events, are the most traditional and conservative, with the strongest ties to China's history, just like expatriate Irishmen or Scots. In China itself, you will find many different points of view, from the Yunnan farmer who still hankers after Mao, to the makers of the *River Elegy* calling into question the whole historical basis of Chinese society. But whatever their viewpoints, they are still looking over their shoulders at the past; loving it or hating it, but still with one eye on it.

Businesses and managers going into China need to know something about China's ancient and recent past. They need this knowledge for the obvious reasons of finding a context for the present and attempting to understand the future. They also need to know what is driving their Chinese partners and competitors. No other people on earth are so strongly influenced by their past as the Chinese.

Similarly, ways of thinking change very slowly. Tolerance for ambiguity, 'and' thinking, paradoxes flow from Daoism. The Chinese do not have the haste to solve problems that Westerners exhibit. This is likely to lead to Chinese advantage in the twenty-first century race for competitive business knowledge or organisational learning.

The visiting business person should not flaunt any historical expertise: it would seem odd. All we propose is awareness and sensitivity. The 'pillar' reflects an unconscious sense of continuity: what is done now must be in harmony with what has gone before. Many things in China change rather slowly: identity, culture, etiquette and business practices all reflect the lessons of history. If you find yourself in business with someone who does *not* have those roots, beware. Continuity may slow things down; it may be frustrating; but it also gives confidence in a relationship that the past is a reliable guide to the future.

The third pillar: the market

Whilst some things change slowly, it took China about one nano-second to revert to the market concept, though the reality is taking a little longer. Trading and bargaining are as natural to China as complaining about the weather is in England: both are national pastimes. We concluded in Chapter 7 that the cost of market research in China was more or less whatever you were prepared to pay. To Coke it was expensive, to others it is quite cheap. You do not necessarily get what you pay for. Those on a cheap holiday are quite likely to end up in the same hotel as those on an expensive holiday. Both paid what they could be persuaded to part with and both got what was available. The West does much the same with airline seats.

The fourth pillar: rén and organisations

Guànxì does not always imply equal relationships. In China, the family relationship system is consciously replicated in businesses, organisations and governments.

Rén, the obligation of a leader's responsibility for all of his or her subordinates, is a strong force in Chinese organisations which are often dominated by strong leaders, with obedience expected of the workers below. In return for obedience, the leader is expected to listen to the opinions of subordinates and care for the lives of their employees, but at the same time is also expected to make decisions and exercise leadership alone. Workers and juniors are not expected to use their initiative or use their entrepreneurial skills. The leader is expected to be flexible, responsible and entrepreneurial, but always in a way which keeps his or her actions within the overall framework of the Chinese economy and society.

Obviously there are many variations of this model which, anyway, does not always work. Some Chinese are critical of their own way of doing things and would like to see wider adoption of Western models. But equally, there is evidence that Western organisational models applied literally to China are unsuccessful as well. The flat hierarchies and devolving responsibility which are popular in the West seem to lead to lower levels of employee loyalty, and the higher salaries paid by Western companies are not always a substitute for the social and other benefits paid by Chinese enterprises. It seems to us that a compromise system, with the organisational freedom of Western businesses but with the strong leadership and strong loyalty inducements Chinese fashion, may be the best model for China. It may also be a model we could usefully look at in the West as well.

When setting up a JV or WFOE organisation, these differences may become incompatibilities. The inequality (or lack thereof) in the relationships between partners, each of whom may *privately* consider themselves the senior, management styles and staff loyalties are all potentially destructive.

The fifth pillar: obstacles

China has long been seen as an impenetrable mass, protected by real and chauvinistic barriers, including the Great Wall and the Bamboo Curtain. American writers in particular, during the Cold War, were fond of seeing China as gigantic and amorphous. They noted the uniformity of fashion during the Cultural Revolution and coined empty phrases such as 'Mao's blue hordes'. Nothing could be further from the real picture.

From Heilongjiang to Yunnan, from Shanghai to Xinjiang, there are vast variations in geography, climate, economy, language, food, dress, occupation, mental and social outlook … and in business conditions. The Chinese government is trying hard, paradoxically, to create more equal conditions throughout the country and spread economic development. Until it does so, China will continue to be a land of variety.

The physical barriers are gone; tourists are the only invaders on the Great Wall now, and there is unrestricted travel throughout most of the country. However, there are still some intangible barriers for a Western businessman. Chinese language, culture and regulations may scare away many faint hearts. Laozi tells us that there is always a trade-off between advantages and disadvantages.

Conclusion

We have met quite a few expatriates during our sojourns in China and they fall broadly into two groups: those who love China and the Chinese and those who will soon be going home. There are dangers in both points of view, not to mention being so crass as to offend Daoist thinking with the dichotomy.

On the one hand, the world economy is not a zero-sum game. China's gain will help the rest of the world too, just as Japan has provided immense benefit to us all in the thirty years, or so, from 1960. On the other hand, we are in competition. Relative wealth depends on our relative skills and endeavours. Working hard is being replaced by working smart. This is no longer a matter of how many white overalled ladies are turning out how many microchips. That was then. Tomorrow is about the depth of under-standing from which creativity and innovation can gain competitive advantage. If this book has helped, in however small a way, to improve the understanding of business in China, then we have done our part.

Note

1 W.F. Jenner (1989) *The Tyranny of History*, Cambridge: Cambridge University Press.

Bibliography

A.T. Kearney Inc. (1994) 'Capturing the Southeast Asian Potential', Chicago: A.T. Kearney Inc. Useful research report, concentrating mostly on China despite the title.

Ambler, Tim (1994) 'Marketing's Third Paradigm: Guànxì', *Business Strategy Review* 5(4): 69–80. Describes a marketing strategy approach using *guànxì* rather than traditional Western modes.

—— (1999) 'Marketing Rights and Consumer Responsibilities', paper presented at the Second Sino-British Conference on Business Ethics, Gresham College, London. Interesting and possibly controversial look at Western and Chinese approaches to ethics in marketing.

Ambler, Tim, Chris Styles and Wang Xiucun (1999) 'The Effect of Channel Relationships and *Guànxì* on the Performance of Inter-province Export Ventures in the People's Republic of China', *International Journal of Research in Marketing* February: 75–87. Academic study of *guànxì* and channel management in China.

Becker, Gerhold K. (ed.) (1996) *Ethics in Business and Society: Chinese and Western Perspectives*, Berlin: Springer. Mostly academic views from Hongkong but a refreshing miscellany of topics.

Berger, Mark and Douglas Borer (1997) *The Rise of East Asia*, London: Routledge. Mostly readable collection of accounts of the rise of East Asia over the past thirty years; written just before the Asia crisis, so a bit behind the times now.

Boisot, M. (ed.) (1994) *East West Business Collaboration*, London: Routledge. Academic but readable study.

Bond, Michael Harris (ed.) (1986) *The Psychology of the Chinese People*, Oxford: Oxford University Press. Good academic overview of what is really known. Usefully separates ethnic from environment components of culture.

—— (1991) *Beyond the Chinese Face: Insights from Psychology*, Oxford: Oxford University Press. Abbreviated version of Bond 1986; the former is better.

Brown, David H. and Porter, Robin (eds) (1996) *Management Issues in China*, vol. 1, *Domestic Enterprises*, London: Routledge. Academic but invaluable, companion to Child and Yuan 1996.

Brown, R. Ampalavanar (1996) *Chinese Business Enterprise: Critical Perspectives on Business and Management*, London: Routledge, 4 vols. Academic and historical, but worth browsing through if you see it in a library; look for the chapters on relationships and on branding.

Burstein, Daniel, and de Keijzer, Arne (1998) *Big Dragon*, New York: Touchstone. Brave and surprisingly optimistic look at China's future, which sees the Asia crisis as a passing event.

Campbell, N.C.G. (ed.) (1990–93) *Advances in Chinese Industrial Studies*, Greenwich, Conn: JAI Press, 4 vols. Important source series.

Chai, Joseph, C.H. (1997) *China: Transition to a Market Economy*, Oxford: Clarendon. Good update, though some of the material on trade regulations has been overtaken by events.

Chang, Y. N. (1976) 'Early Chinese Management Thought', *California Management Review* Winter, p. 74.

Chen Min (1995) *Asian Management Systems*, London: Routledge. Academic but well-written comparison of four business systems: Chinese family, Chinese state-owned enterprise, Korean and Japanese.

Chen Min and Winston Pan (1993) *Understanding the Process of Doing Business in China, Taiwan and Hong Kong: A Guide for International Executives*, New York: Edwin Mellen. Good but basic; Chen 1995 is preferred.

Cheng, Paul M. F. (1994) 'China Trade and Marketing in China: The World Wakes Up!', in *Doing Business With China*, consultant editor J. Reuvid, London: Kogan Page. Assessment of the potential of the China market; now getting a little out of date.

Child, J. (1994) *Management in China During the Age of Reform*, Cambridge: Cambridge University Press. One of the classics on the subject, a very detailed and well-written study; essential for managers as well as academics.

Child, J. and Yuan Lu (1996) *Management Issues in China*, vol. 2, *International Enterprise*, London: Routledge. Very useful collection of academic but relevant articles.

Chong, Alan (1995) *The Art of Management: Sixteen Strategies of Zhuge Liang*, Singapore: Asiapac. Application to management of the sayings and deeds of the Three Kingdoms hero, Zhuge Liang. One of Asiapac's bizarre comic book guides to management; fun.

Chu Chin-ning (1991) *The Asian Mind Game*, New York: Rawson Associates. Whilst some aspects show their age, this is a splendid idiosyncratic tour of three separate areas: Chinese strategic thinking (Sun Tzu, 36 Strategies etc.), a tirade against Japan (her Manchurian and Taiwanese background shows up) and easy-to-read synopsis of Chinese philosophy and customs, plus some sensitive insights on Korea. Written for American executives. Overall, an excellent read.

Clifford Chance (1994) *Establishing a Representative Office in China*, London: Clifford Chance. A how-to-do-it guide by one of the largest legal firms in China.

Craddock, Sir Percy (1994) *Experiences of China*, London: John Murray. Memoirs of a former ambassador, special adviser on Hongkong and 'China hand'; an excellent 'whiff of gunsmoke'.

Crow, Carl (1937) *400 Million Customers*, New York: Halcyon. CC set up first as an agency in China in 1916. Less has changed since than you might think.

Cua, A.S. (1998) 'Confucian Philosophy, Chinese', in E. Craig (ed.) *Routledge Encyclopedia of Philosophy*, vol. 2: 536–49.

De Keijzer, A.J. (1992) *China: Business Strategies for the 90's*, Berkeley, CA: Pacific View Press. Good, easy-to-read introduction. Despite its age, still one of the best books for managers on this subject.

Deacon, R. (1974) *A History of the Chinese Secret Service*, London: Frederick Muller. Interesting insights on organisation and the reverse Opium War (Vietnam).

Deng Xiaoping (1987) *Fundamental Issues in Present-Day China*, Beijing: Foreign Languages Press. Not an easy read, but useful for the reader who wants to know more about why Deng inaugurated China's third great revolution of the century.

Dong, S.H., D. Zhang and M.R. Larson (1992) *Trade and Investment Opportunities in China*, London: Quorum Books. Covers exactly what the title suggests; getting on in years now, but worth a look.

Economist Intelligence Unit (1994) *Investing, Licensing and Trading Conditions Abroad for China*, London. Showing its age now, but still more detailed than most contemporary publications.

—— (1995) *Moving China Ventures out of the Red into the Black*, London: Economist Intelligence Unit/Andersen Consulting. Good study, again getting on in years, but has some useful advice for companies.

EIU (1994) *China Market Atlas*, London: Economist Intelligence Unit. Badly needs updating, but again, no comparable publication has yet emerged.

Euromonitor, *China: A Directory and Sourcebook 1994*, London: Euromonitor. This could be regarded as essential for any company doing, or aiming to do, business in China. Sections 1 and 2 cover economic and consumer market surveys, 3 provides guidance on doing business in China, including law, formation, investment and addresses, 4 provides sources of marketing information, 5 has profiles of more than 400 state and local enterprises and 6 is a statistical fact file. Needs updating, but still very valuable.

Fang, Tony (1998) *Chinese Business Negotiating Style*, Thousand Oaks, CA: Sage Books. Good summary of the subject; recommended.

Financial Times (1999) 'Financial Times Survey: The Philippines', 28 September. Special insert with up-to-date information on the Philippines economy.

Gao Shangquan and Chi Fulin (1995) *Theory and Reality of Transition to a Market Economy*, Beijing: Foreign Languages Press. Heroic attempt at making economic policy sound interesting. Available from Friendship Stores, should you wish to make the attempt.

Hall, David and Roger Ames (1987) *Thinking Through Confucius*, Albany, NY: State University of New York Press. Sometimes technical but mostly highly readable account of Confucianism by two of the world's foremost Confucian scholars.

—— (1997) *Thinking from the Han: Self, Truth and Transcendence in Chinese and Western Cultures*, Albany, NY: State University of New York Press. Sequel to the above; intense but very important comparison of East–West systems of thought. Some philosophical background required.

—— (1998) 'Li'. in E. Craig (ed.) *Routledge Encyclopedia of Philosophy*, London: Routledge, 594–5. Encyclopedia article summing up a key concept in Chinese philosophy; referred to frequently in our text.

Hansen, Chad (1996) 'Chinese Philosophy and Human Rights: An Application of Comparative Ethics', *Ethics in Business and Society*, in Becker 1996: 99–127. Academic but useful comparison of approaches to ethics and human rights.

Ho, D. and Leigh, N. (1994) 'A Retail Revolution', *The China Business Review*, January–February: 22–27. Describes changes in retailing following relaxation of state controls on the retail trade.

Hofstede, Geert (1991) *Cultures and Organizations: Software of the Mind*, Beverly Hills, CA: Sage. An updated version of Hofstede's classic (if flawed) research on organisation behaviour.

Hsieh Tsun-yan (1996) 'Prospering through Relationships in Asia', *The McKinsey Quarterly* 4: 4–13. Another look at the importance of *guànxì* in commerce.

Huang Quanyu, Joseph Leonard and Chen Tong (1997) *Business Decision Making in China*, London: Haworth Press. Strongly recommended as one of the few English-language works on the subject.

Huang, Ray (1990) *A Macro History of China*, Armonk, NY: M.E. Sharpe. Excellent overview but not a quick read. Particularly good at drawing inferences (some debatable) from period to period and looking at underlying causes.

Hucker, C.O. (1978) *China to 1850. A Short History*, Stanford, CA: Stanford University Press. Probably the best short history; recommended for background reading. Unfortunately uses Wade-Giles romanisation which gives it an elderly look. Less academic than Huang but perhaps the best history of its type.

Hughes, Richard (1972) *Foreign Devil*, London: Century. Highly recommended; despite its date, many of Hughes's reflections remain as valuable as ever. The perfect airport read for the Far East-bound traveller.

Huo Da (1992) *The Jade King*, Beijing: Panda. Novel about the Chinese Muslim community in Beijing; a unique glimpse into an all-but-forgotten Chinese community.

I Ching (1992) trans. Thomas Cleary, Boston and London: Shambhala. Pocket version of a Chinese classic; initially impenetrable, but worth dipping into.

International Journal of Advertising (1997) special issue on advertising and branding in China, 16(4). Recommended for a number of articles, especially the distinction between 'name' and 'real' agencies (Swanson) and brand naming (Huang and Chan).

Jiang Wei (1994) *Chinese Business Strategies*, Singapore: Asiapac. A surprisingly useful introduction to Chinese approaches to business strategy, with examples from the literary classics and real case studies; we say 'surprisingly' because this is in fact a 'graphic novel' ('comic book' to older readers). This is one of a series of similar works from Asiapac.

Jianguang Wang (ed.) (1995) *Westerners Through Chinese Eyes*, Beijing: Foreign Languages Press. Interesting, though some of the stories are best taken with a pinch of salt.

Jones, Stephanie (1997) *Managing in China: An Executive Survival Guide*, Singapore: BH Asia. The best informal guide currently on the subject.

Kelley, Lane and Oled Shenkar (eds) (1993) *International Business in China*, New York and London: Routledge. Well-regarded textbook which discusses the key issues facing foreign companies in China.

Kenna, Peggy and Sondra Lacy (1994) *Business China: A Practical Guide to Understanding Chinese Business Culture*, New York: NTC Group. Useful, but getting dated and others preferred.

Laozi (1990) *Tao Teh Ching*, Boston and London: Shambhala. Good pocket translation of the work now usually known as the *Daodejing*; very valuable for understanding Chinese thought, today as in classical times.

Lardy, Nicholas R. (1994) *China in the World Economy*, Washington, DC: Institute for International Economics. Probably the most authoritative macro view, Lardy is well regarded inside and outside China.

Latourette, Kenneth Scott (1934) *The Chinese: Their History and Culture*, London: Macmillan. Good cultural history, complements Hucker, above.

Lemoine, P. (1994) 'Mediation Prospers in China', *Dispute Resolution Journal* 49(2). Useful description of the mediation process, common for settling disputes in China.

Li Cheng (1994) 'University Networks and the Rise of Qinghua Graduates in China's Leadership', *The Australian Journal of Chinese Affairs* 30 (April): 1–30. Interesting look at one form of relationship-building in China.

Lieberthal, Kenneth and Michael Oksenberg (1991) *Policy Making in China: Leaders, Structures and Processes*, Princeton, NJ: Princeton University Press. Academic, but worth a look; in some respects, not much has changed since this book went to press.

Luo Yadong and Min Chen (1997) 'Does *Guànxì* Influence Firm Performance?', *Asia Pacific Journal of Management* 14: 1–16. Assessment of how *guànxì* matters to businesses.

Mann, J. (1989) *Beijing Jeep*, New York: Simon & Schuster. Excellent story from the boardroom, though remember to update the story; Beijing Jeep is now a considerable success.

Meisner, Maurice (1997) *The Deng Xiaoping Era: An Inquiry into the Fate of Chinese Socialism*, New York: Hill and Wang, 1997. A negative view of Deng's reforms. The elite enriched themselves at the expense of the poor, Meisner claims. Not to be taken too seriously but useful for balance.

Meridian Resources (1998) *Managing in China: Recruiting and Retaining Employees*, Washington, DC: Meridian. One of a useful series of small pamphlets, with a good bibliography.

Moise, Edwin E. (1994) *Modern China: A History*, London: Longman. The most recent and in some ways the best, for our purposes, of the three histories. Unfortunately it does not do justice to earlier history, a basic understanding of which is necessary; see Hucker or Huang, above, for this.

Murray, G. (1994) *Doing Business in China: The Last Great Market*, Sandgate, Kent: China Library. Written by a journalist for the serious business reader. Better on economic development and relationships than how to create business (marketing). Uses Beijing Jeep story.

Negotiating: Opening Moves, Negotiating: The Middle Game and *Negotiating: Closing the Deal?*, Videos 3–5 in the Working with China Series, Intercultural Training Resources, Inc., n.d.

Ng Sek Hong and Warner, Malcolm (1997) *China's Trade Unions and Management*, London: Macmillan. Up-to-date study by two leading China business scholars; focuses in particular on the role of unions in state enterprise.

Porter R. and Robinson M. (1994) *The China Business Guide*, Keele: Ryburn Publishing/Keele University Press. Keele's China Business Centre and CBTG's joint production for teaching use.

Purves, W. (1991) *Barefoot in the Boardroom*, Sydney: Allen & Unwin. This is a light but real, tells it as it is, guide book. Hardly academic but a clear Western view of life as a JV general manager.

Pye, Lucian W. (1992) *Chinese Negotiating Style: Commercial Approaches and Cultural Principles*, Westport, Conn. and London: Quorum Books. Overview of negotiating attitudes and problems from US point of view.

Rae, Ian (1997) 'Westerners Need Patience to Crack Chinese Puzzle', *Sunday Times*, 9 November.

Reuvid, Jonathan and Li Yong (eds) (1988) *Doing Business With China*, London: Kogan Page, 2nd edition. Practical (though large) need to know cross section. MOFTEC and Motorola have blessed it. Contributions from Coopers & Lybrand and Baker & Mackenzie. Probably the closest thing to a bible for businessmen/women going from Britain to China. Covers foreign and JVs, regions and sectors, rules and regulations.

Rice, D. (1992) *The Dragon's Brood: Conversations with Young Chinese*, London: Harper-Collins. Interesting insights, not strictly relevant to business but good for attitudes.

Robison, Richard and David S.G. Goodman (eds) (1995) *The New Rich in Asia*, London: Routledge. Pre-1997/98 crash of course, a useful multi-cultural study of the new elites in what used to be called 'tiger economies'.

Schneiter, Fred (1992) *Getting Along with the Chinese for Fun and Profit*, Hongkong: Asia 2000. Humorous, affectionate if not terribly rigorous look at East–West personal relations. Light reading.

Seagrave, Sterling (1996) *The Soong Dynasty*, London: Corgi. Recent Chinese history as family quarrel; terrific read with some insights.

Seligman, S.D. (1990) *Dealing with the Chinese: A Practical Guide to Business Etiquette*, London: W.H. Allen. Informal, easy to read for incoming business person.

Shabad, T. (1972) *China's Changing Map*, London: Methuen. Geography of China; out of date in terms of demography, but useful physical overview.

Shaw, S., and Meier, J. (1993) 'Second Generation MNCs in China', *The McKinsey Quarterly* 4. Useful look at the development of foreign ventures in China in the 1990s.

Shenkar, Oled (1990) 'International "JV" Problems in China: Risks & Remedies', *Long Range Planning*. Although old, the JV management problems this article describes continue to occur in China today.

—— (ed.) (1991) *Organization and Management in China 1979 – 1990*, Armonk NY and London, M.E. Sharpe. Good description of changing forms of management during the first waves of economic reform.

Shih, C.Y. (1990) *The Spirit of Chinese Foreign Policy: A Psycho-Cultural View*, Basingstoke: Macmillan. Very academic, but has some valuable pieces on Chinese decision-making processes.

Spence, Jonathan (1997) *God's Chinese Son: the Taiping Heavenly Kingdom of Hong Xiuquan*, London: Flamingo. Account of the Taiping Rebellion, which began the downfall of the empire and the sequence of events that led to today; some interesting observations on the impact of foreign cultures on China.

Starr, John Bryan (1997) *Understanding China*, New York: Hill and Wang. Fairly up-to-date text by an American sinologist; hypercritical and very pessimistic about China's future, but does have some useful chapters.

Stewart, S. (1990) 'Where the Power Lies: A Look at China's Bureaucracy', *Advances in Chinese Industrial Studies*, vol. 1, New York: JAI Press. Dated but still valuable.

Stewart, S. and Ip Kam Tim (1994) 'Professional Business Services in the People's Republic of China', The University of Hong Kong, unpublished monograph, November. Very useful, though difficult to find.

Strange, Roger (1998) *Management in China: The Experience of Foreign Businesses*, London: Frank Cass. Academic but useful, with some case studies.

Sun Li and Yu Xiaohui (1992) *Metropolis*, Panda Press, 1992. Novel about a north Chinese city in the throes of economic and social reform; no direct business relevance, but an extraordinarily fine account of life in modern China; hard to find.

Tang Y.M. and M. Rice (1992) 'The development of marketing in China: 1979–1990', in *Advances in Chinese Industrial Studies*, Volume 3. Good, but now largely superseded by events.

Tao, Julia (1996) 'The Moral Foundation of Welfare in Chinese Society: Between Virtues and Rights', in Becker 1996: 9–24. Very good account of the subject.

Tsang, Eric W.K. (1998) 'Can *Guànxì* be a Source of Sustained Competitive Advantage for Doing Business in China?', *Academy of Management Executive* 12(2): 64–73. Another useful look at the importance of *guànxì* in commerce.

Tseng, C., Kwan, P. and Cheung, F. (1995) 'Distribution in China: A Guide Through the Maze', *Long Range Planning* 28(1): 81–91. Academic but important, in a field where not enough has been written.

—— (1996) 'Business Strategies, East Asian', *International Encyclopedia of Business and Management*, London: ITBP. Good generic work, with plenty of relevance to China.

Tucker, Spencer C. (1999) *Vietnam*, London: UCL Press. Long-overdue updating of Vietnam's situation; should be required reading for anyone interested in the country.

Wang, Guiguo (1994) *Business Law in China: Cases, Texts and Commentary*, Singapore: Butterworth Law Asia. Sketchy and hard to find but important for lawyers.

Wank, David L. (1996) 'The Institutional Process of Market Clientelism: *Guànxì* and Private Business in a South China City', *The China Quarterly* 137: 820–37. Worth looking for; good example of how a *guànxì* system works.

Warner, Malcolm (1992) *How Chinese Managers Learn*, London: Macmillan. A bit dated but useful for approaches and attitudes to formal and informal management education programmes in China. Warner and John Child, mentioned above, are probably the two best British-based writers on China.

White, Theodore H. (1978) *In Search of History*, New York: Warner Books. Account by veteran journalist of his years in China with Mao, Zhou Enlai *et al.*

Wilson, Dick (1995) *The Big Tiger*, London. One of the better, and certainly bigger, Western journalist surveys of modern China. Not popular with Chinese readers as he plays to the Western liberal gallery.

Wing, R.L. (1988) *The Art of Strategy: A New Translation of Sun Tzu's Classic, The Art of War*, New York: Doubleday.

Witzel, M. (1998) 'Guànxì East and West', in Yuanhui Lin and Oliver Lau (eds) *Proceedings of the 1998 Annual Conference of the Academy of International Business Southeast Asia Region*, Nanning: Guangxi People's Publishing House, 190–223. Conference paper summarising current writings on *guànxì*.

—— (1999) 'Guànxì East and West', *Financial Times Mastering Management Review*, January. More accessible version of 1998, above.

—— (1999) 'China: The World's Oldest Brand', *Financial Times Mastering Management Review*, September. Account of British–Chinese trade in the eighteenth century, when 'China' had many of the connotations of quality that Chinese now associate with the West.

Wu Jie (1996) *On Deng Xiaoping Thought*, Beijing: Foreign Languages Press. Good distillation of Deng's economic and social ideas, preferable by far than attempting to tackle the voluminous originals.

Xu Bai Yi (1990) *Marketing to China: One Billion New Customers*, Chicago: NTC Business Books. Perhaps it toes the Party line but it is a comprehensive guide to the 4 Ps in China. Rather out of date now, but not much has come along to supersede it.

Yan R. (1994) 'To Reach China's Consumers, Adapt to Guo Qing', *Harvard Business Review*, September – October. Controversial in places, but worth a read.

Yang Zhongfang (1988) *The Psychology of Advertising*, Yunnan Peoples' Publisher. In Chinese.

Yang, Mayfair Mei-hui (1994) *Gifts, Favors and Banquets*, Ithaca, NY: Cornell University Press. Do not be put off by the title; this is the best work we have seen on the subject of *guànxì*-building.

Yau, Oliver H.M. (1994) *Consumer Behaviour in China*, New York and London: Routledge. Reports on a research study into the effects of Chinese cultural, experiential and environmental on consumer satisfaction. Technical.

Yeung, I. Y. M. and R. L. Tung (1996) 'Achieving Business Success in Confucian Societies: The Importance of *Guànxì* (Connections)', *Organizational Dynamics* 25(2): 54–65. Another useful, if academic, look at the role of *guànxì*.

Young, Susan (1995) *Private Business and Economic Reform in China*, New York, M.E. Sharpe. Useful and interesting.

Index